DevOps for Serverless Applications

Design, deploy, and monitor your serverless applications using DevOps practices

Shashikant Bangera

Packt>

BIRMINGHAM - MUMBAI

DevOps for Serverless Applications

Commissioning Editor: Gebin George
Acquisition Editor: Rahul Nair
Content Development Editor: Nithin George Varghese
Technical Editor: Mohit Hassija
Copy Editor: Safis Editing
Project Coordinator: Drashti Panchal
Proofreader: Safis Editing
Indexer: Priyanka Dhadke
Graphics: Tom Scaria
Production Coordinator: Aparna Bhagat

First published: September 2018

Production reference: 1280918

Published by Packt Publishing Ltd.
Livery Place
35 Livery Street
Birmingham
B3 2PB, UK.

ISBN 978-1-78862-344-5

www.packtpub.com

To my lovely grandmother, Nemu, and my sweet mom, Padmavati.
There are no words to describe their love and sacrifice.

Mapt

Mapt is an online digital library that gives you full access to over 5,000 books and videos, as well as industry leading tools to help you plan your personal development and advance your career. For more information, please visit our website.

Why subscribe?

- Spend less time learning and more time coding with practical eBooks and Videos from over 4,000 industry professionals

- Improve your learning with Skill Plans built especially for you

- Get a free eBook or video every month

- Mapt is fully searchable

- Copy and paste, print, and bookmark content

packt.com

Did you know that Packt offers eBook versions of every book published, with PDF and ePub files available? You can upgrade to the eBook version at www.packt.com and as a print book customer, you are entitled to a discount on the eBook copy. Get in touch with us at customercare@packtpub.com for more details.

At www.packt.com, you can also read a collection of free technical articles, sign up for a range of free newsletters, and receive exclusive discounts and offers on Packt books and eBooks.

Contributors

About the author

Shashikant Bangera is a DevOps architect with 18 years of IT experience. He has vast experience with DevOps tools across the platform, with core expertise in CI, CD, the cloud, and automation. He has helped his customers adopt DevOps; architected and implemented enterprise DevOps for domains such as banking, e-commerce, and retail; and also contributed to many open source platforms. He has designed an automated on-demand environment with a set of open source tools and also contributed to the open source arena with an environment booking tool, which is available on GitHub.

Writing a book is harder than I thought and more rewarding than I could have ever imagined. None of this would have been possible without the support of my family. I would like to especially thank my wife, Rekha; daughter, Lishika; and my son, Dhruv, for having patience with me for taking yet another challenge that decreases the amount of time I can spend with them. I would like to thank the whole team at Packt, and especially Nithin, for all their effort, and also would like to thank Abbas Attarwala for the technical help.

About the reviewer

Ifemakin Olasupo is a certified systems and cloud expert with over a decade of IT experience. His background is in infrastructure engineering and he has a strong passion for automation. He has worked on and delivered cutting-edge projects for various multinational institutions and currently consults as the lead DevOps engineer for HM Revenue and Customs. He enjoys building event-driven automations and helping organizations build bespoke platforms for application delivery.

Packt is searching for authors like you

If you're interested in becoming an author for Packt, please visit `authors.packtpub.com` and apply today. We have worked with thousands of developers and tech professionals, just like you, to help them share their insight with the global tech community. You can make a general application, apply for a specific hot topic that we are recruiting an author for, or submit your own idea.

Table of Contents

Preface

Serverless development provides developers with the freedom to just concentrate on development and not worrying about the server-side aspects. This book aims to simplify your serverless deployment experience by showing you how to effectively apply DevOps principles to serverless applications. At each step along the way, you will be introduced to best practices for effectively building a complete Continuous Integration and Continuous Delivery pipeline and log management for serverless applications.

Who this book is for

DevOps for Serverless Applications is for DevOps engineers, architects, or anyone interested in understanding the DevOps ideology in the serverless world. You will learn how to use DevOps with serverless and apply continuous integration, continuous delivery, testing, logging, and monitoring with serverless development.

What this book covers

Chapter 1, *Introducing Serverless*, describes what serverless is with simple words, covering its benefits and drawbacks. It talks about different service providers of serverless and provides an introduction to the serverless services they provide.

Chapter 2, *Understanding Serverless Frameworks*, talks about different deployment frameworks for serverless and also dives into the Serverless Framework, which is used in most of the chapters in the book.

Chapter 3, *Applying DevOps to AWS Lambda Applications*, deep dives into AWS Lambda with respect to DevOps. It sails through multiple hands-on tutorials on the continuous integration and continuous deployment pipeline with the Serverless Framework and Jenkins, as well as monitoring and logging. It also covers how to set up canary and blue/green deployments for AWS Lambda.

Chapter 4, *DevOps with Azure Functions*, talks about Azure functions. It starts with how to create and deploy Azure functions, then teaches how to set up a continuous integration and continuous deployment pipeline through Jenkins. It also covers monitoring and logging and talks about best practices for DevOps with Azure functions.

Chapter 5, *Integrating DevOps with IBM OpenWhisk*, introduces Openwhisk and covers setting up a deployment pipeline with Serverless Framework and Jenkins. Monitoring and dynamic dashboard of OpenWhisk on IBM cloud are also covered.

Chapter 6, *DevOps with Google Functions*, starts with an introduction to Google functions. It walks through multiple tutorials, from creating a function to setting up an automated deployment pipeline. It also talks about how to monitor and log with the Google stack driver.

Chapter 7, *Adding DevOps Flavour to Kubeless*, explains that Kubeless is an open source serverless architecture that sits on Kubernetes. This chapter introduces Kubeless and explains how to set up continuous integration and continuous deployment for Kubeless.

Chapter 8, *Best Practices and the Future of DevOps with Serverless*, discusses how we all deal with performance issues with our applications in the journey of development, and this leads us to best practices. So, this chapter outlines the best practices for serverless and DevOps so that we can develop and deploy with ease.

Chapter 9, *Use Cases and Essentials*, covers some popular use cases for serverless and also essential tit-bits that can improve development and deployment.

Chapter 10, *DevOps trends with Serverless*, covers how serverless will the shape DevOps and how DevOps has to change its track with the adoption of serverless.

To get the most out of this book

The main focus of this book is to shed light on serverless and different service provider for serverless. It also teaches how to adopt an automated way to set up DevOps for serverless functions.

You have an understanding of DevOps, continuous integration, and continuous deployment, and should have some knowledge of popular DevOps tools such as Jenkins, ELK (Elasticsearch, Logstash, and Kibana). It is an added advantage if you know about different cloud service providers, such as AWS, Azure, and Google.

Most of my tutorials are build on top of MacBook and Docker containers, so I would recommend using some form of Linux for the tutorials.

Download the example code files

You can download the example code files for this book from your account at www.packt.com. If you purchased this book elsewhere, you can visit http://www.packt.com/support and register to have the files emailed directly to you.

You can download the code files by following these steps:

1. Log in or register at www.packt.com.
2. Select the **SUPPORT** tab.
3. Click on **Code Downloads & Errata**.
4. Enter the name of the book in the **Search** box and follow the onscreen instructions.

Once the file is downloaded, please make sure that you unzip or extract the folder using the latest version of:

- WinRAR/7-Zip for Windows
- Zipeg/iZip/UnRarX for Mac
- 7-Zip/PeaZip for Linux

The code bundle for the book is also hosted on GitHub at https://github.com/PacktPublishing/DevOps-for-Serverless-Applications. In case there's an update to the code, it will be updated on the existing GitHub repository.

We also have other code bundles from our rich catalog of books and videos available at https://github.com/PacktPublishing/. Check them out!

Download the color images

We also provide a PDF file that has color images of the screenshots/diagrams used in this book. You can download it here: https://www.packtpub.com/sites/default/files/downloads/9781788623445_ColorImages.pdf.

Conventions used

There are a number of text conventions used throughout this book.

`CodeInText`: Indicates code words in text, database table names, folder names, filenames, file extensions, pathnames, dummy URLs, user input, and Twitter handles. Here is an example: "In the statement, we pass the parameter to the CLI and the `stage` value is populated in the `serverless.yml` file."

A block of code is set as follows:

```
# serverless.yml
service: myService
provider:
  name: aws
  runtime: nodejs6.10
  memorySize: 512 # will be inherited by all functions
```

Any command-line input or output is written as follows:

```
$ pip install zappa
```

Bold: Indicates a new term, an important word, or words that you see onscreen. For example, words in menus or dialog boxes appear in the text like this. Here is an example: "Click on **Users** on the left-hand sidebar, then click on the **Add User** button and add the username `adm-serverless`."

Warnings or important notes appear like this.

Tips and tricks appear like this.

Get in touch

Feedback from our readers is always welcome.

General feedback: Email customercare@packtpub.com and mention the book title in the subject of your message. If you have questions about any aspect of this book, please email us at customercare@packtpub.com.

Errata: Although we have taken every care to ensure the accuracy of our content, mistakes do happen. If you have found a mistake in this book, we would be grateful if you would report this to us. Please visit www.packt.com/submit-errata, selecting your book, clicking on the Errata Submission Form link, and entering the details.

Piracy: If you come across any illegal copies of our works in any form on the Internet, we would be grateful if you would provide us with the location address or website name. Please contact us at copyright@packt.com with a link to the material.

If you are interested in becoming an author: If there is a topic that you have expertise in and you are interested in either writing or contributing to a book, please visit authors.packtpub.com.

Reviews

Please leave a review. Once you have read and used this book, why not leave a review on the site that you purchased it from? Potential readers can then see and use your unbiased opinion to make purchase decisions, we at Packt can understand what you think about our products, and our authors can see your feedback on their book. Thank you!

For more information about Packt, please visit packt.com.

Introducing Serverless

1

This book will introduce us to the world of the serverless approach to information technology, looking at multiple different cloud service providers, such as AWS, Azure, Google, OpenWhisk, and a few others. We will look in detail at each cloud service, as well as the different methods that are used to apply DevOps to them. We will look at the different use cases and learn the best practices for each of them.

The following topics will be covered in this introductory chapter:

- Introduction to serverless
- Core concept
    - **Backend as a service (BaaS)**
    - **Function as a service (FaaS)**
    - AWS Lambda
    - Azure functions
    - Google functions
    - OpenWhisk
- Pros and cons of serverless
- DevOps with serverless

Introduction to serverless

When we hear the word **serverless**, the first thing that comes to mind is, *oh, my code will magically run without any server!*. In a way, this is right: the serverless approach is a process where we deploy the code into a cloud and it is executed automatically, without worrying about the underlying infrastructure, renting or buying servers, scaling, monitoring, or capacity planning. The service provider will take care of all these things. Also, you won't believe how cheap it is and how much easier it is to manage. Now, you are probably thinking, *how is that possible?*. To look at its workings in more detail, let's compare the serverless approach with something we do in our daily lives.

The serverless approach is a bit like dealing with our laundry. We all need to wash our clothes, and for this, we need to buy a washing machine. But the usage of this washing machine will be about 10 to 15 hours per week, and the rest of the time the washing machine will be idle. Interestingly, we buy servers to host our application, and most of the time, our servers are idle when waiting for requests and sit unused. We have piles of servers that are hardly managed or decommissioned. As they are not properly used or managed, resources, such as the power supply, capacity, storage, and memory, are wasted.

Also, while doing the laundry, the washing machine will allow only a certain load and volume. The same applies to servers: They too allow only a certain volume and load. The more the load or traffic, the slower the processing will be, or it may stop completely. Now, to take care of our extra load, we might decide to buy a bigger washing machine, which will allow a bigger volume of laundry and support a larger load. But again, this high-end machine will take the same resources if we have to wash a huge pile of clothes or just one piece of clothing, which is wasteful. The same is the case in our server analogy. When catering for higher traffic or requests, we could buy a high-end server. But we will end up using the same resources for 10 requests a day as we would for 10,000 requests, even with a high-end server.

Also, to use the washing machine, we have to separate our clothes before washing, select the program, and add the detergent and softener, and if these elements are not handled properly, we might ruin our clothes. Similarly, when using a server, we have to make sure we install the right software—as well as the right version of the software—make sure that it is secure enough, and always monitor whether the services are running.

Also, if you are renting an apartment, then you might not have a washing machine, or perhaps you might find launderettes to be cheaper when you wash you laundry in bulk, and also less worrisome. So launderettes or coin-operated laundry machines can be rented whenever you need to wash your clothes. Likewise, many companies, such as AWS, Azure, or Google, started by renting their servers. So we too can rent a server, and the provider will take care of the storage, memory, power, and basic setup.

Say that we've decided that a coin-operated washing machine at the local launderette is our best option. Now we just put the coin in and wash our clothes, but we still need to make sure we add detergent and fabric softener, and set the right program, otherwise we will end up ruining our clothes. Likewise, when we rent a server on the cloud, we might not bother dealing with the power, storage, and memory. But we still need to install the required software, monitor the application service, and upgrade the software version from time to time, as well as monitor the performance of the application.

Say that I found a new launderette, one that has a delivery service and that would charge me per item of clothing, so I can send clothes in bulk or one piece at a time. They will wash and iron my clothes too. Now, I don't need to worry about which detergent or comforter to use, or what cleaning program to use, and I also don't need to own an iron. But in the case of the world of information technology, companies are still using the rental coin laundry system. They still lease servers and manage them through **Platform as a Service (PaaS)**, still manage application downtime, upgrade the software version, and monitor services.

But this can all be changed by adopting a serverless approach. Serverless computing will automatically provision and configure the server and then execute the code. As the traffic rises, it will scale automatically, apply the required resources, and scale down once the traffic eases down.

Core concept

In earlier days, the term *serverless* referred to an application that was dependent on third-party applications or services to manage server-side logic. Such applications were cloud-based databases, such as Google Firebase, or authentication services, such as Auth0 or AWS Cognito. They were referred to as **Backend as a Service (BaaS)** services. But serverless also means code that is developed to be event-triggered, and which is executed in stateless compute containers. This architecture is popularly known as **Function as a Service (FaaS)**. Let's look at each type of service in a bit more detail.

Backend as a Service

The BaaS was conceptualized by Auth0 and Google Firebase. Auth0 started as authentication as a service, but moved to FaaS. So basically, BaaS is third-party service through which we can implement our required functionality, and it will provide server-side logic for the implementation of the application.

The common approach is that most web and mobile application developers code their own authentication functionality, such as login, registration, and password management, and each of these services has its own API, which has to be incorporated into the application. But this was complicated and time consuming for developers, and BaaS providers made it easy by having a unified API and SDK and bridging them with the frontend of the application so that developers did not have to worry about developing their own backend services for each service. In this way, time and money was saved.

Say, for example, that we want to build a portal that would require authentication to consume our services. We would need login, signup, and authentication systems in place, and we would also need to make it easy for the consumer to sign in with just a click of a button using their existing Google or Facebook or Twitter account. Developing these functionalities individually requires lots of time and effort.

But by using BaaS, we can easily integrate our portal to sign up and authenticate using a Google, Facebook, or Twitter account. Another BaaS service is Firebase, provided by Google. Firebase is a database service that is used by mobile apps, where database administration overhead is mitigated, and it provides authorization for different types of users. In a nutshell, this is how BaaS works. Let's look at the FaaS side of the serverless approach.

Function as a Service

As mentioned at the start of chapter, FaaS is essentially a small program or function that performs small tasks that are triggered by an event, unlike a monolithic app, which does lots of things. So, in FaaS architecture, we break our app into small, self-contained programs or functions instead of the monolithic app that runs on PaaS and performs multiple functions. For instance, each endpoint in the API could be a separate function, and we can run these functions on demand rather than running the app full time.

The common approach would be to have an API coded in a multi-layer architecture, something like a three-tier architecture where code is broken down into a presentation, business, and data layer. All the routes would trigger the same handler functions in the business layer, and data would be processed and sent to the data layer, which would be a database or file. The following diagram shows this three-tier architecture:

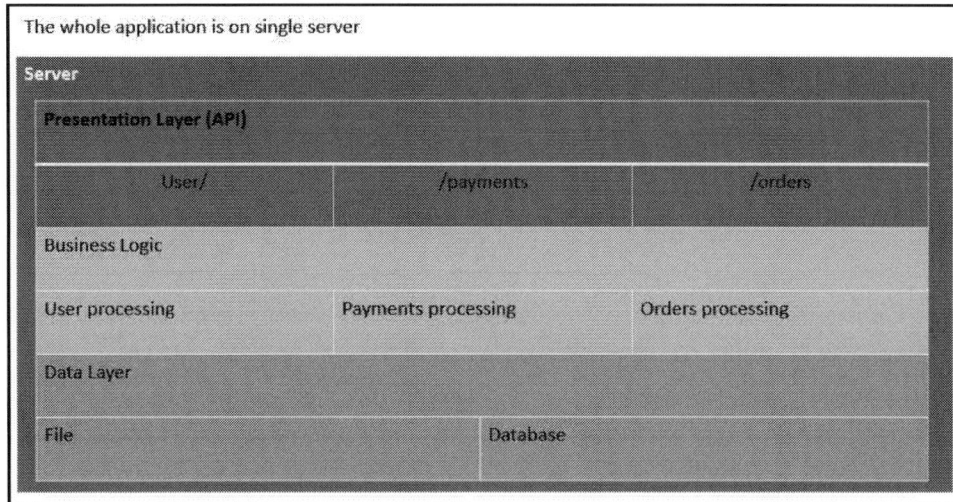

The whole application is on single server		
Server		
Presentation Layer (API)		
User/	/payments	/orders
Business Logic		
User processing	Payments processing	Orders processing
Data Layer		
File	Database	

That might work fine for small numbers of simultaneous users, but how would we manage this when traffic grows exponentially? The application will suddenly become a computing nightmare. So, to resolve this problem, ideally, we would separate the data layer, which contains the database, into the separate server. But the problem is still not solved, because the API routes and business logic is within one application, so the scaling would still be a problem.

A serverless approach to the same problem is painless. Instead of having one server for application API endpoints and business logic, each part of the application is broken down into independent, auto-scalable functions. The developer writes a function, and the serverless provider wraps the function into a container that can be monitored, cloned, and distributed on any number of servers, as shown in the following diagram:

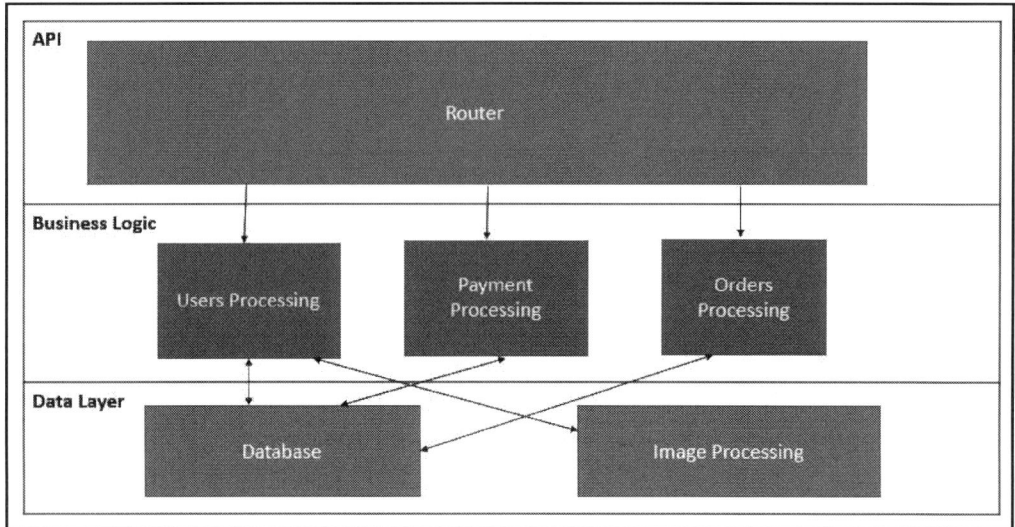

The benefit to breaking down an application into functions is that we can scale and deploy each function separately. For instance, if one endpoint in our API is where 90 percent of our traffic goes, or our image-processing code is eating up most of the computing time, that one function or bit code can be distributed and scaled more easily than scaling out the entire application.

In a FaaS system, the functions are expected to start within milliseconds in order to allow the handling of individual requests. In PaaS systems, by contrast, there is typically an application thread that keeps running for long periods of time, and handles multiple requests. FaaS services are charged per execution time of the function, whilst PaaS services charge per running time of the thread in which the server application is running.

In the microservices architecture, the applications are loosely coupled, fine grained, and light weighted. The reason for the birth of microservices is to break down the monolithic application into small services so that it can be developed, managed, and scaled independently. But FaaS takes that a step further by breaking things down into even smaller units called functions.

The trend is pretty clear: The unit of work is getting smaller and smaller. We'are moving from monoliths to microservices, and now to functions, as shown in the following diagram:

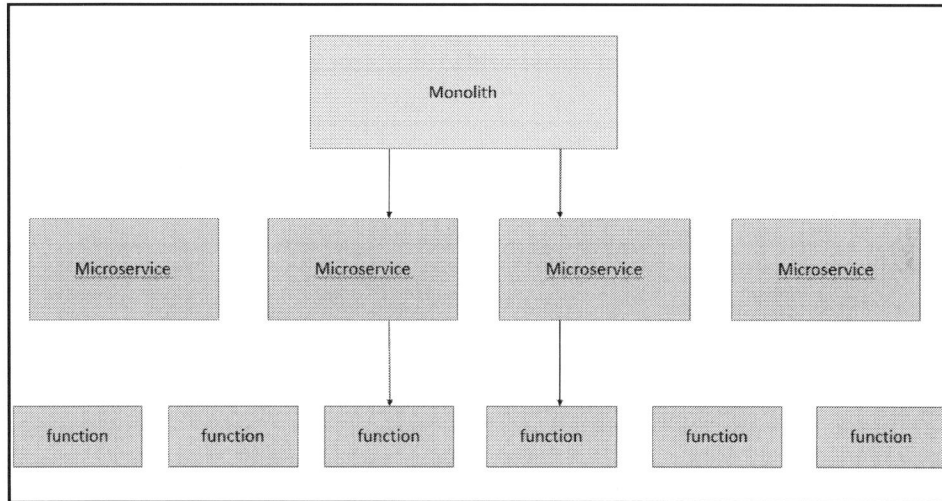

With the rise of containers, many cloud vendors saw that serverless functions architecture will provide better flexibility for developers to build their applications without worrying about the ops (operations). AWS was first to launch this service with the name Lambda, then other cloud providers followed the trend, such as Microsoft Azure with Azure Functions and Google Cloud with Google Functions. But this popularity also gave an opportunity for some vendors to build open source versions. Some popular versions are IBM's OpenWhisk, which is Apache licensed, Kubeless, which is built over the top of Kubernetes, and OpenFaaS, which is built over the Docker container. Even Oracle jumped into the foray with Oracle Fn. Let's briefly look at each vendor in this chapter, learning about how they work. We will then travel with them over the rest of the book, looking at their approach to DevOps.

AWS Lambda

Amazon Web Services (**AWS**) were the first to launch a FaaS, or serverless, service in 2014, called Lambda. They are currently the leaders in this kind of serverless provision. AWS Lambda follow the event-driven approach. At the trigger of an event, Lambda executes the code and performs the required functionality, and it can automatically scale as the traffic rises, as well as automatically descale. Lambda functions run in response to events, such as changes to the data in an Amazon S3 bucket, an Amazon DynamoDB table change, or in response to an HTTP request through the AWS API Gateway. That's how Lambda helps to build the triggers for multiple services, such as S3 DynamoDB, and the stream data store in Kinesis.

So, Lambda helps developers only worry about the coding—the computing part, such as the memory, CPU, network, and space, is taken care of by Lambda automatically. It also automatically manages the patching, logging, and monitoring of functions. Architecturally, a Lambda function is invoked in a container, which is launched based on the configuration provided. These containers might be reused for subsequent invocations for functions. As the demand dies, the container is decommissioned, but this is all managed internally by Lambda, so users do not have to worry about it as they do not have any control over these containers. The languages supported by AWS Lambda functions are Node.js, Java, C#, and Python.

While building serverless applications, the core components are functions and the event source. The event source is the AWS service or custom application, and the Lambda function processes the events. The execution time for each Lambda function is 300 seconds.

Let's look at an example of how AWS Lambda actually works. In a photo-sharing application, people upload their photos, and these photos need to have thumbnails so that they can be displayed on the user's profile page. In this scenario, we can use the Lambda function to create the thumbnails, so that the moment the photo gets uploaded in the AWS S3 bucket, S3, which supports the events source, can publish the object-created events and invoke the Lambda function. The Lambda function code reads the latest photo object from the S3 bucket, creates a thumbnail version, and saves it in another S3 bucket.

In `Chapter 3`, *Applying DevOps on AWS Lambda Applications*, we will look at how we can create, run, and deploy Lambda functions in an automated way, and we will also monitor and perform root-cause analysis through logging.

Azure Functions

Azure Functions is Microsoft's venture into serverless architecture. It came onto the market in March 2016. Azure Functions allows functions to be coded in C#, F#, PHP, Node.js, Python, and Java. Azure Functions also supports bash, batch, and PowerShell files. Azure Functions has seamless integration with **Visual Studio Team System** (**VSTS**), Bitbucket, and GitHub, which will make continuous integration and continuous deployment easier. Azure Functions supports various types of event triggers, timer-based events for tasks, OneDrive, and SharePoint, which can be configured to trigger operations in functions. Real-time processing of data and files adds the ability to operate a serverless bot that uses Cortana as the information provider. Microsoft has introduced **Logic Apps**, a tool with a workflow-orchestration engine, which will allow less technical users to build serverless applications. Azure Functions allows triggers to be created in other Azure cloud services and HTTP requests. The maximum execution time is five minutes per function. Azure Functions provides two types of app service plan: **Dynamic** and **Classic**. **App Service** is a container or environment for a set of Azure functions to run in. The Dynamic option is similar to Lambda, where we pay for the time and memory our function uses to run. The Classic option is about allocating your own existing or provisioned app resources for the functions at no extra cost. The memory allotted is as per App Service, whereas in AWS Lambda, the memory allocation is per function. Azure Functions allows just 10 concurrent executions per function

Azure Functions follows a similar pricing model to AWS Lambda. The total cost is based on number to triggers executed and time. So the first one million requests are free, and beyond that, it will cost $0.02 for every 100,000 executions.

We will be looking at automating the deployment of Azure Functions in `Chapter 4`, *DevOps with Azure Functions*, and also at how different DevOps processes will fit in to give Azure Functions a faster time to market.

Google Functions

Google joined the party a little late compared to AWS Lambda and Azure Functions. They came onto the market with a beta version of Cloud Functions in March 2017. Currently, we can write Google Functions through Node.js; they will be supporting other languages soon. They support internal event bus triggers and also HTTP triggers, which respond to events such as GitHub WebHooks, slack, or any HTTPS requests, and also mobile backend for events from Firebase analytics, a real-time database.

In terms of scalability, there is in-built provision for autoscaling. Google Functions supports 1,000 functions per project and allows 400 executions per function, which is claimed to be a soft limit. Google Functions allows an execution time of 540 seconds (9 minutes). Deployment is supported through ZIP upload, cloud storage, and cloud store repositories. The event source is through cloud pub/sub or cloud storage objects. The logging of function executions is managed through Stackdriver logging, which is Google Cloud's logging tool.

We will sail through Google Functions's DevOps approach in Chapter 5, *Integrating DevOps with IBM – OpenWhisk*, and will also look at the best practices around DevOps using Google Functions.

OpenWhisk

OpenWhisk is an open source FaaS platform that can be deployed to the cloud or on an on-premise data center. It is driven by IBM, and they have open sourced using the Apache licence. We can sign up for OpenWhisk through **Bluemix** (Bluemix is IBM's cloud platform) or we can set it up locally through a vagrant. It works in a similar way to any FaaS technology, such as AWS Lambda , Azure Functions, or Google Functions. But OpenWhisk supports open events providers. So if we have a custom event provider, then we can incorporate it with OpenWhiz, because, unlike other cloud platforms, OpenWhiz allows events within its service. One example would be that a function can be triggered through OpenWhiz upon the arrival of a new item appearance in an RSS feed. OpenWhiz will allow an organisation to set up their own FaaS platform within their premises if they are not happy to allow their data to go out of their organisation. The language support in OpenWhiz is Swift, along with JavaScript or Node.js. OpenWhiz has integrated Docker support for binary code execution within functions.

Other serverless architectures

There are many other serverless options, such as OpenFaaS, Fission, and Iron.io. I won't cover them in this book, but let's scheme through the features. **OpenFaaS** is an open source alternative for serverless architecture. It is built over Docker containers, Swarm, and Kubernetes. It has its own UI portal and also has CLI support to deploy functions. OpenFaaS supports Node.js, Python, GO, and C# on Windows and Linux. We can set it up over a cloud, a local laptop, or an on-premise server. We can write functions for almost everything—that is what is claimed by OpenFaas. OpenFaaS is written in Golang. It allows events through HTTP/HTTPS requests.

Fission is yet another open source version of serverless architecture—the underlying technology is Kubernetes and Docker containers, which can be deployed on both cloud and on-premise infrastructures. It is designed as a set of microservices, and its components are the controller, router, and pool manager. The router manages HTTP requests, the controller manages functions, event triggers, and environment images, and the pool manager manages the pool of containers and loads the functions into these containers. The functions are written with Python.

Serverless benefits

There are a number of pros and cons of using serverless architecture. Let's look at the bright side first. Why would anyone build their application using a serverless architecture such as AWS Lambda or OpenWhiz? The main reason is how efficiently the application performs, how fast it will scale, and, most importantly, its cost. Let's look at a few important pros and then move on to the cons.

Faster time to market

We can push the application to market much faster, as OPS becomes much simpler, and will help the developer to concentrate only on their development. The OPS team does not have to bother about writing code that could handle scaling or worry about the underlying infrastructure.

Also, teams can build the application much faster with the help of third-party integration, such as API services such as OAuth, Twitter, and Maps.

Highly scalable

Every company wants their application to perform better, have zero downtime, and scale quickly and easily with rising traffic, but with monolithic application development, it can become very difficult. The Ops team has to be vigilant in scaling the underlying infrastructure as the load on the application rises. A huge amount of time and money is wasted over downtime due to rises in traffic. But serverless computing is highly scalable, and the applications can be scaled and descaled within seconds.

Low cost

In serverless computing, developers are billed only for the time that the function is running, unlike IaaS and PaaS, which are billed 24/7 for each server. This is good for companies with a huge setup of apps, APIs, or microservices that are currently running 24/7 and using resources 100 percent of the time, whether they are required or not. But with serverless, instead of running the application 24/7, we can execute functions on demand and share the resources, so we can reduce the idle time substantially and still make the application run faster.

Latency and geolocation improvement

The scalability of the application depends on three factors: the number of users, the location of the users, and the latency of the network. In today's world, applications have a global audience, which can add to latency. But the danger of latency can be highly mitigated with the serverless platform. With serverless, a container is instantiated to run a function at every event call, and this container can be created close to the user's geographical region, which will automatically improve the performance of the app.

Serverless drawbacks

Although there are upsides to using serverless, there are also downsides. Let's look at the other side of the coin of the serverless function.

Increased complexity

The more granular we go with the application, the more complex it becomes. The code for each function might get simpler, but the application as a whole will get more complex. Say, for example, that we break the application into 10 different microservices. We would have to manage 10 different apps, whereas in a monolithic application, it is just one app that has to be managed.

Lack of tooling

Let's say that we break our monolithic application into 50 different functions. There are still a variety of processes and tools to manage, log, monitor, and deploy the monolithic application. As serverless is pretty new in the market, monitoring or logging an application that runs for a few seconds is limited and challenging as of now, but over time, there will be many efficient ways to do this.

Complexity with architecture

It is hard to make a decision as to how granular a function should be, and it is time consuming to assess, implement, and test to check our preferences. It would be cumbersome to manage too many functions, and at the same time, ignoring granularity would result in us setting up mini monoliths.

Drawback in implementation

The biggest challenge with serverless is integration tests. We will write many functions for an application, but how would we integrate them to work as an application? Of course, before that, how do we test how efficiently they work together? As serverless is new and still maturing, the options that are added through testing are still limited. But we will be covering a few aspects of deployment and testing in future chapters.

DevOps with serverless

DevOps is another buzzword that has been around for quite a long time. Like serverless, DevOps is also a confusing term. Lots of people have lots of different perspectives on DevOps. Some say that DevOps is just tools, some feel that DevOps consists of a few processes—even IaaS and PaaS falls under the umbrella of DevOps. As per my understanding, DevOps is a collaboration of tools, processes, and feedback. They all go hand in hand for the successful implementation of DevOps. But why are we talking about DevOps here? In short, because we would need DevOps for a smooth transition to production, to log or monitor the serverless functions, and to test them before they reach users.

With DevOps functional prospective, I will be covering version control, continuous integration, continuous deployment, monitoring, and logging for AWS Lambda functions, Azure Functions, Google Functions, and OpenWhiz. Version control is a process where we version the code so that we can branch it, package it, deploy it, and also roll back to a previous version. Continuous integration is the practice where code is integrated together by developers with automated builds to detect and mitigate problems early on. Continuous deployment is basically a bus or pipeline where code is continuously refined using automated testing, and is then deployed to the environment. This pipeline moves smoothly towards production, with minimal manual intervention.

Summary

We will evaluate a few serverless frameworks in the next chapter, and then use one of them through the book with various DevOps implementation tutorials. In most of these DevOps implementations, we will be using the more popular DevOps tools, such as Jenkins, which is used for orchestrating, and GitHub, which is used for versioning. We will also cover automated units, integration, and system testing. We will also look at the adoption of monitoring and logging best practices, as well as many more DevOps processes and features.

2
Understanding Serverless Frameworks

In the previous chapter, we looked into the world of serverless computing, how it works, what the purpose of it is, the benefits of adopting it, the different service providers, and how they fare in terms of the services they offer. We also learned about the pros and cons of adopting a serverless architecture. The goal of this chapter is to teach us different serverless deployment frameworks, and how they will eventually help us to achieve continuous integration and continuous delivery. Furthermore, we will also look at the various features provided by the frameworks and talk in more detail about the serverless framework, learning what it does under the hood.

In the world of application development, the process of developing an application is usually the same. The developer develops the code on their local machine, and compiles and pushes the changes to the source code management repository. The tester then tests and publishes reports, and the ops team plays the role of deploying the code into various different environments and manages the infrastructure.

But there is a chance that the same code will fail on production. Now, to get this code working again, the developer, tester, and operations teams have to work overtime to get the production live again. During root-cause analysis, the developer will say that his code works fine on his PC, the tester will claim that she has tested everything and will provide reports supporting this fact, and the operations guy will say that his job is just to deploy the code. So the challenges we have here are as follows:

- Make the code run perfectly on production every time it is deployed
- Speed up the deployment cycle
- Make the team work together and own their responsibility
- Have tensionless production deployment

The solution to all these problems is adopting DevOps, automating both the process and team collaboration.

> *"DevOps is a set of practices that automate the processes between the software development and IT teams, so that they can build, test, and release software faster and more reliably."*

-Definition of DevOps on Atlassian

DevOps rides on the wheels of tools, people, processes, and feedback loops. But tools and processes are the front wheel of DevOps, and play a very important role in driving faster release cycles on non-production and production environments, and in continuous integration, continuous testing, and continuous deployment.

Using serverless architecture to implement DevOps is much easier, as we do not have to worry about the underlying infrastructure. However, we still need continuous integration, monitoring, logging, and continuous deployment for smoother-sailing code to production. As serverless is still in its infancy, there are quite a few newly developed tools and frameworks that are available, but these numbers will eventually grow. We will be looking at the more popular tools or frameworks, and finally focus on one framework, looking at it in detail and learning about the features that it offers.

All the tools that we will be looking at in this book are open source frameworks. They each serve a particular function on an as-per-need basis. We will consider four popular serverless frameworks and look at what they have to offer.

ClaudiaJS

ClaudiaJS is one of the earliest of the deployment frameworks and tools. It is licensed under open source, and, at the time writing, it only supports AWS Lambda. ClaudiaJS is a Node.js library that helps to deploy Node.js projects on to AWS Lambda and API Gateway. It currently supports just the Node.js language. ClaudiaJS claims that it is not a framework, but a deployment tool, so the developer just calls it ClaudiaJS within their code and does not have to change their code structure. ClaudiaJS is built on top of AWS SDK and AWS CLI. It flags three types of JavaScript libraries:

- Command-line library
- API builder library
- Bot builder library

Command-line library

The first JavaScript library is a command-line tool or library. The command-line tool helps to deploy, update, roll back, package, invoke or test, and destroy Lambda functions, and it also works seamlessly with AWS API Gateway. It uses the standard npm packaging conventions, which just means that you can call it without making changes to your actual code structure. So the really interesting features with ClaudiaJs's command-line library are as follows:

- `claudia create` : This command will create a function and a related security role on the AWS portal
- `claudia update` : This command will update the function by deploying a new version of the function and update the associated API
- `claudia test-lambda`: This command will execute the Lambda function
- `claudia set-version`: This command will point the Lambda API stage to the latest deployment version
- `claudia add-scheduled-event`: This command can add the scheduled recurring events for the Lambda function to run, so through this, we can keep the Lambda function warm
- `claudia destroy`: This command will destroy the function and associated API and security roles

API builder library

The second type of library is the API builder library. It is the extension of the ClaudiaJS library, and it helps in setting up the AWS API Gateway endpoint. It also helps to route multiple API gateways to a single Lambda function. It automatically enables the CORS for the endpoints.

Bot builder library

This library is one of the most interesting libraries provided by ClaudiaJS. This library helps to create different types of bots within minutes. It has out-of-the-box features to integrate with Facebook Messenger, Telegram, and Skype. It is pretty easy to set up a bot using ClaudiaJS bot libraries.

To summarize, ClaudiaJS is great tool when using the AWS Cloud provider. It also supports Node.js. The documentation link provided in the following information box is up to date; the documentation explains each and every CLI command very well. There are lots of tutorials available, ranging from simple development to advanced tasks. The bot libraries are one of the best things that ClaudiaJS can provide. However, there is no support for multiple serverless providers, nor for multiple languages.

> More information on Claudia.JS can found at the following link:
> `https://claudiajs.com`

Apex

Apex is yet another serverless framework that is built on the Go to manage AWS Lambda functions. It is an open source framework and uses Terraform for bootstrapping the resources, which makes it faster to execute. The features provided by the frameworks are the ability to deploy, test functions, roll back deployment, view metrics, and tail logs.

Although it does not support invoking the function locally, it does support multiple languages, such as Node.js, Python, Java, Rust, and Go. We can create various environments through Apex. It has good documentation and helps you to quickly get started with using the frameworks. However, Apex currently only supports AWS Lambda.

> More information on Apex can be found at the following link:
> `http://apex.run/#function-hooks`

Zappa

If you decide to write your functions in Python, then you can use Zappa to deploy them. **Zappa** is a CLI/command-line framework, and it is open source. Zappa currently supports Python WSGI applications, which are basically Flask and Django applications. It can deploy macro and micro applications. Zappa has a wide variety of features, such as the ability to deploy functions like API to AWS lambda and AWS API Gateway respectively. It can also configure AWS events sources.

Once deployed, we can also invoke the function through Zappa. It can fetch or tail the logs from the AWS. It also allows rollback to the previous version. We can set up multistage deployment (by **stage**, it means multiple environment deployments, such as `dev`, `qa`, `uat`, and `prod`).

Zappa also has the cool feature of being able to keep the Lambda function warm. This makes for better performance and decreases latency, to an extent. It allows us to schedule deployment, which means that we can set up deployment earlier on in the day so that it does not interfere with regular traffic. It has the ability to undeploy the purging of logs from the CloudWatch. We can also use it to package the Lambda functions for future deployment. Post deployment status can also be checked through Zappa. Zappa allows us to deploy the Lambda function to any region in AWS. Let's look at a few of Zappa's features:

- **Installation of Zappa:** To install Zappa, you need to make sure that you have Python 2.7 or older, and that you have PIP installed and configured on your local machine or laptop. You also need to make sure that your AWS credentials are set up (`https://aws.amazon.com/blogs/security/a-new-and-standardized-way-to-manage-credentials-in-the-aws-sdks/`). We need Python and pip to install Zappa on the local environment:

  ```
  $ pip install zappa
  ```

- **Zappa init:** The `init` code phrase will set up deployment settings. It should automatically detect the Flask/Django application and it will create a JSON file named `zappa_settings.json` within the project directory:

  ```
  $ zappa init
  ```

- **Packaging and deployment:** Once the settings are configured, we can package and deploy the application using the following command. By default, it uses the production stage, but we can create multiple different stages:

  ```
  $ zappa deploy production
  ```

Zappa is an awesome framework, but there are a few cons about it, such as the fact that it does not support other cloud providers, such as Azure, Google, and OpenWhisk. It only supports Python-WSGI-based applications and no other languages, such as Node.js.

> You can find more information about the Zappa framework at the following link:
> `https://www.zappa.io/`

Serverless Framework

Serverless Framework is one of the most popular frameworks for building serverless architectures. It is an open source CLI, with about 23,000 stars on GitHub. There is also an enterprise edition that helps in setting up templates and providing support. This framework has been used by many companies, such as EA, Coca Cola, Expedia, and Reuters. It is a framework that supports lots of cloud service providers, such as AWS, Azure, Google, OpenWhisk, Kubeless, Oracle Fn, and many others. It has a very well-documented user guide containing quite a large number of examples to help you start using it. It supports lots of languages, such as Node.js, Python, Java, Scala, C#, Go, F#, Groovy, Kotlin, PHP, and Swift.

It supports the life cycle of serverless architecture, which can build, deploy, update, and delete. It supports function grouping for easy management of code, processes, and resources across large projects, and also provides fairly good support for CD/CI. It has far better community support compared to other frameworks. It provides lots of plugins to support framework functionality. There are a lot of blogs to help us build the best practices in using the framework. It has a support forum and slack rooms for resolving issues and problems. It supports lots of features, such as deploying functions and events, invoking functions, tailing logs, integration testing, and packaging for future deployment. Let's take a closer look at the features of Serverless Framework.

Framework features

There are many features available in Serverless Framework, although they vary with the cloud provider. I will list and describe a few of the more important and more common ones.

Services and deployment

A service is a project where we define the functions, the events that trigger them, and any infrastructure resources that are required for the function to perform. They are collected together into one file, which is called `serverless.yml`:

```
eg.
 myServerlessService/
         serverless.yml
```

When we start using Serverless Framework for deployment, we will be using one single service. But as the application grows, it is recommended that you have multiple services as shown in the following code:

```
users/
        serverless.yml # Contains 4 functions
posts/
            serverless.yml # Contains 4 functions
```

Having multiple services can isolate the infrastructure resources that are to be used. But it also has a drawback, as currently each service creates a separate REST API on API Gateway. This is a limitation with API Gateway. But there is a workaround to resolve this, which we will look into in future chapters.

To create the service, we have to use the create command, and we must pass the runtime language in which you would like to write the service. We can also provide the path, as shown in the following example:

```
$ serverless create --template <runtimes> --path myService
```

The main purpose of Serverless Framework is to deploy functions, events, and infrastructure resources into the remote cloud without much hassle, and that is done through the deploy plugin. There are various features that this deploy plugin provides. Let us look at a few of them:

- **Deploy to different stages and regions:**
  ```
  $ serverless deploy --stage production --region us-east-1
  ```
- **Deploying single function from the service:**
  ```
  $ serverless deploy function <function_name>
  ```
- **Deploying package to cloud:**
  ```
  $ serverless deploy --package <path to package>
  ```

This deploy plugin works in the following ways:

- The framework packages up the targeted AWS Lambda function into a .zip file
- The framework fetches the hash of the already uploaded function .zip file and compares it to the local .zip file hash
- The framework terminates if both hashes are the same
- That .zip file is uploaded to your S3 bucket using the same name as the previous function, which is the CloudFormation stack it is pointing to

Functions and events

Functions are the properties that are defined within the service, and they are defined within the `serverless.yml`, so we name the function and provide the handler property to the function, and this property points to the function file, which could be Node.js or Python. We can add multiple functions within the property. The functions can inherit the properties from the provider or we can define the properties at function level. These function properties vary as per the cloud provider, as shown in the following code:

```
# serverless.yml
service: myService
provider:
  name: aws
  runtime: nodejs6.10
  memorySize: 512 # will be inherited by all functions
functions:
  usersAdd:
    handler: handler.userAdd
    description: optional description for your function
userModify:
    handler: handler.userModify
userDelete:
    handler: handler.userDelete
    memorySize: 256 # function specific
```

The functions can be listed as arrays if we create a separate file for each function:

```
# serverless.yml

functions:
    - ${file(../user-functions.yml)}
  - ${file(../post-functions.yml)}
 # user-functions.yml
addUser:
    handler: handler.user
deleteUser:
      handler: handler.user
```

An environment object property can also be added to the function within the service, and it should be a key–pair value. Also, the function-specific environment variable overrides the provider-specific environment variable:

```
# serverless.yml
service: service-name
provider: aws

  functions:
```

```
hello:
    handler: handler.hello
    environment:
        TABLE_NAME: tableName
```

Events are things that trigger the function, such as the S3 bucket upload. There are multiple events supported by Serverless Framework, but they vary as per the cloud provider. We can define multiple events for a single function, as shown in the following code:

```
events:
  - http:
     path: handler
     method: get
```

> The types of events provided for AWS Lambda by Serverless Framework are shown at the following link:
> https://serverless.com/framework/docs/providers/aws/events/

Variables and plugins

Variables are the values that can be passed to the configuration values within the `serverless.yml` while running the Serverless Framework command. They need to pass reference values enclosed in `${}` brackets, but you can use variables in property values rather than in the property keys. The following code shows how this is added in the `serverless.yml` file:

```
provider:
    name: aws
      stage: ${opt:stage, 'dev'}
```

In the following statement, we pass the parameter to the CLI and the `stage` value is populated in the `serverless.yml` file:

```
$ serverless deploy --stage qa
```

The variables can be used recursively as reference properties—that is, we can combine multiple values and variable sources, as shown in the following environment variable:

```
environment: SERV_SECRET:
${file(../config.${self:provider.stage}.json):CREDS}
```

We can reference environment variables as well (as shown in the following code), but it is insecure to add sensitive data to environment variables, because they can be accessed through build logs or in the serverless CloudFormation templates:

```
functions:
    myfunction:
        name: ${env:FUNC_PREFIX}-myfunction
        handler: handler.myfunction
```

Let's look at a few tutorials for doing this. Make sure that you have the latest Serverless Framework installed and working:

1. Create a simple `hello` project with the Serverless AWS template, then open this project in your favorite editor:

    ```
    $ serverless create --template aws-nodejs --path env-variable-
    service
    ```

2. Replace the `serverless.yml` file and handler, as shown in the following code. Here, we are adding an environment variable by the name of MY_VAR, and in the handler, we display the environment variable in the message output:

    ```
    $ cat serverless.yml
    service: env-variable-service
    # You can pin your service to only deploy with a specific
    Serverless version
     # Check out our docs for more details
     # frameworkVersion: "=X.X.X"
    provider:
        name: aws
        runtime: nodejs6.10
    # you can define service wide environment variables here
        environment:
            MY_VAR: Lion
        functions:
            hello:
                handler: handler.hello
     $ less handler.js
    'use strict';
    module.exports.hello = (event, context, callback) => {
    const response = {
      statusCode: 200,
      body: JSON.stringify({
        message: `my favourite animal is ${process.env.MY_VAR}`,
        input: event,
      }),
    };
    ```

```
callback(null, response);
};
```

3. Let's invoke locally and look at the result. If you look in the message section, you can see the value of the environment variable that we defined, as shown in the following code:

```
$ serverless invoke local -f hello
{
"statusCode": 200,
"body": "{\"message\":\"my favourite animal is
Lion\",\"input\":\"\"}"
}
```

As we discussed earlier for nonsensitive data, adding a variable into the `serverless.yml` file should be fine, but how do we add sensitive data into an environment variable, like a database connection. Let's look into the steps needed to do this:

1. Create a new file in the `env-variable-service` folder and name it `serverless.env.yml`. Then add the following details into it, as shown in the following code. Here, we are creating a secret variable as per the environment:

```
$ less serverless.env.yml
dev:
    MYSECRET_VAR: 'It is at secret den'
```

2. Let's add one more environment variable in the `serverless.yml` file, but this time the value will be pulled from the file, so you need to add the highlighted line as the environment variable. This way, Serverless Framework will read through the file and refer it to the specific environment:

```
# serverless.yml
 # you can define service wide environment variables here
environment:
    MY_VAR: Lion
    MYSECRET_VAR: ${file(./serverless.env.yml):dev.MYSECRET_VAR}
```

3. Let's change the response of the handler to display the secret through the message. Ideally, we should be displaying the secret over the screen, but for this tutorial, I am doing it manually. So let's replace the message body with the one displayed in the following code:

```
# handler.js
message: `my favourite animal is ${process.env.MY_VAR} and
${process.env.MYSECRET_VAR}`,
```

4. Invoke the function locally and look at the output:

```
$ serverless invoke local -f hello
{
"statusCode": 200,
"body": "{\"message\":\"my favourite animal is Lion and It is at
secret den\",\"input\":\"\"}"
}
```

Finally, like I said, we can have multiple environment variables for each deployment stage, such as dev, sit,uat, and prod. The following steps show us how we can add them:

1. Let's add one more environment variable for prod to the serverless.env.yml file. Then, we can use them dynamically within the serverless.yml file, as shown in the following code:

```
$ less serverless.env.yml
dev:
    MYSECRET_VAR: 'It is at secret dev den'
prod:
    MYSECRET_VAR: 'It is at secret prod den'
```

2. Now, we need to makes changes to the serverless.yml file to dynamically pick up the environment variable on the basis of the stage that we set at the time of the invocation or deployment of the function, which is the replacement of the MYSECRET_VAR line with the following line:

```
#serverless.yml
MYSECRET_VAR:
${file(./serverless.env.yml):${opt:stage}.MYSECRET_VAR}
```

3. We will now invoke the function locally and look at the output for a different stage:

```
$ serverless invoke local -f hello -s dev
{
"statusCode": 200,
"body": "{\"message\":\"my favourite animal is Lion and It is at
secret dev den\",\"input\":\"\"}"
}

$ serverless invoke local -f hello -s prod
{
"statusCode": 200,
"body": "{\"message\":\"my favourite animal is Lion and It is at
secret Prod den\",\"input\":\"\"}"
}
```

I have uploaded the preceding tutorials into the following GitHub repository as well, so you can use them at your leisure:
`https://github.com/shzshi/env-variable-service.git`

The plugins are custom JavaScript code that provide extension to existing CLI commands within Serverless Framework. The framework itself is a group of plugins that is provided in the core. We can build our own custom plugin; Serverless Framework provides documentation for this plugin as well. The plugin can be installed using the following code:

```
$ npm install --save custom-serverless-plugin
```

We also need to call them within the `serverless` service, using the following code:

```
serverless.yml file
 plugins:
    - custom-serverless-plugin
```

A list of existing Serverless plugins can be found at the following link:
`https://github.com/serverless/plugins`

Resources

When we create Lambda functions, they might be dependent on many different types of infrastructure resources, such as AWS, DynamoDB or AWS S3, so we can define these resources within the `serverless.yml` file and deploy them. When we add these resources, they get added to the `serverless.yml` file, and when they are deployed, they get added to the CloudFormation stack and are executed at serverless deploy. We can look at the following example to see how these resources are defined:

```
resources:
  Resources:
    NewResource:
        Type: AWS::S3::Bucket
        Properties:
          BucketName: my-s3-bucket
```

You can refer to the following link for more details on resources and to see which resources are available using only AWS Lambda: `https://serverless.com/framework/docs/providers/aws/guide/resources/`

Let's look at a simple example of Serverless Framework using AWS Lambda. You will need the following prerequisites for this:

- A free AWS account needs to be created
- Nodejs 4.0 and higher must be installed on the local machine
- AWS CLI can also be installed, but this is optional

Setting up AWS access keys

Go through the following steps:

1. Log in to the AWS account and go to the **IAM (Identity & Access Management)** page.
2. Click on **Users** on the left-hand side bar, then click on the **Add User** button and add the username `adm-serverless`. Then enable **programmatic access** by clicking the checkbox. Then click on the **Next:Premissions** button.
3. On this page, select **Attach existing policies directly**, search for and select the **AdministratorAccess** checkbox, then click on **Next:Review**.
4. Now check whether everything is good, then click **Create User**. This will create a user and show us the access key ID and secret access key. Copy and store these keys somewhere, temporarily.

5. Now that we have the keys, we export them as an environment variable so that they will be accessed by the framework to perform their required function:

   ```
   $ export AWS_ACCESS_KEY_ID=<access-key-id>
   $ export AWS_SECRET_ACCESS_KEY=<secret-key-id>
   ```

Installation of Serverless Framework

Go through the following steps:

1. Install Node.js 4.0 or higher from `https://nodejs.org/en/download/`. Once installed, we can verify installation through the following command:

   ```
   $ node --version
   ```

2. Now we need to install Serverless Framework globally through the following command:

```
$ npm install -g serverless
```

3. Once installed successfully, we can verify the installation by using the following command. It will show all the framework commands and documentation:

```
$ serverless
```

4. We can also see the version of Serverless Framework installed by using the following command:

```
$ serverless --version
```

Lambda service and function deployment

In the following step, we will be create a simple Node.js service and Lambda function, and then deploy and invoke them:

1. Create a new service using the Node.js template by Serverless Framework. We need to make sure that the name is unique and add the path to the service, which is optional. This command will create two files—handler.js and serverless.yml:

```
$ serverless create --template aws-nodejs --path my-serverless-
service
Serverless: Generating boilerplate...
 Serverless: Generating boilerplate in
"/Users/shashi/Documents/packt/chapter2/serverless/my-serverless-
service"
 _____ __
| _ .-----.----.--.--.-----.----| .-----.-----.-----.
| |___| -__| _| | | -__| _| | -__|__ --|__ --|
|____ |_____|__| \___/|_____|__| |__|_____|_____|_____|
| | | The Serverless Application Framework
| | serverless.com, v1.26.1
 _____'
Serverless: Successfully generated boilerplate for template: "aws-
nodejs"
```

A service is the framework's unit of organization. It can be considered as a project file. It's where we can define functions, the events that trigger them, and the resources of the function that we will use. All of these are placed into one file serverless.yml. In this .yaml file, we define the service called my-serverless-service. Then we define the provider; as I mentioned earlier, Serverless Framework supports a lot of other cloud service providers. We can list the provider details in this tag and also mention the runtime, which in our case is Node.js. The runtime will change depending on the language we use to write the function. We can define the environment or stage we are deploying to—which in our case is dev—as well as the respective region. Then, in the functions section, we define the function name—which in our case is hello—which has an attribute called handler, and this handler will call the handler.js file. We can also define the memory size. Next, I have added an HTTP event, which, in addition to the Lambda function, provisions the AWS API Gateway. It will create and provide an endpoint for the handler. So, using one script, we can provision a Lambda function and an API endpoint. We can define various other attributes and parameters; we will look into these in more detail in the next chapter.

> Please make sure the .yaml files are properly indented, otherwise they will fail. You can also use the one that I have put on the following GitHub link:
> https://github.com/shzshi/my-serverless-service.git

```
$ cat serverless.yml
# Welcome to Serverless!
#
# This file is the main config file for your service.
# It's very minimal at this point and uses default values.
# You can always add more config options for more control.
# We've included some commented out config examples here.
# Just uncomment any of them to get that config option.
#
# For full config options, check the docs:
# docs.serverless.com
#
# Happy Coding!
service: my-serverless-service
# You can pin your service to only deploy with a specific Serverless
version
# Check out our docs for more details
# frameworkVersion: "=X.X.X"
provider:
name: aws
runtime: nodejs6.10
stage: dev
region: us-east-1
functions:
```

```
hello:
handler: handler.hello
memorySize: 128
events:
- http:
path: handler
method: get
```

The `handler.js` code phrase is the Node.js Lambda function for `Hello, World!`, which is referenced in the `serverless.yml` file. It is a pretty simple function that will just display the message `My Serverless World` on execution, as shown in the following code:

```
$ cat handler.js
'use strict';
module.exports.hello = (event, context, callback) => {
const response = {
statusCode: 200,
body: JSON.stringify({
message: 'My Serverless World',
input: event,
}),
};
callback(null, response);
// Use this code if you don't use the http event with the LAMBDA-PROXY
integration
// callback(null, { message: 'Go Serverless v1.0! Your function executed
successfully!', event });
};
```

Invoking locally

Pushing the code to AWS Lambda and testing every time would be expensive and time consuming. So with Serverless Framework, we can invoke or test functions locally and then deploy them to the cloud. We can have this as part of the continuous deployment pipeline, where we can set the local invocation for `dev` stage deployment, set up automated testing, and then move them further down the pipeline to deploy and test remotely. The following command is used to invoke the function locally:

```
$ serverless invoke local --function hello
{
"statusCode": 200,
"body": "{\"message\":\"My Serverless World\",\"input\":\"\"}"
}
```

Deploying and invoking locally

As we are now able to successfully invoke and test the function locally, we should be fine to deploy and test it remotely. First, we need to make sure that we have retrieved and exported the access and secret access keys as environment variables, as shown in the following code:

```
$ export AWS_ACCESS_KEY_ID=<access-key-id>
$ export AWS_SECRET_ACCESS_KEY=<secret-key-id>
```

Now I am deploying the function and API to the AWS Cloud through a simple `deploy` command. Behind the scenes, the deployment process will create a `.serverless` folder with `CloudFormation` JSON templates. The serverless code is packaged into a `.zip` file and a serverless state JSON file. If we look into the `create-stack` JSON template, Serverless Framework will create an S3 bucket on the AWS Cloud and deploy the function and API package on to the bucket with the `CloudFormation` template JSON file. It will also keep the state of the deployment in the form of a JSON file. The successful deployment will provision an API endpoint that is tied to an AWS Lambda function and creates a service as mentioned in the provider:

```
$ serverless deploy

  Serverless: Packaging service...
  Serverless: Excluding development dependencies...
  Serverless: Creating Stack...
  Serverless: Checking Stack create progress...
  .....
  Serverless: Stack create finished...
  Serverless: Uploading CloudFormation file to S3...
  Serverless: Uploading artifacts...
  Serverless: Uploading service .zip file to S3 (417 B)...
  Serverless: Validating template...
  Serverless: Updating Stack...
  Serverless: Checking Stack update progress...
  .............................
  Serverless: Stack update finished...
  Service Information
  service: my-serverless-service
  stage: dev
  region: us-east-1
  stack: my-serverless-service-dev
  api keys:
  None
  endpoints:
  GET - https://kn6esoolgi.execute-api.us-east-1.amazonaws.com/dev/handler
```

```
functions:
hello: my-serverless-service-dev-hello
```

Postdeployment, we will go to the AWS portal and see whether the function is deployed. Then we will invoke it through the portal and then again invoke the remote function through the serverless CLI, using the following steps:

1. Log in to the AWS portal, then select the correct region where the function and API was deployed.
2. Select the service as **Lambda**. The Lambda portal page will show the function name deployed. Select the function that you test using the radio button, then go to the drop-down marked **Actions** and select the option marked **Test**. The window will pop up to configure the event. You can add your own event or keep the default, and then click on **Save**. The event will be saved and the page will be redirected to the **Function** page. Now click on the **Test** button. The function will be executed, and the execution status and results will be displayed.

As I mentioned earlier, we can invoke the remote function locally as well. We will now look at the various commands for the remote Lambda function:

To invoke the function and get the logs, use the following command:

```
$ serverless invoke -f hello -l
{
"statusCode": 200,
"body": "{\"message\":\"My Serverless World\",\"input\":{}}"
}
--------------------------------------------------------------
START RequestId: c4bdc7f8-60e1-11e8-9846-f5267af11144 Version: $LATEST
END RequestId: c4bdc7f8-60e1-11e8-9846-f5267af11144
REPORT RequestId: c4bdc7f8-60e1-11e8-9846-f5267af11144 Duration: 44.37 ms
Billed Duration: 100 ms Memory Size: 128 MB Max Memory Used: 20 MB
```

To just get the logs for the previous invocation, enter the following code. We can do this in a separate console to test the working:

```
$ serverless logs -f hello -t
START RequestId: 75139847-60dc-11e8-8c0b-4f4996ceffb3 Version: $LATEST
END RequestId: 75139847-60dc-11e8-8c0b-4f4996ceffb3
REPORT RequestId: 75139847-60dc-11e8-8c0b-4f4996ceffb3 Duration: 9.04 ms
Billed Duration: 100 ms Memory Size: 128 MB Max Memory Used: 20 MB
START RequestId: 675574ec-60de-11e8-bbd5-8bf1c1e7f05c Version: $LATEST
END RequestId: 675574ec-60de-11e8-bbd5-8bf1c1e7f05c
REPORT RequestId: 675574ec-60de-11e8-bbd5-8bf1c1e7f05c Duration: 18.15 ms
Billed Duration: 100 ms Memory Size: 128 MB Max Memory Used: 20 MB
```

The command will undeploy the function from the Lambda and also remove the package details from the S3 bucket. Once `serverless remove` runs successfully (as shown in the following code), you can log in to the AWS portal and check the S3 bucket and the Lambda function for the specific region—it should be removed:

```
$ serverless remove
Serverless: Getting all objects in S3 bucket...
 Serverless: Removing objects in S3 bucket...
 Serverless: Removing Stack...
 Serverless: Checking Stack removal progress...
 .........
 Serverless: Stack removal finished...
```

Summary

In this chapter, we learned about different frameworks, such as ClaudiaJS, Zappa, and Apex. We also looked into a few examples of using them, but we mostly covered Serverless Framework extensively. We will be using Serverless Framework extensively in most of our tutorials while going through the book, because Serverless Framework fairs far better than other frameworks because it has better community support and support for multiple cloud providers. This means that you don't have vendor locking, as you do with some other frameworks. It also has a huge list of plugins for different types of cloud service, good blog support, and finally, some really good features for easy deployment into various different cloud providers.

3
Applying DevOps to AWS Lambda Applications

Let's briefly look at what we learned about AWS Lambda functions. Amazon Web Services was the first web service platform to launch the serverless computing module Lambda, written in **Lambda functions**. Lambda functions are stateless and have no affinity with the underlying infrastructure. Lambda functions are executed in response to the events. These events could be an HTTP request, a change of the data in the S3 bucket, a change in a DynamoDB table, or a change in Kinesis or SNS. Lambda functions replicate faster in response to events, and descale as the number of events goes down.

In this chapter, we will be covering various methods of deploying Lambda functions, looking at how we can painlessly deploy to multiple environments, unit test, system test, and integration test the Lambda function. We will also learn various deployment best practices and go through a few example recipes using these best practices. We will see how we can manage the AWS Lambda logs and move them to the ELK stack.

We will explore the following topics in this chapter:

- Manual deployment of a Lambda function
- AWS Lambda with DevOps
- Serverless with CodeStar
- Blue and green deployment with AWS Lambda
- The GitHub and Jenkins pipeline using Serverless Framework
- Setting up Jenkins for a serverless application
- Unit testing a deployed application
- Integrating CloudWatch with ELK

I will be creating a simple application that is used in our day-to-day work. The application is a thumbnail creator, and is a Node.js application that uses two S3 buckets. One bucket is for uploading the actual images and the other is for the thumbnails. The moment an image is uploaded into the images bucket, an event is triggered that calls a function to resize the image and upload it to the thumbnails bucket. We will first look at how we can manually execute this sequence of events, and then we will learn how we can streamline the process by automating the deployment process. In the section dealing with DevOps, we will talk about setting up an assembly line with the development environment, automated testing and deployment, applying a CI/CD pipeline, logging, and monitoring.

Manual deployment of a Lambda function

The Node.js Lambda application that we will be using here is already part of AWS tutorials. We will learn how to create, deploy, and execute a Lambda application via the AWS portal. The prerequisite for this tutorial is for you to have an AWS account; we will be using a free AWS subscription throughout this chapter. The next step is to set up AWS CLI.

> You can create an AWS free account and an AWS CLI through the
> following links:
> `https://portal.aws.amazon.com/billing/signup#/start`
> `https://docs.aws.amazon.com/cli/latest/userguide/cli-chap-`
> `welcome.html`

Go through the following steps:

1. Once the AWS account and CLIs are in place, sign in to AWS Console (`https://aws.amazon.com/console/`), and then we will create an IAM user with the name `adminuser` by logging into your AWS account then either clicking on the IAM link or searching for the link through the services:

2. Then we click on the **Users** link on the left-hand side, where a new page will open. Then we click on **Add User**. Add a user with the name **adminuser** and select both the access type **Programmatic access** and **AWS Management Console access**. In the console's **Password** field, add your custom password, uncheck the **Require password reset** checkbox, and then click **Next:Permissions**. Let's create a group by clicking on the **Create Group** button. We will give the group the name of administrators. Next, let's select the **AdminstrativeAccess** checkbox to provide full access to the group and then click on **Create Group**. Now that we have a group created, let's click on **Next:Review**. Then, we will review the user, which the user have created and has been added to the administrator group. Now click on the **Create User** button. Once the user is created, we should be able to see the user in the list, as shown in the following screenshot:

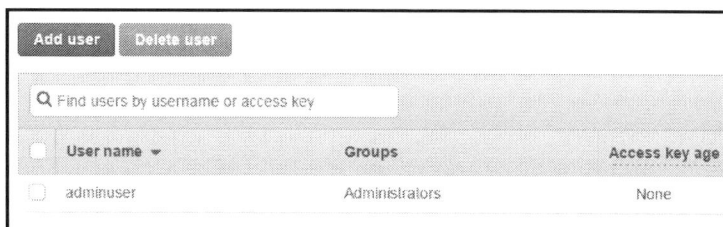

Add user	Delete user	
Q Find users by username or access key		
User name ▾	Groups	Access key age
adminuser	Administrators	None

> We have created a user with administrative rights just for our tutorials, but in the real world the role and policies will be more restricted for the sake of security.

3. We need to create two buckets in AWS S3. The buckets need to be created through the adminuser login, so let's log in to AWS Console using the new user that we have created. Click on the **adminuser** and select the **Security credentials** tab. Next, let's copy the Console URL for logging in, then open it on the new browser tab. Feed in the username and password for the new user that we have created and click on **Sign In**. Once you are logged in, search for **S3** in the **AWS Services**. Then go to **S3 Console Management** and click on the **Create bucket** button, as shown in the following screenshot:

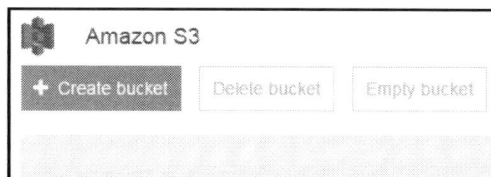

Amazon S3

+ Create bucket | Delete bucket | Empty bucket

Let's add a unique bucket and region name of **US East** by default. The two buckets should be named `Source` and `SourceResized`. Source is the placeholder name that should be replaced with the actual bucket name—for example, `my-image-bucket76` and `my-image-bucket76resized`. So, `my-image-bucket76` will be the source bucket and `my-image-bucket76resized` will be the target bucket, as shown in the following screenshot:

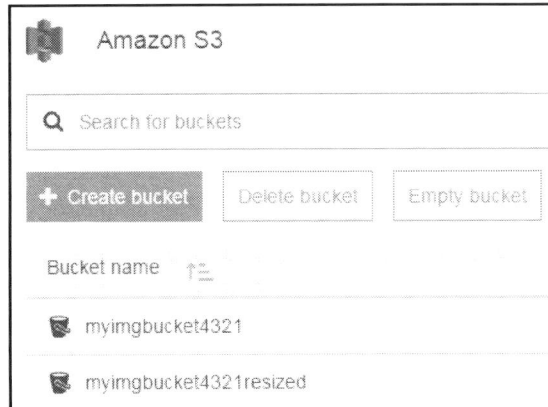

The bucket name must be unique, as AWS allows only universally unique bucket names.

4. Once both the buckets are successfully created, we can upload an image for the Lambda function to resize and push to the resized bucket. Let's upload a JPG image into the `my-source-bucket76` source. Click on the bucket name, then upload an image to this bucket. This will redirect you to the bucket page. Click on the **Upload** button and a popup will pop up. Then, select **Add files** to browse for an image file from the local directory and then upload the image to the S3 bucket.

5. The next step is to create a Lambda function and run it manually. Here, we have to first follow three steps to create the deployment package, and then create the execution role (IAM role) and a Lambda function and test them. The deployment package is a ZIP file containing the Lambda function and its dependencies:

   - Let's create a deployment package. I will be using Node.js as the language for this practice application, but we can use Java and Python as well (it depends on the developer's preference).

- A prerequisite for creating this deployment package is to have Node.js version 6.0 (`https://nodejs.org/en/download/`) or later installed on you local environment. You should also make sure that npm is installed.
- Then go through the following steps. We are downloading the npm libraries for the image resizing of the Node.js Lambda function, using the first of the two following commands. The second command will download the required libraries:

```
$ mkdir tutorial1; cd tutorial1
$ npm install async gm
```

  - Open your favorite editor and copy the following script into the file named `CreateThumbnails.js`:

```
// dependencies
var async = require('async');
var AWS = require('aws-sdk');
var gm = require('gm')
            .subClass({ imageMagick: true }); // Enable
ImageMagick integration.
var util = require('util');
// constants
var MAX_WIDTH  = 100;
var MAX_HEIGHT = 100;
// get reference to S3 client
var s3 = new AWS.S3();
exports.handler = function(event, context, callback) {
    // Read options from the event.
    console.log("Reading options from event:\n",
util.inspect(event, {depth: 5}));
    var srcBucket = event.Records[0].s3.bucket.name;
    // Object key may have spaces or unicode non-ASCII
characters.
    var srcKey    =
decodeURIComponent(event.Records[0].s3.object.key.replace(/
\+/g, " "));
    var dstBucket = srcBucket + "resized";
    var dstKey    = "resized-" + srcKey;
```

You can find the gist for `CreateThumbnails.js` at `https://gist.github.com/shzshi/6e1cf435a4c1aa979e3a9a243c13c44a`.

- As a sanity check, validate that the source and destination are different buckets:

```
if (srcBucket == dstBucket) {
    callback("Source and destination buckets are the
same.");
    return;
}
```

- Infer the image type:

```
var typeMatch = srcKey.match(/\.([^.]*)$/);
    if (!typeMatch) {
        callback("Could not determine the image type.");
        return;
    }
    var imageType = typeMatch[1];
    if (imageType != "jpg" && imageType != "png") {
        callback('Unsupported image type: ${imageType}');
        return;
    }
```

- Download the image from S3, transform it, and upload it to a different S3 bucket:

```
async.waterfall([
        function download(next) {
            // Download the image from S3 into a buffer.
            s3.getObject({
                    Bucket: srcBucket,
                    Key: srcKey
                },
                next);
            },
        function transform(response, next) {
            gm(response.Body).size(function(err, size) {
```

- Infer the scaling factor to avoid stretching the image unnaturally:

```
var scalingFactor = Math.min(
                    MAX_WIDTH / size.width,
                    MAX_HEIGHT / size.height
                );
                var width  = scalingFactor * size.width;
                var height = scalingFactor * size.height;
```

- Transform the image buffer in memory:

```
this.resize(width, height)
                .toBuffer(imageType, function(err,
buffer) {
                    if (err) {
                        next(err);
                    } else {
                        next(null,
response.ContentType, buffer);
                    }
                });
        });
    },
    function upload(contentType, data, next) {
```

- Stream the transformed image to a different S3 bucket:

```
s3.putObject({
                Bucket: dstBucket,
                Key: dstKey,
                Body: data,
                ContentType: contentType
            },
            next);
        }
    ], function (err) {
        if (err) {
            console.error(
                'Unable to resize ' + srcBucket + '/' +
srcKey +
                ' and upload to ' + dstBucket + '/' +
dstKey +
                ' due to an error: ' + err
            );
        } else {
            console.log(
                'Successfully resized ' + srcBucket +
'/' + srcKey
+
                ' and uploaded to ' + dstBucket + '/' +
dstKey
            );
        }
        callback(null, "message");
    }
    );
};
```

Now we should see two items in our `tutorials1` folder, namely the `CreateThumbnail.js` and `node_modules` folders. Let's zip all these into a file named `tutorialsimg.zip`. This will be our Lambda function deployment package:

```
$ cd tutorials1
$ zip -r ../tutorialsimg.zip *
```

6. Next, we will create the execution role for the Lambda function in IAM. Log into AWS Console, search for **IAM services**, and then go into IAM and click on the **Roles** button. Click on **Create Role**, select the **AWS service,** and then choose **Lambda** as the service. Then click on the **Next: Permission** button. Then search for **AWSLambda** in the **Policy Type** box and check the **AWSLambdaExecute** checkbox. Then search for **AmazonS3FullAccess** and select it. Then click on the **Next:Review** button. Next, on the **Create Role** page, add the role name **myLambdaRole**, add a description, and then click on **Create Role**. Now we have the role that contains the policies that we can use to execute the Lambda function in order to make changes to the content of the S3 bucket.

7. The next step is to deploy the Lambda functions and node modules on the AWS Lambda portal. Let's go to the AWS Console's home page, and under **Services**, let's search for Lambda. We will be redirected to the Lambda home page. Click on **Create Function**, then choose **Author from scratch** in the **Functions Information** section. Let's add the function name of `myfirstLambdafunction`, **Runtime** as **Node.js 6.10**. Choose the existing role name of **myLambdaRole** and click on **Create Function**. Now we will be redirected to the Lambda function designer page. We will upload our Lambda function to the portal. Scroll down a bit and go to the **Function Code** section, then select **Code entry type** as **Upload a .ZIP file**, **Runtime** as **Node.js 6.10**, and type into the **Handler** field the text **CreateThumbnail.handler**. Now let's click on the **Upload** button, select the file named **tutorialsimg.zip** and upload it. Once the package is uploaded successfully, we should be able to see the **CreateThumbnail.js** file in the function editor with the **node_modules** folder, as shown in the following screenshot:

8. Now that the function and node modules are uploaded, we will create an event to trigger the function. If we scroll to the top right-hand side of the screen, we will see a drop-down menu appear that we can use to add the event. Select **Configure Test Events.** A pop-up box will appear. Give the event the name of `myThumbnailEvent` and in the text field, add the following listed JSON file. Make sure that you replace `my-source-bucket76` with your source bucket's name and `Baby.jpg` with your image name. Then go ahead and click **Save**:

> 8. You can find the event JSON file at `https://gist.github.com/shzshi/7a498513ae43b6572c219843bbba277d`.

```
{
  "Records": [
    {
      "eventVersion": "2.0",
      "eventSource": "aws:s3",
      "awsRegion": "us-west-2",
      "eventTime": "1970-01-01T00:00:00.000Z",
      "eventName": "ObjectCreated:Put",
      "userIdentity": {
        "principalId": "AIDAJDPLRKLG7UEXAMPLE"
      },
      "requestParameters": {
        "sourceIPAddress": "127.0.0.1"
      },
      "responseElements": {
```

```
          "x-amz-request-id": "C3D13FE58DE4C810",
          "x-amz-id-2":
"FMyUVURIY8/IgAtTv8xRjskZQpcIZ9KG4V5Wp6S7S/JRWeUWerMUE5JgHvANOjpD"
        },
        "s3": {
          "s3SchemaVersion": "1.0",
          "configurationId": "testConfigRule",
          "bucket": {
            "name": "my-source-bucket76",
            "ownerIdentity": {
              "principalId": "A3NL1KOZZKExample"
            },
            "arn": "arn:aws:s3:::my-source-bucket76"
          },
          "object": {
            "key": "Baby.jpg",
            "size": 1024,
            "eTag": "d41d8cd98f00b204e9800998ecf8427e",
            "versionId": "096fKKXTRTtl3on89fVO.nfljtsv6qko"
          }
        }
      }
    ]
  }
```

9. Now we have deployed the function, and have created S3 buckets and an event. Now let's invoke the function and see if our image in the source bucket is resized and pushed to the resized S3 bucket. To do this, click on **Test**. We should see that the function has successfully executed in the logs (as shown in the following log text). If you refresh the resized named S3 bucket, you should be able to see resized image file. You can just download the resized file and see whether the resizing worked. We can also add the S3 put trigger to automatically trigger this CreateThumbnail function when any image file is uploaded to the source S3 bucket.

eTag: 'd41d8cd98f00b204e9800998ecf8427e', versionId: '096fKKXTRTtl3on89fVO.nfljtsv6qko' } } }] } 2018-06-14T21:07:25.469Z ea822830-7016-11e8-b407-9514918aacd8

Successfully resized my-source-bucket76/Baby.jpg and uploaded to my-source-bucket76resized/resized-Baby.jpg END RequestId: ea822830-7016-11e8-b407-9514918aacd8

In this exercise, we learned how to create, build, deploy, and invoke the Lambda function manually, and we had to go through number of steps to get this working. Now let's say that we need to deploy hundreds or thousands of such Lambda functions for a banking application to the portal. To do this task manually, we would require lots of resources and time. This is where DevOps comes in really handy to make our life faster and more easy. Let's look closer at how we can use DevOps to automate all of the steps involved and make it much simpler to build, test, and deploy our Lambda functions.

AWS Lambda with DevOps

To start implementing DevOps for AWS Lambda, we first create an assembly line. An assembly line outlines the stages involved when a developer creates code, tests the code, and then commits the code into a repository. The source code is pulled from the repository, and is then built and tested. After this, the static code analysis takes place. Once it is deployed into a production-like environment, acceptance tests are run against it. This is how the application is monitored, and how logging is managed. We will look at these stages using the recipes in this section. We will also look at two perspectives of DevOps—one through AWS's own set of tools, and the other through serverless frameworks, such as GitHub, Jenkins, Mocha (for testing), and JSHint (for source code analysis).

So the first step is to set up a local development environment where we can create a folder structure, add and change the source code, add images, and so on. We can run the source code locally, execute tests, and debug them for errors and failures. We will do this using a Node.js tutorial. We will set up a Node.js project from scratch with unit testing, source code analysis, and acceptance testing.

The Node.js application that I have created is a simple task manager. The underlying architecture is AWS Lambda functions with an API gateway to add, update, delete, and list the DynamoDB table. In short, we will be doing the `create`, `read`, `update`, and `delete` functions through AWS Lambda functions.

Serverless frameworks with AWS CodePipeline

As I have mentioned, our first approach will be through AWS's own DevOps tools. We will start with CodePipeline, which is an indigenous cloud-based tool of AWS that can help you to build, develop, and deploy applications quickly on AWS. We can set up continuous delivery very quickly with CodePipeline. It has its own dashboard, and it integrates easily with tools such as JIRA, Jenkins, GitHub, and other project-management tools. Let's look how we can use this for Lambda functions. We will be using the thumbnail application that was created earlier in the chapter.

The prerequisites for these recipes are as follows:

- **AWS account and login credentials for AWS Console:** Most of the setup for the first part of the tutorials will be done through AWS Console. We will using the same **adminuser** account that we created earlier in the chapter.
- **GitHub repository:** You need to create a repository and copy all the files and folders from the following repository into your repository: `https://github.com/shzshi/aws-lambda-thumbnail.git`
- **CloudFormation service role:** Go to the home page of AWS Console and search for **IAM.** On the **IAM** page, select **Roles** and then click on **Create role**. On the **Create role** page, select **AWS Service** and choose **CloudFormation** as the service. Then click on **Next:Permission**, and on the permission policy page, select the **AWSLambdaExecute** policy and click on **Next:Review**. Once the review page is open, name the role as `myCloudFormationRole` and then click on **Create role**. Now, for this service role, we need to add additional policies to execute the pipeline, so let's go to the roles. We will see our role in the list; let's click on it. In the **Role Summary** page, click on **Add inline policy**, and in the **Create Policy** page, click on the **JSON** tab and then replace the existing JSON script with the script within `cloudformationpolicy.json`, which is in the `aws-lambda-thumbnail` repository. Click on **Review policy**. Now let's name the policy `myThumbnailPipelinePolicy`, so that we have a service role for CloudFormation.
- **Bucket for the CloudFormation package:** We need to create a bucket for the CloudFormation package, so let's go to the home page of AWS Console and search for **S3** in services. Next, let's create a bucket with the name of **my-cloud-formation-bucket**. This bucket is used for packaging our artifacts when we run the pipeline.

Let's go through the following steps:

1. To add and retrieve CodeStar permission for the **adminuser**, go to AWS Console (`https://console.aws.amazon.com/console/home`) and log in with your root account credentials. This means that we need to log in as a free account user (we created this free account at the start of the chapter). If you go to the **adminuser** login page, you will see a link at the bottom named **Sign-in using root account credentials**. Once you are logged in, go to **IAM services** and click on **Users**. You should be able to see the **adminuser** in the list. Now click on the **adminuser** link to the **Security credentials** tab. Scroll down to find the **HTTPS Git credentials for AWS CodeCommit** section and click on the **Generate** button. The credentials to authenticate AWS CodeCommit will then be generated. Copy or download the credentials. If you have not copied the access key ID and the secret access key, please generate new ones using the **Create access key** button. Save the details for both of these somewhere for later use.

2. Let's now log into the console as **adminuser**. Search for **CodePipeline** from the home page. A page will open. On this page, click on **Create pipeline**. You will then be redirected to the **Create Pipeline** page. Let's name the pipeline **myServerlessThumbnailPipeline** and click on **Next Step**.

3. In **Source Provider**, let's select **GitHub**. We will then be asked to connect to GitHub; go ahead and connect using your credentials. The **Repository** should be the one that we created as a prerequisite, and the **Branch** should be the branch where our files are residing (for example, master). Once the details are added, click on **Next step**. While setting up **CodeBuild**, a role was created, so we need to add an extra policy for this.

4. In the **Build provider,** select **AWS CodeBuild**, and then in the **Configure your Project** section, select **Create a new build project**. Let's add the project details: The project name should be `myThumbnailCodeBuild`, the environment image should be **Use an image managed by AWS CodeBuild**, the operating system should be **Ubuntu**, the runtime should be **Node.js**, and the version should be **Node.js 6.3.1**. Keep the rest of the details as their default values and click on **Save build project**. We have successfully created a AWS CodeBuild project. However, it has also created a service role, and we need to add an additional policy for the CodeBuild project role. So let's open a new tab on the browser and log into AWS Console as **adminuser**. Then, in services, search for **IAM,** and on the **IAM** page, go to **Roles** and select the service role with the name **code-build-myThumbnailCodeBuild-service-role** or something similar.

Now click on **Add inline policy** and then click on the **Create Policy** page. Choose the **S3** service and the **PubObject** action from the **Write** access level, and select the **Resources** as **All resources**. Finally, click **Review Policy**. Name the policy `myThumbnailCodeBuildPolicy`. In the **Summary** section, we should be able to see S3. Click on **Create Policy**. Now we have a new policy for **S3** that has been added to the **CodeBuild** role. Let's go back to the create CodePipeline page. Click **Next step**.

5. In the **Deploy** template, let's set **Deployment provider** as **AWS CloudFormation**. Now that we're in the CloudFormation section, let's add all the details as shown in the following screenshot. The template file is basically an export file that will be used by CloudFormation:

AWS CloudFormation ⓘ

Configure your action to create, update CloudFormation stacks or change sets. Learn more

Action mode*	Create or replace a change set
Stack name*	mythumbnailstack
Change set name*	mythumbnailchangeset
Template file*	template-export.yml
Configuration file	configuration.json
Capabilities	CAPABILITY_IAM
Role name*	myCloudFormationRole

6. Next, we will create a role to give permission to the AWS CodePipeline to use the resources. Click on **Create role** and go through the steps as it prompts you. Once the role is created, click on **Next**. Then review the pipeline, and click on **Create pipeline**. Our pipeline will trigger automatically. Our first stages of the pipeline worked fine. If we go to CloudFormation (**Services | CloudFormation**), we should be able to see the stack for the thumbnail that was created. If you tick the checkbox and select the events, you should be able to see the events that ran, as well as some other details. Let's go ahead and add more stages to the pipeline that we can approve, and then deploy the function.

7. Now, we will edit the pipeline and add some stages to deploy the thumbnail Lambda function. Let's click on **Edit** and scroll to the bottom. Click on **+ Stage**. Let's add a stage called **Approval**, so that we can review and approve our work before deployment. Click on **Action** and select **approval** from the **Action** category of the drop-down list. Let's name it as Approval. We can also add an SNS topic to get approval emails. To do this, let's go ahead and use the default values for the rest and click on **Add action**.

8. The next stage to add is the deployment of the function from the Git repository to the Lambda function. Click on **+ Stage**. Let's add a stage named **Deploy**, click on **Action**, and select **Deploy** from the **Action** category drop-down list. Next, let's name the action **myDeploy** and select **AWS CloudFormation** as the **Deployment Provider**. In the **CloudFormation** section, let's add an action mode called **execute a change set** and select the stack name **mythumbnailstack** and the change set name **mythumbnailchangeset**. Let's leave the rest of the details as their defaults and click on **Add action**.

9. Now we have added two stages, let's save the pipeline by clicking **Save Pipelineline changes**. We will be asked to continue; let's go ahead and click **Save and Continue**. This time, the pipeline won't trigger automatically, so let's click on **Release change** to start the pipeline. Once the pipeline has successfully completed, we should see all the stages in green, as shown in the following screenshot:

myImgThumbnailPipeline
View pipeline history
View progress and manage your pipeline.
Edit
Release change
Source
Source
10e5adf
Source: this is t...
Build
CodeBuild
Details
Source: this is t...
Staging
mythumbnailstack
Details
Source: this is t...
Approval
Approval
Details
Source: this is t...
Deploy
myDeploy
Details
Source: this is t...

10. Let's check whether the function has been created, and try executing it. Let's go to the AWS Console home page and search for Lambda. We should be able to see that a **thumbnail** function has been created. Let's open the Lambda function. On the **Function** page, let's scroll to the top right-hand side of the page, where we will see a drop-down menu that we can use to add the event. Select **Configure Test Events**. A pop-up box will appear containing the name of the **myThumbnailEvent** event and a text field. In the text field, add the following JSON file. Make sure that you replace the `my-source-bucket76` with your source bucket name and `Baby.jpg` with your image name. Then go ahead and click on **Save**:

> The event JSON file can be found at
> https://gist.github.com/shzshi/7a498513ae43b6572c219843bbba277d.

11. Now we have deployed our function, and created our S3 buckets and an event. Let's invoke the function. Click on **Test**. Now you should see that the function has successfully executed. You will see the details in the logs, and if you refresh the S3 bucket named **resized**, we should be able to see a resized image file. You can just download the resized file and see whether the resizing worked. We can also add an S3 put trigger in order to automatically trigger this **CreateThumbnail** function when any image file is uploaded to the source S3 bucket.

In this tutorial, we learned how to use CodePipeline, which is a CD platform of AWS, to deploy Lambda functions. It was pretty quick in deploying a function from GitHub into Lambda using different combinations of tools by AWS. But the cons of these tools are that you are charged for their use, and we have to really get our heads around CloudFormation and the roles. Now let's look at how to set up a pipeline using open source tools.

Continuous integration and continuous deployment with Lambda

In this section, we will be using Jenkins, a serverless framework, and other open source software to set up Continuous Integration and Continuous Deployment. I have the whole project set up in a Git repository (`https://github.com/shzshi/aws-lambda-dynamodb-mytasks.git`), or we can go through the following steps listed in this section.

The application that we are using for this tutorial will create a Lambda function and an AWS API gateway for the task where we can test our Lambda function, which will manage tasks using CRUD operations to DynamoDB.

First, let's create a folder structure using a serverless framework to create a template function, as shown in the following code. I am assuming that you are using Linux Terminal, and that all the instructions are Linux-Terminal-based:

```
$ serverless create --template aws-nodejs --path AWSLambdaMyTask
$ cd AWSLambdaMyTask
```

We will see three files created within the AWSLambdaMyTask folder. This is a sample template for Node.js using a serverless framework. We will be modifying these files as per our example's need, as shown in the following code:

```
$ ls -la
total 10
drwxr-xr-x 1 417910 1049089    0 Nov 12 13:24 ./
drwxr-xr-x 1 417910 1049089    0 Nov 12 13:24 ../
-rw-r--r-- 1 417910 1049089   86 Nov 12 13:24 .gitignore
-rw-r--r-- 1 417910 1049089  466 Nov 12 13:24 handler.js
-rw-r--r-- 1 417910 1049089 2820 Nov 12 13:24 serverless.yml
```

1. Let's create two more folders within the AWSLambdaMyTask folder, namely src and test. The src phrase is our source code folder and test is the folder for our test cases, as shown in the following code:

    ```
    $ mkdir test
    $ mkdir src
    ```

2. Then we will create a file called package.json using the editor. This file will hold the metadata that is relevant to the project. Copy the following content into the file. Please make whatever changes you need:

    ```
    {
      "name": "AWS-serverless-with-dynamodb",
      "version": "1.0.0",
      "description": "Serverless CRUD service exposing a REST HTTP interface",
      "author": "Shashikant Bangera",
      "dependencies": {
        "uuid": "^3.0.1"
      },
      "keywords": [
        "AWS",
        "Deployment",
    ```

```
      "CD/CI",
      "serverless",
      "task"
    ],
    "repository": {
      "type": "git",
      "url": ""
    },
    "bugs": {
      "url": ""
    },
    "author": "Shashikant Bangera <shzshi@gmail.com>",
    "license": "MIT",
    "devDependencies": {
      "AWS-sdk": "^2.6.7",
      "request": "^2.79.0",
      "mocha": "^3.2.0",
      "serverless": "^1.7.0"
  },
    "scripts": {
      "test": "./node_modules/.bin/mocha"
    }
  }
```

3. Let's edit the `serverless.yml` file, as per our needs, as shown in the following snippet. You can find the file in the mentioned GitHub repo: https://github. com/shzshi/aws-lambda-dynamodb-mytasks/blob/master/serverless.yml:

```
# Welcome to Serverless!
#
# This file is the main config file for your service.
# It's very minimal at this point and uses default values.
# You can always add more config options for more control.
# We've included some commented out config examples here.
# Just uncomment any of them to get that config option.
#
# For full config options, check the docs:
#    docs.serverless.com
#
# Happy Coding!
service: AWSLambdaMyTask
frameworkVersion: ">=1.1.0 <2.0.0"
provider:
  name: AWS
  runtime: nodejs4.3
  environment:
    DYNAMODB_TABLE: ${self:service}-${opt:stage,
self:provider.stage}
```

```
      iamRoleStatements:
        - Effect: Allow
          Action:
            - dynamodb:Query
            - dynamodb:Scan
            - dynamodb:GetItem
            - dynamodb:PutItem
            - dynamodb:UpdateItem
            - dynamodb:DeleteItem
          Resource: "arn:AWS:dynamodb:${opt:region,
self:provider.region}:*:table/${self:provider.environment.DYNAMODB_
TABLE}"
functions:
  create:
    handler: src/mytasks/create.create
---
  list:
    handler: src/mytasks/list.list
---
  get:
    handler: src/mytasks/get.get
---
  update:
    handler: src/mytasks/update.update
---
  delete:
    handler: src/mytasks/delete.delete
---
resources:
  Resources:
    mytasksDynamoDbTable:
      Type: 'AWS::DynamoDB::Table'
      DeletionPolicy: Retain
      Properties:
        AttributeDefinitions:
          -
            AttributeName: id
            AttributeType: S
        KeySchema:
          -
            AttributeName: id
            KeyType: HASH
        ProvisionedThroughput:
          ReadCapacityUnits: 1
          WriteCapacityUnits: 1
        TableName: ${self:provider.environment.DYNAMODB_TABLE}
```

4. Let's move the `src` directory, and create a file named `package.json` and a folder named `mytasks`, as shown in the following code. The `mytasks` folder will have Node.js files to create, delete, get, list, and update the DynamoDB table on the AWS:

```
$ cd src
$ mkdir mytasks
$ vim package.json
```

5. Copy the following content to `package.json`:

```
{
  "name": "src",
  "version": "1.0.0",
  "description": "",
  "main": "index.js",
  "scripts": {
    "test": "echo \"Error: no test specified\" && exit 1"
  },
  "keywords": [],
  "author": "",
  "license": "MIT",
  "dependencies": {
    "uuid": "^2.0.3"
  }
}
```

Go to the `mytasks` folder and create a `create.js` file to create, update, list, get, and delete the DynamoDB tables. The `create.js` files are handlers for functions in Lambda.

6. Add the following content to `src\mytasks\create.js`:

```
'use strict';
const uuid = require('uuid');
const AWS = require('AWS-sdk');
const dynamoDb = new AWS.DynamoDB.DocumentClient();
module.exports.create = (event, context, callback) => {
  const timestamp = new Date().getTime();
  const data = JSON.parse(event.body);
  if (typeof data.text !== 'string') {
    console.error('Validation Failed');
    callback(null, {
      statusCode: 400,
      headers: { 'Content-Type': 'text/plain' },
      body: 'Couldn\'t create the task item.',
    });
```

```
        return;
      }
      const params = {
        TableName: process.env.DYNAMODB_TABLE,
        Item: {
          id: uuid.v1(),
          text: data.text,
          checked: false,
          createdAt: timestamp,
          updatedAt: timestamp,
        },
      };
      // write the task to the database
      dynamoDb.put(params, (error) => {
        // handle potential errors
        if (error) {
          console.error(error);
          callback(null, {
            statusCode: error.statusCode || 501,
            headers: { 'Content-Type': 'text/plain' },
            body: 'Couldn\'t create the task item.',
          });
          return;
        }
        // create a response
        const response = {
          statusCode: 200,
          body: JSON.stringify(params.Item),
        };
        callback(null, response);
      });
    };
```

7. Add the following content to `src\mytasks\delete.js`:

```
'use strict';
const AWS = require('AWS-sdk'); // eslint-disable-line import/no-
extraneous-dependencies
const dynamoDb = new AWS.DynamoDB.DocumentClient();
module.exports.delete = (event, context, callback) => {
  const params = {
    TableName: process.env.DYNAMODB_TABLE,
    Key: {
      id: event.pathParameters.id,
    },
  };
  // delete the task from the database
  dynamoDb.delete(params, (error) => {
```

```
      // handle potential errors
      if (error) {
        console.error(error);
        callback(null, {
          statusCode: error.statusCode || 501,
          headers: { 'Content-Type': 'text/plain' },
          body: 'Couldn\'t remove the task item.',
        });
        return;
      }
      // create a response
      const response = {
statusCode: 200,
        body: JSON.stringify({}),
      };
      callback(null, response);
    });
  };
```

8. Add the following content to src\mytasks\get.js:

```
'use strict';
const AWS = require('AWS-sdk'); // eslint-disable-line import/no-
extraneous-dependencies
const dynamoDb = new AWS.DynamoDB.DocumentClient();
module.exports.get = (event, context, callback) => {
  const params = {
    TableName: process.env.DYNAMODB_TABLE,
    Key: {
      id: event.pathParameters.id,
    },
  };
  // fetch task from the database
  dynamoDb.get(params, (error, result) => {
    // handle potential errors
if (error) {
      console.error(error);
      callback(null, {
        statusCode: error.statusCode || 501,
        headers: { 'Content-Type': 'text/plain' },
        body: 'Couldn\'t fetch the task item.',
      });
      return;
    }
    // create a response
    const response = {
      statusCode: 200,
      body: JSON.stringify(result.Item),
```

```
      };
      callback(null, response);
    });
  };
```

9. Add the following content to `src\mytasks\list.js`:

```javascript
'use strict';
const AWS = require('AWS-sdk'); // eslint-disable-line import/no-
extraneous-dependencies
const dynamoDb = new AWS.DynamoDB.DocumentClient();
const params = {
  TableName: process.env.DYNAMODB_TABLE,
};
module.exports.list = (event, context, callback) => {
  // fetch all tasks from the database
  dynamoDb.scan(params, (error, result) => {
    // handle potential errors
    if (error) {
      console.error(error);
      callback(null, {
        statusCode: error.statusCode || 501,
        headers: { 'Content-Type': 'text/plain' },
        body: 'Couldn\'t fetch the tasks.',
      });
      return;
    }
    // create a response
    const response = {
      statusCode: 200,
      body: JSON.stringify(result.Items),
    };
    callback(null, response);
  });
};
```

10. Add the following content to `src\mytasks\update.js`:

```javascript
'use strict';
const AWS = require('AWS-sdk'); // eslint-disable-line import/no-
extraneous-dependencies
const dynamoDb = new AWS.DynamoDB.DocumentClient();
module.exports.update = (event, context, callback) => {
  const timestamp = new Date().getTime();
  const data = JSON.parse(event.body);
  // validation
  if (typeof data.text !== 'string' || typeof data.checked !==
'boolean') {
```

```
      console.error('Validation Failed');
      callback(null, {
        statusCode: 400,
        headers: { 'Content-Type': 'text/plain' },
        body: 'Couldn\'t update the task item.',
      });
      return;
    }
  const params = {
    TableName: process.env.DYNAMODB_TABLE,
    Key: {
id: event.pathParameters.id,
    },
    ExpressionAttributeNames: {
      '#task_text': 'text',
    },
    ExpressionAttributeValues: {
      ':text': data.text,
      ':checked': data.checked,
      ':updatedAt': timestamp,     },
    UpdateExpression: 'SET #task_text = :text, checked = :checked,
updatedAt = :updatedAt',
    ReturnValues: 'ALL_NEW',
  };
  // update the task in the database
  dynamoDb.update(params, (error, result) => {
    // handle potential errors
    if (error) {
      console.error(error);
      callback(null, {
        statusCode: error.statusCode || 501,
        headers: { 'Content-Type': 'text/plain' },
        body: 'Couldn\'t fetch the task item.',
      });
      return;
    }
// create a response
    const response = {
      statusCode: 200,
      body: JSON.stringify(result.Attributes),
    };
    callback(null, response);
  });
};
```

Now we will create test cases to unit test the code that we created. We will be using Mocha for unit testing and run the APIs again. Let's create a file called `data` in the `test` folder, as shown in the following screenshot. This will have the JSON data that the unit test will run on:

```
$ mkdir test/data
```

11. Next, let's add the `test/createDelete.js` file, which will create DynamoDB data and delete it, once the test is complete, as shown in the following code:

```
var assert = require('assert');
var request = require('request');
var fs = require('fs');
describe('Create, Delete', function() {
        this.timeout(5000);
    it('should create a new Task, & delete it', function(done) {
                    // Build and log the path
                    var path = "https://" +
process.env.TASKS_ENDPOINT + "/mytasks";
                    // Fetch the comparison payload
                    require.extensions['.txt'] = function
(module, filename) {
                         module.exports =
fs.readFileSync(filename, 'utf8');
                    };
                    var desiredPayload =
require("./data/newTask1.json");
                    // Create the new Task
                    var options = {'url' : path, 'form':
JSON.stringify(desiredPayload)};
                    request.post(options, function (err, res,
body){
                             if(err){
                                    throw new
Error("Create call failed: " + err);
                             }
                             assert.equal(200,
res.statusCode, "Create Status Code != 200 (" + res.statusCode +
")");
                             var task =
JSON.parse(res.body);
                             // Now delete the task
                             var deletePath = path + "/" +
task.id;
                             request.del(deletePath, function
(err, res, body){
                                    if(err){
```

```
                                                                     throw
new Error("Delete call failed: " + err);
                                                          }
                                              assert.equal(200,
res.statusCode, "Delete Status Code != 200 (" + res.statusCode +
")");
                                              done();
                              });
                      });
      });
});
```

12. Now add the `test/createListDelete.js` file, which will create the DynamoDB data, list it, and then delete it once the test is complete, as shown in the following code:

```
var assert = require('assert');
var request = require('request');
var fs = require('fs');
describe('Create, List, Delete', function() {
            this.timeout(5000);
    it('should create a new task, list it, & delete it',
function(done) {
                              // Build and log the path
----
                              // Fetch the comparison payload
                              require.extensions['.txt'] = function
(module, filename) {
----
                              // Create the new Task
                              var options = {'url' : path, 'form':
JSON.stringify(desiredPayload)};
                              request.post(options, function (err, res,
body){
                                      if(err){
                                              throw new
Error("Create call failed: " + err);
                                      }
                                      assert.equal(200,
res.statusCode, "Create Status Code != 200 (" + res.statusCode +
")");
// Read the list, see if the new item is there at the end
                                      request.get(path, function
(err,
res, body){
                                              if(err){
                                                      throw
new Error("List call failed: " + err);
```

```
                                                             }
                                              assert.equal(200,
res.statusCode, "List Status Code != 200 (" + res.statusCode +
")");
                                                  var taskList =
JSON.parse(res.body);
if(taskList[taskList.length-1].text = desiredPayload.text)     {
                                                   // Item
found, delete it
-----
assert.equal(200, res.statusCode, "Delete Status Code != 200 (" +
res.statusCode + ")");
done();
                                                         });
                                      } else {
                                                   // Item
not found, fail test
assert.equal(true, false, "New item not found in list.");
                                                     done();
                                           }
});
                          });
      });
});
```

13. Let's add the `test/createReadDelete.js` file, which will create the DynamoDB data, read it, and then delete it once the test is complete, as shown in the following code:

```
var assert = require('assert');
var request = require('request');
var fs = require('fs');
describe('Create, Read, Delete', function() {
            this.timeout(5000);
    it('should create a new Todo, read it, & delete it',
function(done) {
                        // Build and log the path
                        var path = "https://" +
process.env.TASKS_ENDPOINT + "/mytasks";
                        // Fetch the comparison payload
                        require.extensions['.txt'] = function
(module, filename) {
                            module.exports =
fs.readFileSync(filename, 'utf8');
                        };
                        var desiredPayload =
require("./data/newTask1.json");
                        // Create the new todo
```

```
                                var options = {'url' : path, 'form':
JSON.stringify(desiredPayload)};
                                request.post(options, function (err, res,
body){
if(err){
                                                        throw new
Error("Create call failed: " + err);
                                }
                                assert.equal(200,
res.statusCode, "Create Status Code != 200 (" + res.statusCode +
")");
                                var todo =
JSON.parse(res.body);
                                // Read the item
                                var specificPath = path + "/" +
todo.id;
                                request.get(path, function
(err, res, body){
                                        if(err){
                                                throw
new Error("Read call failed: " + err);
                                        }
                                        assert.equal(200,
res.statusCode, "Read Status Code != 200 (" + res.statusCode +
")");
                                        var todoList =
JSON.parse(res.body);
                                        if(todoList.text =
desiredPayload.text)

                                                // Item
found, delete it
request.del(specificPath, function (err, res, body){
if(err){
throw new Error("Delete call failed: " + err);
}
assert.equal(200, res.statusCode, "Delete Status Code != 200 (" +
res.statusCode + ")");
done();
                                                });
} else {
                                                // Item
not found, fail test
assert.equal(true, false, "New item not found in list.");
                                                done();
                                        }
                                });
                        });
```

```
        });
    });
```

Now we will create two test data files—`newTask1.json` and `newTask2.json`—that can be used for unit testing.

14. Let's create `data/newTask1.json` using the aforementioned data, as follows:

    ```
    { "text": "Learn Serverless" }
    ```

15. Add the following JSON data to `data/newTask2`:

    ```
    { "text": "Test Serverless" }
    ```

The project folder should now look like the following screenshot:

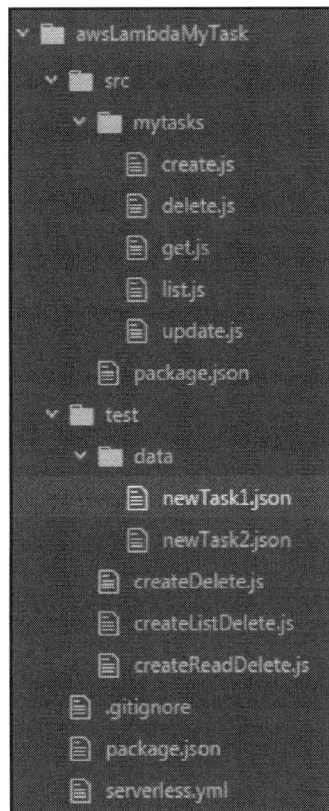

We need to create a repository on Git to push all the code that we created previously so that we can set up CI to the serverless project. I am assuming that Git has already been installed on the local server and that the Git repository is already in place. In my case, I have the following Git repository set up. I will `git clone`, add files and folders, and then push everything to the Git repository:

```
$ git clone https://github.com/shzshi/AWS-lambda-dynamodb-mytasks.git
```

There will be a folder with the name `AWS-lambda-dynamodb-mytasks`. Go into that directory, copy all the files that we created earlier, and then push it to the repository, as shown in the following code:

```
$ git add .
$ git commit -m "my first commit"
$ git push origin master
```

Setting up Jenkins for a serverless application

Assuming that we already have Jenkins up and running, we need to install Node.js, and then we need to install Mocha on the Jenkins server for unit testing. After this, we need to install a serverless framework. You can use the Dockerfile (`https://github.com/shzshi/aws-lambda-dynamodb-mytasks/blob/master/Dockerfile`) from the aforementioned GitHub repository for Jenkins and serverless frameworks. If you are using Docker, you don't need to follow the steps for installing Node.js on Jenkins.

Go through the following steps to install Node.js on the Jenkins node:

```
$ curl -sL https://deb.nodesource.com/setup_6.x | sudo -E bash -
$ sudo apt-get install -y nodejs
$ sudo npm install -g serverless
```

Then go to the browser and open the Jenkins home page. Click on the **New item** link. This will open a new page, that will allow you to create a job with a name of your choosing. Select **Freestyle project**, which is the default selection, and click **OK** to go ahead, as shown in the following screenshot:

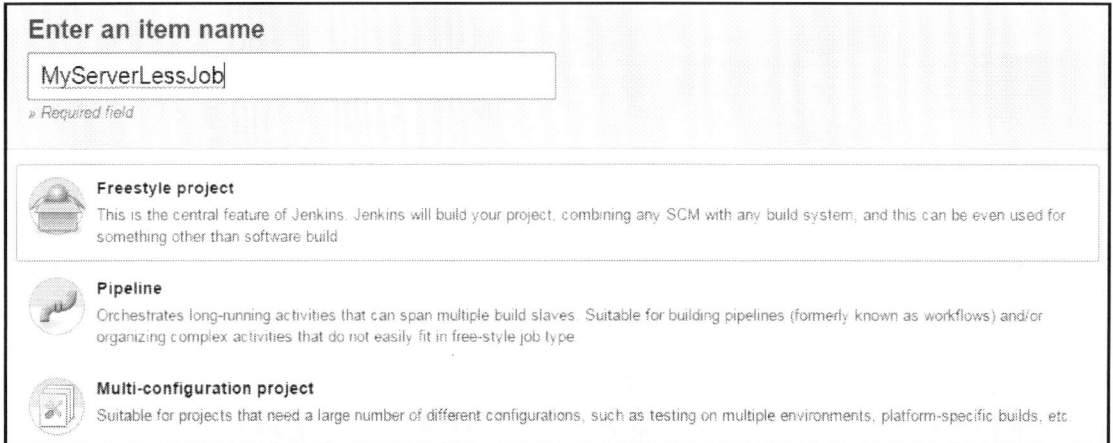

Now, we need to integrate Git source code with Jenkins and then build, deploy, and test our serverless application. First, let's add the Git repository to the Jenkins job, as shown in the following screenshot:

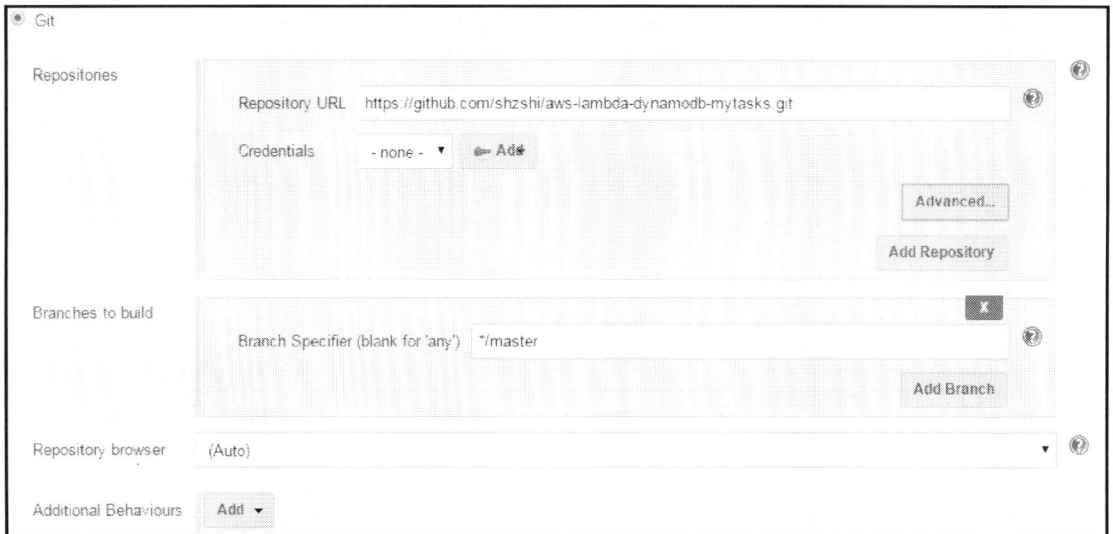

We need to parameterize the build to add `AWS_ACCESS_KEY_ID` and `AWS_SECRET_ACCESS_KEY`, as shown in the following screenshot. We will get `AWS_ACCESS_KEY_ID` and `AWS_SECRET_ACCESS_KEY` after we create an IAM user for the Serverless Framework to work:

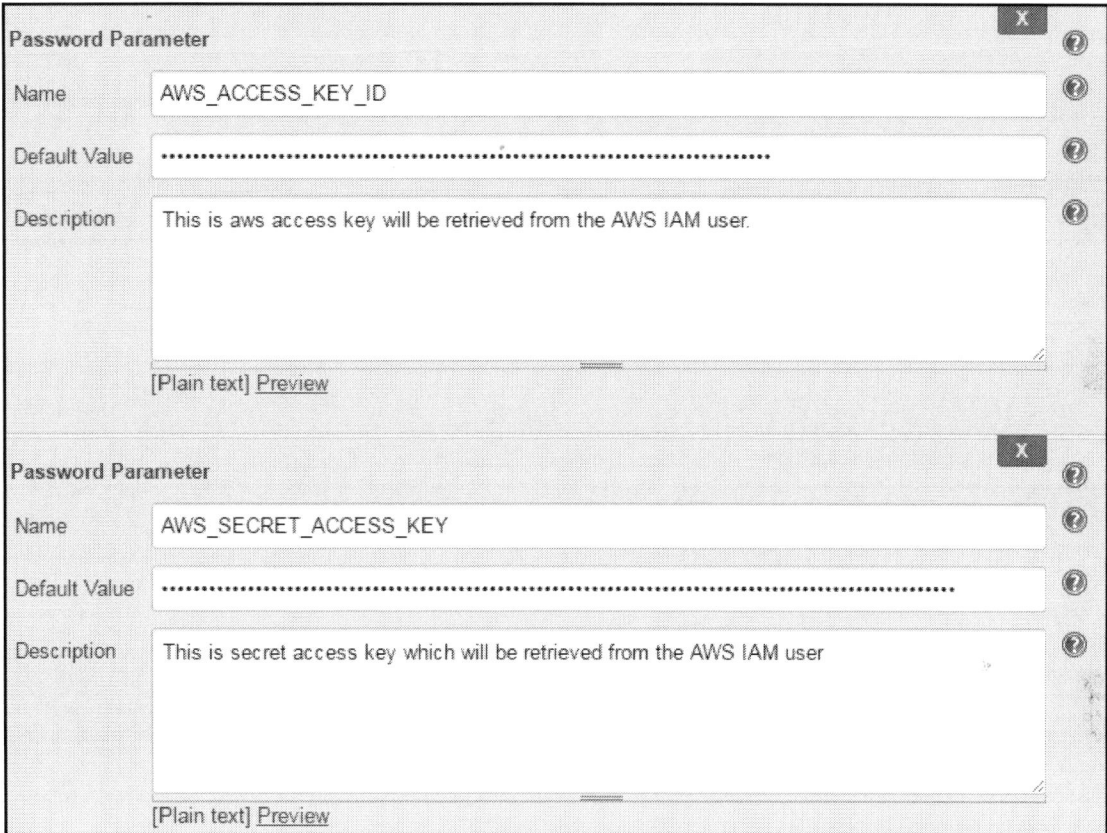

Now go to **Build** | **Add build step** | **Execute shell** | **Execute build step** | **Add build step** from the drop-down menu, which will open Command Prompt, where we will add the command that we need to run, as shown in the following screenshot:

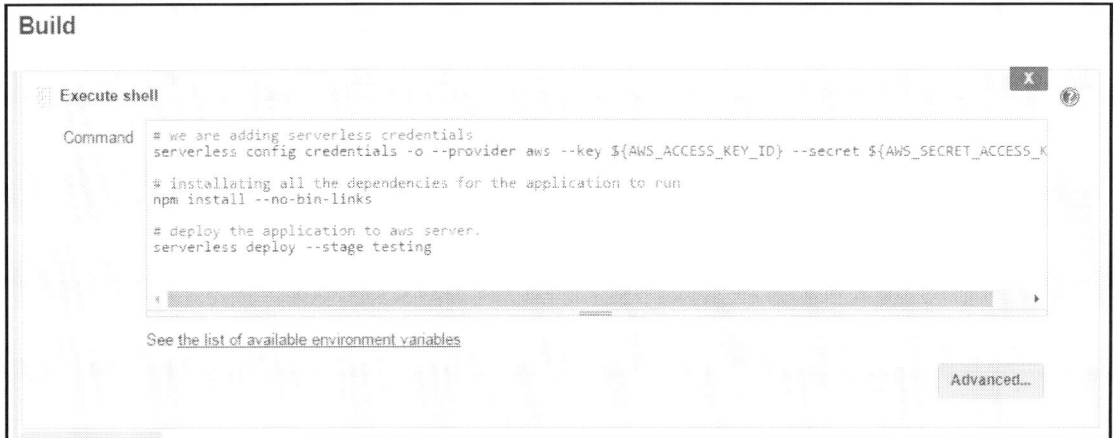

Once the build is successful, we will have successfully deployed the application to the AWS S3 bucket that was created by Serverless Framework. We will also have exposed the API and the functions, allowing them to be used by the application to perform CRUD functions, as shown in the following screenshot:

```
[MyServerLessJob] $ /bin/sh -xe /tmp/jenkins3013495074686274313.sh
+ serverless config credentials -o --provider aws --key AKIAI5WW66EBYFLRFYZA --secret QfhHUa6iRpfv6hujwRC7ZbLNHjaMo2YeZeeDpB0
Serverless: Setting up AWS...
Serverless: Saving your AWS profile in "~/.aws/credentials"...
Serverless: Success! Your AWS access keys were stored under the "default" profile.
+ npm install --no-bin-links
npm WARN package.json aws-rest-with-dynamodb@1.0.0 Normalized value of bugs field is an empty object. Deleted.
+ serverless deploy --stage testing
Serverless: Packaging service...
Serverless: Excluding development dependencies...
Serverless: Uploading CloudFormation file to S3...
Serverless: Uploading artifacts...
Serverless: Uploading service .zip file to S3 (21.78 KB)...
Serverless: Validating template...
Serverless: Updating Stack...
Serverless: Checking Stack update progress...
.....................................
Serverless: Stack update finished...
Service Information
service: serverless-rest-api-with-dynamodb
stage: testing
region: us-east-1
stack: serverless-rest-api-with-dynamodb-testing
api keys:
  None
endpoints:
  POST - https://oa62oybbr6.execute-api.us-east-1.amazonaws.com/testing/mytasks
  GET - https://oa62oybbr6.execute-api.us-east-1.amazonaws.com/testing/mytasks
  GET - https://oa62oybbr6.execute-api.us-east-1.amazonaws.com/testing/mytasks/{id}
  PUT - https://oa62oybbr6.execute-api.us-east-1.amazonaws.com/testing/mytasks/{id}
  DELETE - https://oa62oybbr6.execute-api.us-east-1.amazonaws.com/testing/mytasks/{id}
functions:
  create: serverless-rest-api-with-dynamodb-testing-create
  list: serverless-rest-api-with-dynamodb-testing-list
  get: serverless-rest-api-with-dynamodb-testing-get
  update: serverless-rest-api-with-dynamodb-testing-update
  delete: serverless-rest-api-with-dynamodb-testing-delete
Finished: SUCCESS
```

Automated testing for Lambda functions

In the previous recipes, we looked at how we can automate builds and deploy Lambda functions through Jenkins and Serverless Frameworks. But we can also unit test the deployed Lambda functions through Jenkins. In the following recipes, we will see how to unit test the Lambda function to check whether the function is deployed perfectly and works fine.

Unit testing a deployed application

Once the application is deployed, we can run the unit test on it. In order to try out some unit tests, I have created three unit tests in the `test` folder, and we will be testing them using Mocha. Let's create another job in Jenkins for setting up unit testing. Again, it would be a freestyle job in Jenkins, as shown in the following screenshot:

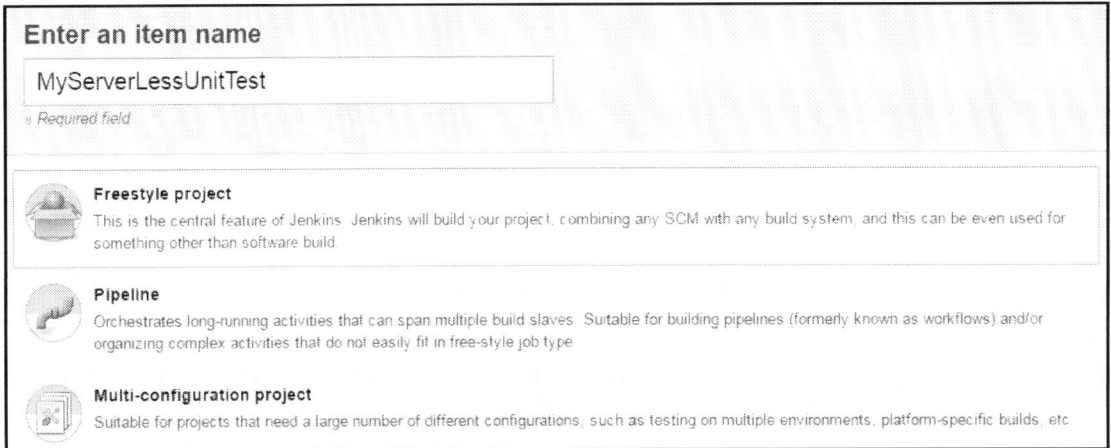

We add the Git repository path to Jenkins where our test cases are residing, as shown in the following screenshot:

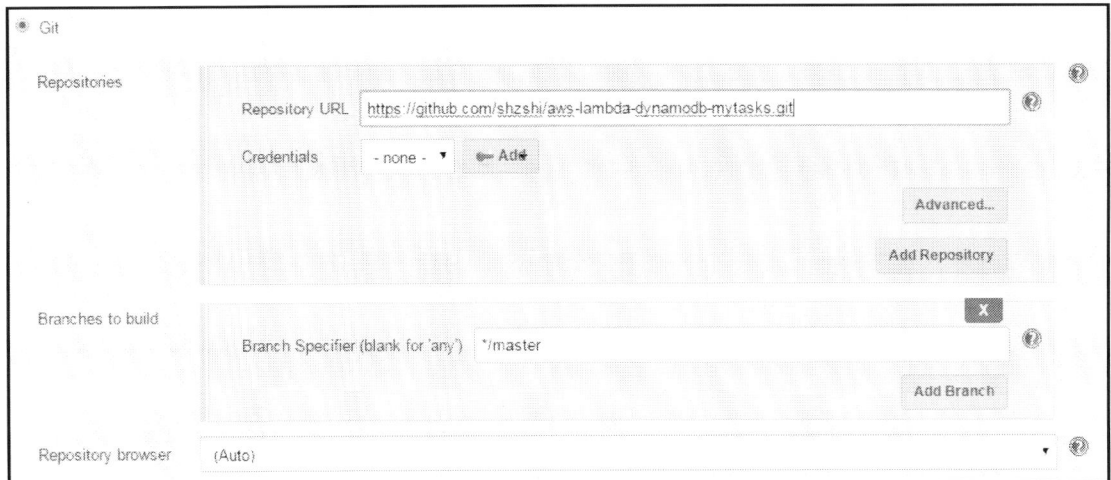

Then we add an execute shell to run the unit test using Mocha, as shown in the following screenshot:

As you can see in the following screenshot, our test cases are passing, which proves that our functions are running perfectly fine:

```
├── json-refs@2.1.7 (slash@1.0.0, commander@2.11.0, native-promise-only@0.8.1, graphlib@2.1.1, uri-js@3.0.2, path-loader@1.0.4)
├── download@5.0.3 (pify@2.3.0, get-stream@3.0.0, filenamify@2.0.0, got@6.7.1, mkdirp@0.5.1, caw@2.0.1, decompress@4.2.0)
├── yaml-ast-parser@0.0.34
├── archiver@1.3.0 (buffer-crc32@0.2.13, archiver-utils@1.3.0, walkdir@0.0.11, readable-stream@2.3.3, tar-stream@1.5.4, glob@7.1.
zip-stream@1.2.0, async@2.6.0)
├── graphql@0.10.5 (iterall@1.1.3)
├── moment@2.19.2
├── @serverless/fdk@0.5.1 (url-parse@1.2.0, isomorphic-fetch@2.2.1, ramda@0.24.1)
├── tabtab@2.2.2 (object-assign@4.1.1, lodash.uniq@4.5.0, lodash.difference@4.5.0, debug@2.6.9, mkdirp@0.5.1, npmlog@2.0.4,
inquirer@1.2.3)
├── lodash@4.17.4
└── apollo-client@1.9.3 (whatwg-fetch@2.0.3, symbol-observable@1.0.4, graphql-anywhere@3.1.0, @types/graphql@0.10.2, apollo-link-
core@0.5.4, redux@3.7.2)
+ ./node_modules/mocha/bin/mocha ./test/createDelete.js ./test/createListDelete.js ./test/createReadDelete.js


  Create, Delete
    ✓ should create a new Task, & delete it (1966ms)

  Create, List, Delete
    ✓ should create a new task, list it, & delete it (1944ms)

  Create, Read, Delete
    ✓ should create a new Todo, read it, & delete it (962ms)


  3 passing (5s)

Finished: SUCCESS
```

AWS Lambda pipeline

In this section of the chapter, we will move to the continuous delivery pipeline and do what we have been doing again: creating different environments, deploying to multiple environments, unit testing, system testing, and adding an approval process. In this pipeline, we will be using Jenkins, Groovy, Serverless Framework, and Docker to set up a Serverless Framework environment. Make sure that you have Docker installed on your machine.

Prerequisites

We need to create a user for each stage or environment so that we can isolate environments and stage the deployment for each environment. To do this, go through the following steps for each user:

1. Log in to an AWS account as the root user, and go to the **IAM (Identity and Access Management)** page.
2. Click on **Users** on the left-hand-side bar, then click on the **Add User** button and add the username **dev-serverless**. Enable **programmatic access** by checking the checkbox. Then click on the **Next:Permissions** button.
3. On the **Permissions** page, select **Attach existing policies directly**, and search for and select the **AdministratorAccess** checkbox. Then click on **Next:Review**.
4. Now check that everything is good and then click on **Create User**. This will create a user and show us the **access key id** and **secret access key**. Copy these these keys somewhere temporarily.
5. Now that we have the keys, we export them as environment variables so that they will be accessed by the framework to perform the required functions.
6. Repeat the preceding five steps for the **sit-serverless** and **prod-serverless** users.
7. CloudBees AWS Credentials Jenkins Plugin.

Now, go through the following steps to create the pipeline:

1. Git clone the following repository into a directory:

   ```
   $ git clone
   https://github.com/shzshi/aws-lambda-dynamodb-mytasks.git
   ```

2. Go into this directory and build the Docker image with the Dockerfile provided. With `docker images`, we should be able to see the Docker image with the name `docker build --rm -f Dockerfile -t aws-lambda-dynamodb-mytasks:latest`, as shown in the following code:

   ```
   $ cd aws-lambda-dynamodb-mytasks
   $ docker build --rm -f Dockerfile -t aws-lambda-dynamodb-
   mytasks:latest .
   $ docker images
   ```

3. Next, we will run the container and open Jenkins on the browser. The initial installation password can be found in the container run logs as shown in the following code:

```
$ mkdir jenkins
$ docker run --rm -it -p 50000:50000 -p 8080:8080 -v
<FULL_PATH_TO_JENKINS_FOLDER>/jenkins:/var/jenkins_home  aws-
lambda-dynamodb-mytasks:latest
```

4. Go to the browser and open `http://localhost:8080`. Copy the password from the container run; it should be something like the following output. Once you are logged in, install the suggested plugin and create a Jenkins user for future logins.

Jenkins initial setup will be required. An admin user will have been created and a password generated. Use the following password to proceed to installation:

6050bfe89a9b463c8e2784060e2225b6

This may also be found at /var/jenkins_home/secrets/initialAdminPassword.

Once Jenkins is up and running, we can go ahead and create a pipeline job, so click on **New Item**, enter the item name as `my-serverless-pipeline`, and select the **pipeline** project. In **Job Configure**, select the **This project is parameterized** checkbox, and then in **Add Parameter**, select **Credentials Parameter** and then go to the **Default Value** section of the **Credentials Parameter** and click on **Add**. Then select **Jenkins**. This will open the **Jenkins Credentials Provider** page. On this page in the **Kind** drop-down menu, select **AWS Credentials** and add the users `dev-serverless`, `sit-serverless`, and `prod-serverless`, as shown in the following screenshot. Then, click **Add**:

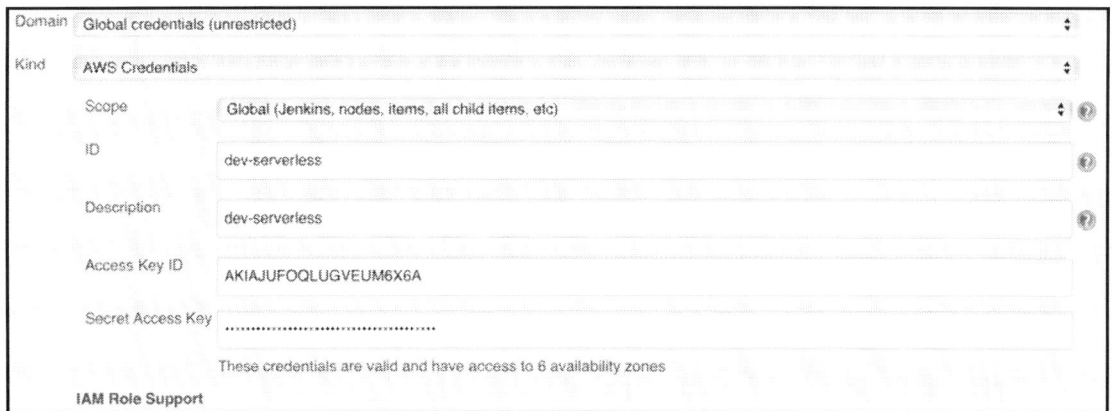

Once all the AWS credentials are added, pull them into the **Credentials** parameter for AWS, as shown in the following screenshot. Make sure that all three types of credential parameter are added, namely `dev`, `sit`, and `prod`:

You need to create your own Git repository and push the files from the repository named `https://github.com/shzshi/aws-lambda-dynamodb-mytasks.git`. Then, open the Jenkins file in your favorite editor and comment in all the system test code for the entire environment, as shown in the following code. The reason we are doing this is because we will be exporting the API gateway endpoint to execute the system test for the entire environment:

```
stage ('System Test on Dev') {
steps {
    withCredentials([[$class: 'AmazonWebServicesCredentialsBinding',
accessKeyVariable: 'AWS_ACCESS_KEY_ID', credentialsId: 'dev-serverless',
secretKeyVariable: 'AWS_SECRET_ACCESS_KEY']]) {
    sh '''
        export TASKS_ENDPOINT=6pgn5wuqeh.execute-api.us-
east-1.amazonaws.com/dev
./node_modules/mocha/bin/mocha ./test/*.js
'''
    }
  }
}
```

Now click on the **Pipeline** tab and select **Pipeline script the SCM** in the definition. Set the **SCM** as **Git** and in the **Repository URL** field, add the Git repository path created by you. This repository has a Jenkins file, a Lambda function, and a test folder. Leave the rest as default and click on **Save**. Now our pipeline is saved. It is time to run the pipeline. Jenkinsfile is a great script that will orchestrate the pipeline for us.

Click **Build with Parameters**. You will then see the environment-based build parameter that will be required for our pipeline to build, test, and deploy our code.

The first run should be without any testing in place, and should only deploy functions and the API gateway for the tasks on the AWS Cloud. The console output will provide us with the endpoints for the tasks, as shown in the following code:

```
endpoints:
  POST - https://6pgn5wuqeh.execute-api.us-east-1.amazonaws.com/dev/mytasks
  GET - https://6pgn5wuqeh.execute-api.us-east-1.amazonaws.com/dev/mytasks
  GET -
https://6pgn5wuqeh.execute-api.us-east-1.amazonaws.com/dev/mytasks/{id}
  PUT -
https://6pgn5wuqeh.execute-api.us-east-1.amazonaws.com/dev/mytasks/{id}
  DELETE -
https://6pgn5wuqeh.execute-api.us-east-1.amazonaws.com/dev/mytasks/{id}
```

Replace the task endpoint in the Jenkinsfile for the entire environment with the API gateway path listed on the console, as shown in the following code. Then save the Jenkinsfile and push it to the Git repository created by you. The reason we are adding the endpoints late in the build is because API gateway endpoints are created dynamically. But we can also have a static endpoint URL with custom domain names featured in the API gateway:

```
export TASKS_ENDPOINT=6pgn5wuqeh.execute-api.us-east-1.amazonaws.com/dev
```

Build the job by clicking on **Build with Parameters**. Here, we should be able to see that the system test is running along the deployment steps, and the pipeline should be green, as shown in the following screenshot:

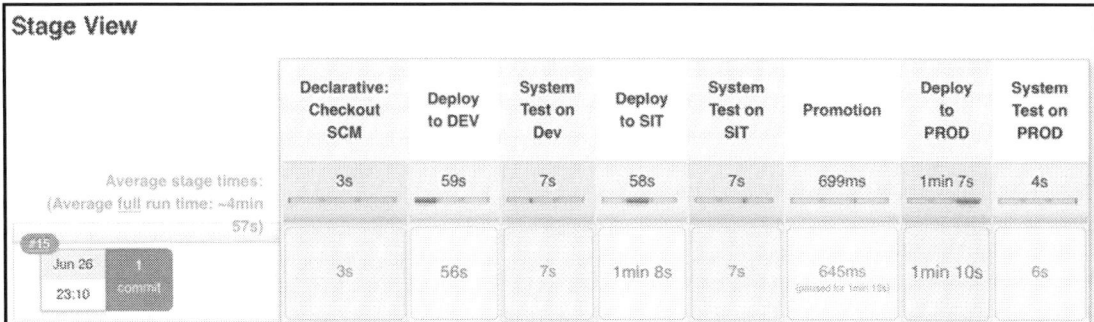

Stage View		Declarative: Checkout SCM	Deploy to DEV	System Test on Dev	Deploy to SIT	System Test on SIT	Promotion	Deploy to PROD	System Test on PROD
Average stage times: (Average full run time: ~4min 57s)		3s	59s	7s	58s	7s	699ms	1min 7s	4s
#15 Jun 26 23:10	1 commit	3s	56s	7s	1min 8s	7s	645ms (paused for 1min 19s)	1min 10s	6s

In the preceding recipe, we learned how Lambda functions and the API gateway call tasks. We also learned how they are deployed to AWS through Serverless Framework and Jenkins via different environments, such as **dev**, **sit**, and **prod**. We also created and tested a system test. The deployment and execution will deploy the Lambda function and API gateway to the AWS cloud, and every system test will execute the Lambda function to perform CRUD operations on DynamoDB. So if you go into DynamoDB, you should see three tables that are created for each environment. You should also be able to see different functions and the API gateway for each environment.

Deployment methods

Deployment into production has its pains. We take a lot of precautions while deploying into production. We introduce lots of testing on lower environments so that most of the bugs and performance problems are taken care of early on. But we are still nervous when deploying into production, as we are never 100 percent sure whether the deployed version will work perfectly fine. If we are using deployment techniques, then we minimize the deployment failure substantially. There are varieties of deployment technique, but canary and blue-green are the most popular ones. We will look at examples of both deployment techniques for AWS Lambda.

Canary deployment

Canary deployment is a deployment technique involving a gradual shift in production traffic from version A to version B, where version B is the latest version and version A is the previous version. AWS has recently introduced traffic shifting for Lambda functions aliases. An alias is a pointer to a specific version of the Lambda functions, which basically means that we can split the traffic of the functions between two different versions by specifying the percentage of incoming traffic that we want to direct to the new release. Lambda will automatically load balance requests between versions when aliases are invoked. So instead of replacing one function with another version, both versions can coexist and can be monitored as to how they perform.

All of this sounds awesome, but doing all this it not that easy. Fortunately, AWS already has a service that will help us with this problem—CodeDeploy. To use canary deployment with the AWS CodeDeploy service, we need to create a variety of resources. We need to create a CodeDeploy application, a deployment group, and aliases for the functions. We also need to create new permissions and replace all the event sources to trigger the aliases instead of the latest functions. But this can be much easier if we use the canary deployment plugin with Serverless Framework. Let's learn how we can achieve this using an example.

> The code that we will be working on in the following recipe is available at : `https://github.com/shzshi/my-canary-deployment.git`.

Setting up a simple environment

Perform the following steps:

1. Let's create a simple serverless service with the following command. Two files will be created named `handler.js` and `serverless.yml`:

   ```
   $ serverless create --template aws-nodejs --path my-canary-
   deployment
   ```

2. Now replace the content of `serverless.yml` with the following code. Make sure that it is indented properly. We are creating a service with a function and an API gateway:

   ```
   service: my-canary-deployment
   provider:
       name: aws
       runtime: nodejs6.10
   ```

```
plugins:
    - serverless-plugin-canary-deployments
functions:
    hello:
        handler: handler.hello
        events:
            - http: get hello
```

3. Let's replace the content of `handler.js` with the following content:

```
module.exports.hello = (event, context, callback) => {
    const response = {
        statusCode: 200,
        body: 'Go Serverless v1.0! Your function executed
successfully!'
    };

    callback(null, response);
};
```

4. Create a `package.json` file, as shown in the following code:

```
{
    "name": "my-canary-deployment",
    "version": "1.0.0",
    "description": "",
    "main": "handler.js",
    "scripts": {
        "test": "echo \"Error: no test specified\" && exit 1"
    },
    "author": "shashikant bangera",
    "devDependencies": {
        "serverless-plugin-aws-alerts": "^1.2.4",
        "serverless-plugin-canary-deployments": "^0.4.0"
    }
}
```

5. Let's deploy this function to the AWS, as shown in the following code. Make sure that you have configured your AWS access and secret key before deploying:

```
$ npm install
$ serverless deploy -v
```

6. Once successfully deployed, let's invoke the function and let it verify the execution. We will be provided with the service endpoint, so let's invoke the function with the endpoint, as shown in the following code:

```
$ curl https://<my-service-endpoint>-east-1.amazonaws.com/dev/hello

Go Serverless v1.0! Your function executed successfully!
```

Setting up canary deployment

Once the initial setup is complete, we will tell the serverless canary deployment plugin to split the traffic between the last two versions and gradually shift more traffic to the new version until it receives all the load.

The following are the three types of gradual deployment that we can implement using AWS's CodeDeploy:

- **Canary:** The traffic is shifted to a new version during a certain period of time, and when the time elapses, all the traffic will have moved to the newer version
- **Linear:** The traffic is shifted to the new version incrementally at intervals until it gets all of the traffic
- **All at once:** All the traffic is shifted to the new version at once

We need to be specific as to which parameter and type of deployment we will use by choosing any of the aforementioned options for using CodeDeploy:

`Canary10Percent30Minutes`, `Canary10Percent5Minutes`, `Canary10Percent10Minutes`, `Canary10Percent15Minutes`, `Linear10PercentEvery10Minutes`, `Linear10PercentEvery1Minute`, `Linear10PercentEvery2Minutes`, `Linear10PercentEvery3Minutes` or `AllAtOnce`.

For our tutorial, we will use `Linear10PercentEvery1Minute`, which means that the traffic that the new version of the function will receive will be increased by 10 percent increments every minute, until it reaches 100%. To do this, we need to set the type and alias (the name of the alias that we want to create) under `deploymentSettings` in the function. Let's update the files, and redeploy and invoke the function to see how the traffic moves:

1. Add the deployment settings within the `serverless.yml`, as shown in the following code:

```
service: my-canary-deployment
provider:
 name: aws
 runtime: nodejs6.10
```

```
plugins:
 - serverless-plugin-canary-deployments
functions:
 hello:
     handler: handler.hello
     events:
         - http: get hello
     deploymentSettings:
         type: Linear10PercentEvery1Minute
         alias: Live
```

2. Update the `handler.js` with the following code:

```
module.exports.hello = (event, context, callback) => {
    const response = {
    statusCode: 200,
    body: 'Hey new version is 1.26.1 !'
    };
    callback(null, response);
};
```

3. Let's deploy the function. You will see from the following code that the deployment will trigger `CodeDeploy` with linear deployment, and requests will be load balanced between the two functions:

```
$ serverless deploy -v

Serverless: Packaging service...
---
Serverless: Checking Stack update progress...
CloudFormation - UPDATE_IN_PROGRESS - AWS::CloudFormation::Stack -
my-canary-deployment-dev
CloudFormation - CREATE_IN_PROGRESS - AWS::IAM::Role -
CodeDeployServiceRole
CloudFormation - CREATE_IN_PROGRESS - AWS::CodeDeploy::Application
- MycanarydeploymentdevDeploymentApplication
CloudFormation - UPDATE_IN_PROGRESS - AWS::Lambda::Function -
HelloLambdaFunction
CloudFormation - CREATE_IN_PROGRESS - AWS::CodeDeploy::Application
- MycanarydeploymentdevDeploymentApplication
CloudFormation - CREATE_IN_PROGRESS - AWS::IAM::Role -
CodeDeployServiceRole
CloudFormation - CREATE_COMPLETE - AWS::CodeDeploy::Application -
MycanarydeploymentdevDeploymentApplication
CloudFormation - UPDATE_COMPLETE - AWS::Lambda::Function -
HelloLambdaFunction
CloudFormation - CREATE_IN_PROGRESS - AWS::Lambda::Version -
HelloLambdaVersionW59z2S8rIu6lAv3dCyvgKLndpEosDs1l1kpbg6Lrg
```

```
CloudFormation - CREATE_IN_PROGRESS - AWS::Lambda::Version -
HelloLambdaVersionW59z2S8rIu6lAv3dCyvgKLndpEosDs1l1kpbg6Lrg
CloudFormation - CREATE_COMPLETE - AWS::Lambda::Version -
HelloLambdaVersionW59z2S8rIu6lAv3dCyvgKLndpEosDs1l1kpbg6Lrg
CloudFormation - CREATE_COMPLETE - AWS::IAM::Role -
CodeDeployServiceRole
CloudFormation - CREATE_IN_PROGRESS -
AWS::CodeDeploy::DeploymentGroup -
HelloLambdaFunctionDeploymentGroup
CloudFormation - CREATE_IN_PROGRESS -
AWS::CodeDeploy::DeploymentGroup -
HelloLambdaFunctionDeploymentGroup
CloudFormation - CREATE_COMPLETE - AWS::CodeDeploy::DeploymentGroup
- HelloLambdaFunctionDeploymentGroup
CloudFormation - CREATE_IN_PROGRESS - AWS::Lambda::Alias -
HelloLambdaFunctionAliasLive
CloudFormation - CREATE_IN_PROGRESS - AWS::Lambda::Alias -
HelloLambdaFunctionAliasLive
CloudFormation - CREATE_COMPLETE - AWS::Lambda::Alias -
HelloLambdaFunctionAliasLive
CloudFormation - UPDATE_IN_PROGRESS - AWS::ApiGateway::Method -
ApiGatewayMethodHelloGet
CloudFormation - UPDATE_COMPLETE - AWS::ApiGateway::Method -
ApiGatewayMethodHelloGet
CloudFormation - UPDATE_IN_PROGRESS - AWS::Lambda::Permission -
HelloLambdaPermissionApiGateway
CloudFormation - UPDATE_IN_PROGRESS - AWS::Lambda::Permission -
HelloLambdaPermissionApiGateway
CloudFormation - CREATE_IN_PROGRESS - AWS::ApiGateway::Deployment -
ApiGatewayDeployment1530401347906
CloudFormation - CREATE_IN_PROGRESS - AWS::ApiGateway::Deployment -
ApiGatewayDeployment1530401347906
CloudFormation - CREATE_COMPLETE - AWS::ApiGateway::Deployment -
ApiGatewayDeployment1530401347906
CloudFormation - UPDATE_COMPLETE - AWS::Lambda::Permission -
HelloLambdaPermissionApiGateway
CloudFormation - UPDATE_COMPLETE_CLEANUP_IN_PROGRESS -
AWS::CloudFormation::Stack - my-canary-deployment-dev
CloudFormation - DELETE_IN_PROGRESS - AWS::Lambda::Permission -
HelloLambdaPermissionApiGateway
CloudFormation - DELETE_IN_PROGRESS - AWS::ApiGateway::Deployment -
ApiGatewayDeployment1530398711004
CloudFormation - DELETE_SKIPPED - AWS::Lambda::Version -
HelloLambdaVersionjAYLrhwIiK3mGoae1oyrqMYfnXsHGIk0IuE6gh2dWdA
CloudFormation - DELETE_COMPLETE - AWS::ApiGateway::Deployment -
ApiGatewayDeployment1530398711004
CloudFormation - DELETE_COMPLETE - AWS::Lambda::Permission -
HelloLambdaPermissionApiGateway
```

```
CloudFormation - UPDATE_COMPLETE - AWS::CloudFormation::Stack - my-
canary-deployment-dev
```

4. Let's invoke the function and see whether it is load balanced, as shown in the following code:

```
$ curl https://<api-gateway-path>.amazonaws.com/dev/hello
Go Serverless v1.0! Your function executed successfully!

$ curl https://<api-gateway-path>.amazonaws.com/dev/hello
Hey new version is 1.26.1!
```

Making sure the deployment works fine

Our function deployed without any hassle, but how do we ensure that whole system is behaving correctly? To ensure everything is working fine, we can provide CodeDeploy with a list of variables to track during the deployment process, then cancel it, and shift all the traffic to the old version if the ALARM is triggered. With serverless, we can set the alarm using another plugin. Let's have a look at how to do this:

1. Update the serverless.yml to set the alarm, as shown in the following code:

```
service: my-canary-deployment
provider:
 name: aws
 runtime: nodejs6.10

plugins:
    - serverless-plugin-aws-alerts
    - serverless-plugin-canary-deployments

custom:
    alerts:
        dashboards: true

functions:
    hello:
        handler: handler.hello
        events:
            - http: get hello
        alarms:
            - name: test
                namespace: 'AWS/Lambda'
                metric: Errors
                threshold: 1
                statistic: Minimum
                period: 60
```

```
                    evaluationPeriods: 1
                    comparisonOperator: GreaterThanOrEqualToThreshold
              deploymentSettings:
                  type: Linear10PercentEvery1Minute
                  alias: Live
                  alarms:
                      - HelloTestAlarm
```

2. Let's deploy the function and see how it works, as shown in the following code:

```
$ serverless deploy -v

Serverless: Packaging service...
Serverless: Excluding development dependencies...
Serverless: Uploading CloudFormation file to S3...
Serverless: Uploading artifacts...
Serverless: Uploading service .zip file to S3 (611 B)...
Serverless: Validating template...
Serverless: Updating Stack...
Serverless: Checking Stack update progress...
CloudFormation - UPDATE_IN_PROGRESS - AWS::CloudFormation::Stack -
my-canary-deployment-dev
CloudFormation - CREATE_IN_PROGRESS - AWS::CloudWatch::Dashboard -
AlertsDashboard
CloudFormation - UPDATE_IN_PROGRESS - AWS::Lambda::Function -
HelloLambdaFunction
CloudFormation - UPDATE_COMPLETE - AWS::Lambda::Function -
HelloLambdaFunction
CloudFormation - CREATE_IN_PROGRESS - AWS::CloudWatch::Alarm -
HelloTestAlarm
CloudFormation - CREATE_IN_PROGRESS - AWS::CloudWatch::Alarm -
HelloTestAlarm
CloudFormation - CREATE_IN_PROGRESS - AWS::Lambda::Version -
HelloLambdaVersionja19jdYXntxmsiUagZLZfDEMTshQJ8ApOagyYwmXE
CloudFormation - CREATE_COMPLETE - AWS::CloudWatch::Alarm -
HelloTestAlarm
CloudFormation - CREATE_IN_PROGRESS - AWS::Lambda::Version -
HelloLambdaVersionja19jdYXntxmsiUagZLZfDEMTshQJ8ApOagyYwmXE
CloudFormation - CREATE_COMPLETE - AWS::Lambda::Version -
HelloLambdaVersionja19jdYXntxmsiUagZLZfDEMTshQJ8ApOagyYwmXE
CloudFormation - CREATE_IN_PROGRESS - AWS::CloudWatch::Dashboard -
AlertsDashboard
CloudFormation - CREATE_COMPLETE - AWS::CloudWatch::Dashboard -
AlertsDashboard
CloudFormation - UPDATE_IN_PROGRESS -
AWS::CodeDeploy::DeploymentGroup -
HelloLambdaFunctionDeploymentGroup
CloudFormation - UPDATE_COMPLETE - AWS::CodeDeploy::DeploymentGroup
```

```
    - HelloLambdaFunctionDeploymentGroup
CloudFormation - UPDATE_IN_PROGRESS - AWS::Lambda::Alias -
HelloLambdaFunctionAliasLive
CloudFormation - UPDATE_IN_PROGRESS - AWS::Lambda::Alias -
HelloLambdaFunctionAliasLive
CloudFormation - UPDATE_COMPLETE - AWS::Lambda::Alias -
HelloLambdaFunctionAliasLive
CloudFormation - CREATE_IN_PROGRESS - AWS::ApiGateway::Deployment -
ApiGatewayDeployment1530403890255
CloudFormation - CREATE_IN_PROGRESS - AWS::ApiGateway::Deployment -
ApiGatewayDeployment1530403890255
CloudFormation - CREATE_COMPLETE - AWS::ApiGateway::Deployment -
ApiGatewayDeployment1530403890255
CloudFormation - UPDATE_COMPLETE_CLEANUP_IN_PROGRESS -
AWS::CloudFormation::Stack - my-canary-deployment-dev
CloudFormation - DELETE_IN_PROGRESS - AWS::ApiGateway::Deployment -
ApiGatewayDeployment1530401797330
CloudFormation - DELETE_COMPLETE - AWS::ApiGateway::Deployment -
ApiGatewayDeployment1530401797330
CloudFormation - DELETE_SKIPPED - AWS::Lambda::Version -
HelloLambdaVersionW59z2S8rIu6lAv3dCyvgKLndpEosDs1l1kpbg6Lrg
CloudFormation - UPDATE_COMPLETE - AWS::CloudFormation::Stack - my-
canary-deployment-dev
```

The deploy step will create an alarm in CodeDeploy and the CloudWatch dashboard, where we can see different graphs representing invocations and errors. You can log into AWS Console and go to CodeDeploy and CloudWatch to see how the alarm is created, and to see what the dashboard looks like.

Deploying CodeDeploy hooks

So now we have all the tools to minimize the impact of possible bugs or failures. However, we can also avoid invoking a function version that contained errors by running the CodeDeploy hooks first. Hooks are Lambda functions triggered by CodeDeploy before and after traffic shifting takes place. It expects to get notified about the success or failure of the hooks, only continuing to the next step if they succeed. They are good for running integration tests and checking that everything fits together in the cloud, since it will automatically rollback at a failure.

Let's have look at how to create hooks by going through the following steps:

1. Let's update the `serverless.yml` to add hook details. We need to grant our functions access to CodeDeploy so that we can use CodeDeploy's SDK in the hooks, as shown in the following code:

```yaml
service: my-canary-deployment
provider:
    name: aws
    runtime: nodejs6.10
    iamRoleStatements:
    - Effect: Allow
    Action:
        - codedeploy:*
    Resource:
        - "*"
plugins:
    - serverless-plugin-aws-alerts
    - serverless-plugin-canary-deployments

custom:
    alerts:
        dashboards: true

functions:
    hello:
        handler: handler.hello
        events:
            - http: get hello
        alarms:
            - name: test
            namespace: 'AWS/Lambda'
            metric: Errors
            threshold: 1
            statistic: Minimum
            period: 60
            evaluationPeriods: 1
            comparisonOperator: GreaterThanOrEqualToThreshold
        deploymentSettings:
            type: Linear10PercentEvery1Minute
            alias: Live
            preTrafficHook: preHook
            postTrafficHook: postHook
            alarms:
                - HelloTestAlarm
    preHook:
        handler: hooks.pre
```

```
      postHook:
          handler: hooks.post
```

2. Next, we will create the hooks. Let's create a new file named `hooks.js` within the service directory and add the following hook content:

```
const aws = require('aws-sdk');
const codedeploy = new aws.CodeDeploy({apiVersion: '2014-10-06'});
module.exports.pre = (event, context, callback) => {
 var deploymentId = event.DeploymentId;
 var lifecycleEventHookExecutionId =
event.LifecycleEventHookExecutionId;

console.log('We are running some integration tests before we start
shifting traffic...');

var params = {
 deploymentId: deploymentId,
 lifecycleEventHookExecutionId: lifecycleEventHookExecutionId,
 status: 'Succeeded' // status can be 'Succeeded' or 'Failed'
 };

return
codedeploy.putLifecycleEventHookExecutionStatus(params).promise()
 .then(data => callback(null, 'Validation test succeeded'))
 .catch(err => callback('Validation test failed'));
};

module.exports.post = (event, context, callback) => {
 var deploymentId = event.DeploymentId;
 var lifecycleEventHookExecutionId =
event.LifecycleEventHookExecutionId;
 console.log('Check some stuff after traffic has been shifted...');
 var params = {
 deploymentId: deploymentId,
 lifecycleEventHookExecutionId: lifecycleEventHookExecutionId,
 status: 'Succeeded' // status can be 'Succeeded' or 'Failed'
 };
 return
codedeploy.putLifecycleEventHookExecutionStatus(params).promise()
 .then(data => callback(null, 'Validation test succeeded'))
 .catch(err => callback('Validation test failed'));
};
```

3. Now that we have created the hooks, let's deploy them and see how they function using the following code:

```
$ serverless deploy -v
Serverless: Packaging service...
Serverless: Excluding development dependencies...
Serverless: Uploading CloudFormation file to S3...
Serverless: Uploading artifacts...
Serverless: Uploading service .zip file to S3 (1.12 KB)...
Serverless: Validating template...
Serverless: Updating Stack...
Serverless: Checking Stack update progress...
CloudFormation - UPDATE_IN_PROGRESS - AWS::CloudFormation::Stack -
my-canary-deployment-dev
CloudFormation - CREATE_IN_PROGRESS - AWS::Logs::LogGroup -
PreHookLogGroup
CloudFormation - CREATE_IN_PROGRESS - AWS::Logs::LogGroup -
PostHookLogGroup
CloudFormation - CREATE_IN_PROGRESS - AWS::Logs::LogGroup -
PreHookLogGroup
CloudFormation - UPDATE_IN_PROGRESS - AWS::IAM::Role -
IamRoleLambdaExecution
CloudFormation - CREATE_IN_PROGRESS - AWS::Logs::LogGroup -
PostHookLogGroup
CloudFormation - UPDATE_IN_PROGRESS - AWS::CloudWatch::Dashboard -
AlertsDashboard
CloudFormation - CREATE_COMPLETE - AWS::Logs::LogGroup -
PreHookLogGroup
CloudFormation - CREATE_COMPLETE - AWS::Logs::LogGroup -
PostHookLogGroup
CloudFormation - UPDATE_COMPLETE - AWS::CloudWatch::Dashboard -
AlertsDashboard
CloudFormation - UPDATE_COMPLETE - AWS::IAM::Role -
IamRoleLambdaExecution
CloudFormation - CREATE_IN_PROGRESS - AWS::Lambda::Function -
PostHookLambdaFunction
CloudFormation - CREATE_IN_PROGRESS - AWS::Lambda::Function -
PreHookLambdaFunction
CloudFormation - UPDATE_IN_PROGRESS - AWS::Lambda::Function -
HelloLambdaFunction
CloudFormation - CREATE_IN_PROGRESS - AWS::Lambda::Function -
PreHookLambdaFunction
CloudFormation - UPDATE_COMPLETE - AWS::Lambda::Function -
HelloLambdaFunction
CloudFormation - CREATE_IN_PROGRESS - AWS::Lambda::Function -
PostHookLambdaFunction
CloudFormation - CREATE_COMPLETE - AWS::Lambda::Function -
PostHookLambdaFunction
```

```
CloudFormation - CREATE_IN_PROGRESS - AWS::Lambda::Version -
HelloLambdaVersionUutX83EhRCt0XFaMjWRyD8vAkoceeNRnZXqaeuCkFo
CloudFormation - CREATE_COMPLETE - AWS::Lambda::Function -
PreHookLambdaFunction
CloudFormation - CREATE_IN_PROGRESS - AWS::Lambda::Version -
PostHookLambdaVersionI0mvapPGCoXwaOw5oaAUMCSPtZYGXKy9YJABLTU
CloudFormation - CREATE_IN_PROGRESS - AWS::Lambda::Version -
HelloLambdaVersionUutX83EhRCt0XFaMjWRyD8vAkoceeNRnZXqaeuCkFo
CloudFormation - CREATE_COMPLETE - AWS::Lambda::Version -
HelloLambdaVersionUutX83EhRCt0XFaMjWRyD8vAkoceeNRnZXqaeuCkFo
CloudFormation - CREATE_IN_PROGRESS - AWS::Lambda::Version -
PostHookLambdaVersionI0mvapPGCoXwaOw5oaAUMCSPtZYGXKy9YJABLTU
CloudFormation - CREATE_COMPLETE - AWS::Lambda::Version -
PostHookLambdaVersionI0mvapPGCoXwaOw5oaAUMCSPtZYGXKy9YJABLTU
CloudFormation - CREATE_IN_PROGRESS - AWS::Lambda::Version -
PreHookLambdaVersionG9WhVjc3o3mP7moxWMFYoj0jCN4eO1jJBUgGLJmcJA
CloudFormation - CREATE_IN_PROGRESS - AWS::Lambda::Version -
PreHookLambdaVersionG9WhVjc3o3mP7moxWMFYoj0jCN4eO1jJBUgGLJmcJA
CloudFormation - CREATE_COMPLETE - AWS::Lambda::Version -
PreHookLambdaVersionG9WhVjc3o3mP7moxWMFYoj0jCN4eO1jJBUgGLJmcJA
CloudFormation - UPDATE_IN_PROGRESS - AWS::Lambda::Alias -
HelloLambdaFunctionAliasLive
CloudFormation - UPDATE_IN_PROGRESS - AWS::Lambda::Alias -
HelloLambdaFunctionAliasLive
```

While the deployment is continuing on the CLI, we should log into the AWS Cloud console and go to **Services** | **CloudFormation**. Select the stack named **my-canary-deployment-dev** and scroll down and select the **CodeDeploy** link in the **Status Reason** column. We should be able to see the gradual shifting of traffic with prehook, traffic shifting, and posthook execution, finally completing the whole stack and, lastly, the deployment.

Here, we learned how we can set up canary deployments using Serverless Framework, various plugins, and AWS CodeDeploy.

Blue-green deployment

Like canary deployment, blue–green deployment is another type of methodology for safe deployment for production. In canary deployment, we shifted the traffic from one version to the next version gradually until we completely moved it to the latest version. But in the case of blue–green deployment, we create two different environments. One environment is used for going live and the other for staging the new version. So a blue–green deployment setup would create a separate region for staging and production and then route the traffic from one region to another with deploying the latest version.

Let's say that I have a **blue** region (`us-east-1`), which is the production region, and that it is live and has the current version of the Lambda functions deployed. Now let's say that I also have a new version out, so I will deploy the Lambda function (the new version) into a **green** region (`us-east-2`), and that this will act as my staging environment. I will perform all the testing, and once satisfied, I will redirect all the traffic to the **green** region (`us-east-2`). Now that my staging is live, I will go ahead and deploy the latest version to the blue region (`us-east-1`), and my functions will be tested for bugs and problems. But let's say that, unfortunately, some serious bugs are discovered in the **blue** region (`us-east-1`).

Then the code is rolled back, all the traffic is once again pointed to the **blue** region (`us-east-1`), and the **green** region (`us-east-2`) becomes the staging environment again:

- **Blue:** `$ serverless deploy --stage prod --region us-east-1`
- **Green:** `$ serverless deploy --stage prod --region us-east-2`

Integration of CloudWatch with ELK

I have been using ELK for quite a long time. It was daily work for me, as AWS Lambda logs are shipped to CloudWatch, but as my company uses ELK for centralized log management, I now like to push all the logs from CloudWatch to ELK.

So I decided to ship the CloudWatch logs to ELK. Lambda logs can be shipped directly to Elasticsearch or to Redis for Logstash to pick it up. There is a plugin available that will help us to ship the Lambda CloudWatch logs to ELK. We will now look at how to configure this. We will be using a Docker ELK image to set up ELK locally and then connect to AWS CloudWatch through the Logstash plugin. Then we will push the logs to Elasticsearch. Let's go through the following steps:

1. Get the Docker image for ELK, as shown in the following code. If you already have an ELK account set up, then you don't need to follow this step:

```
$ docker pull sebp/elk
$ docker run --rm -it -p 5044:5044 -p 5601:5601 -p 9200:9200 -p
9300:9300 sebp/elk:latest
```

Now, if you go to your browser and open the link `http://localhost:5601/`, then you should be able to see the Kibana dashboard.

2. Install the `logstash-input-cloudwatch_logs` plugin. Ssh into your Docker container that was created in the previous step and install the plugin, as shown in the following code:

```
$ docker exec -it <container> bash
$ /opt/logstash/bin/logstash-plugin install logstash-input-
cloudwatch_logs

Validating logstash-input-cloudwatch_logs
Installing logstash-input-cloudwatch_logs
Installation successful
```

3. Once the plugin is successfully installed, we need to create a Logstash config file that will help us in shipping the CloudWatch logs. Let's open the editor and add the following config file and name it `cloud-watch-lambda.conf`. We need to replace `access_key_id` and `secret_access_key` as per the AWS IAM user and also update the log group. I have added three `grok` filters:

   - The first filter matches the generic log message, where we strip the timestamp and pull out the `[lambda][request_id]` field for indexing
   - The second `grok` filter handles the `START` and `END` log messages
   - The third filter handles the `REPORT` messages and gives us the most important fields

```
[lambda][duration]
[lambda][billed_duration]
[lambda][memory_size]
[lambda][memory_used]
input {
    cloudwatch_logs {
        log_group => "/AWS/lambda/my-lambda"
        access_key_id => "AKIAXXXXXX"
        secret_access_key => "SECRET"
        type => "lambda"
    }
}
```

Let's name this `cloud-watch-lambda.conf` and place it in the `/etc/logstash/conf.d` file of the Docker container.

4. Now let's restart the Logstash service, as shown in the following code. Once this is done, you should be able to see that the logs have been pulled into our ELK container:

```
$ /etc/init.d/logstash restart
```

5. Open the browser and go to the page `http://localhost:5601` and we should be able to see the logs streaming into ELK from cloudwatch and this can be refined further with ELK filter and regular expression.

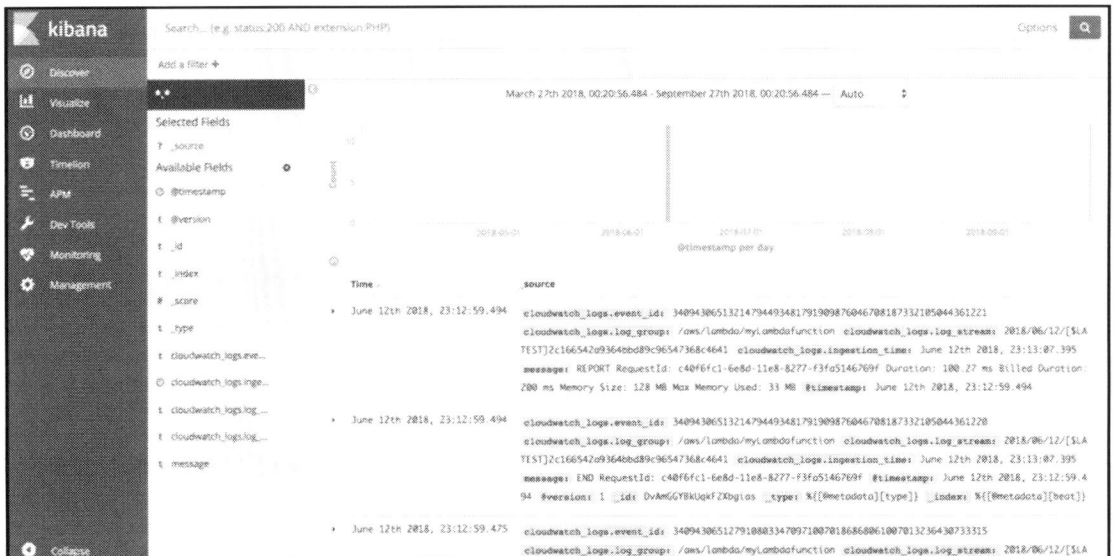

Summary

In this chapter, we learned how to integrate DevOps with various out-of-the-box tools within AWS Lambda and with open source tools. In the next chapter, we will learn how to set up CI and CD with Azure functions with the help of Serverless Framework, as well as how to monitor and log with Azure functions.

DevOps with Azure Functions 4

Microsoft Azure is the number two cloud service provider, just behind AWS. But, until 2015, they hadn't provided API services, but they were excelling in other cloud services like AWS and Google Cloud Functions. Then, eventually, they decided to invest in functions. So, Azure Functions is the answer to AWS Lambda, but the underlying technology is different, which we will cover in upcoming chapters. Azure Functions sit on top of the Azure app service and WebJobs SDK. Azure Functions support a lot of languages like F#, Python, Batch, PHP, and PowerShell, but C# and Node.js are officially supported. We will be using Node.js for all our tutorials throughout this chapter and more details on the Azure Functions can be found on Microsoft link: `https:/ / msdn. microsoft. com/ en- us/ magazine/ mt793269. aspx.`

In this chapter, we will cover the following topics:

- Building a simple Azure function
- Continuous integration and continuous delivery with Azure Functions
- Continuous deployment to Azure Functions
- Blue green deployment in Azure Functions
- Monitoring and logging
- Best practice

Building a simple Azure function

We will first try to create a simple Azure function through the portal and then we will automate the build and deployment process using S tools and framework. So, to start playing with Azure Functions, we need to create an Azure Cloud service account first. Microsoft provides one month of free subscription and we will be using the Node.js scripts for all the DevOps-related examples and demos.

Azure Cloud account creation
`https://azure.microsoft.com/free/?ref=microsoft.comutm_source=`
`microsoft.comutm_medium=docsutm_campaign=visualstudio`

Once the account is created, follow these steps:

1. Log into the Azure portal (Azure portal: `https://portal.azure.com/`).

    On successful login, we will be redirected to the homepage of the Azure portal.

2. Now, we need to create resources for Azure Function. So let's click on the button **Create a Resource**, which will take us to the Azure marketplace page.

3. Here, we need to create a **Compute** by clicking on the link **Compute** within the Azure marketplace.

4. Then we can go ahead to create a function through the link **Function App** (which will open a new window where we have to feed details for the **Function App**.).

The following screenshot gives us the details of how we move through the screen while creating a simple Azure Function:

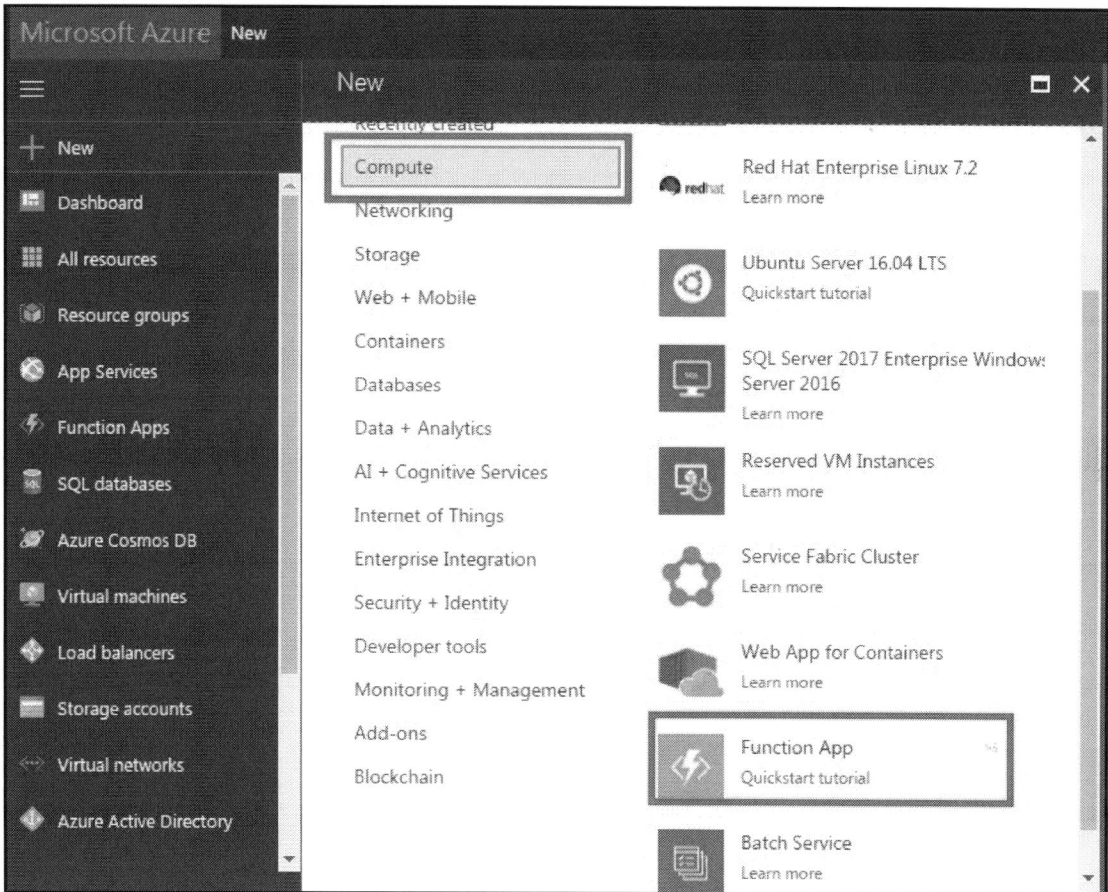

5. After clicking the link, a page will open on which we need to feed in details about the **Function App**. So let's name it `mySampleAppName`. The Function App name must be unique, because the Azure Function does not allow a duplicate app name across the Azure Cloud. On acceptance of the app name, we will see a green tick mark on the **App name** column. Then we will add **Subscription**, **Resource Group** (we can use the default value or add an existing resource group), **OS** , **Hosting Plan**, **Storage** (we can create new storage or use the existing one).

Let's keep the other details as default and create a **Function App**:

This will create a **Function App**, where the function will be residing. After successful creation of the **Function App**, if you click on **All Resources**, you should be able to see the Function App. We will go ahead and create the application, then Azure will create resources for the function which is a storage account and Function App.

6. Let's now go to **Function Apps** and, on the right-hand side at the **Function App** tab, we should be able to see our function. Let's click on it and hover the mouse and we should see **+**. We can create a new function by clicking on the **+**; we can only see **+** after hovering over the **Functions** tab. This will open a tab on the right-hand side which will provide multiple options to create an Azure Function. We will go ahead and choose Scenario as our **Webhook + API** and JavaScript as our language, and then click on **Create this function**:

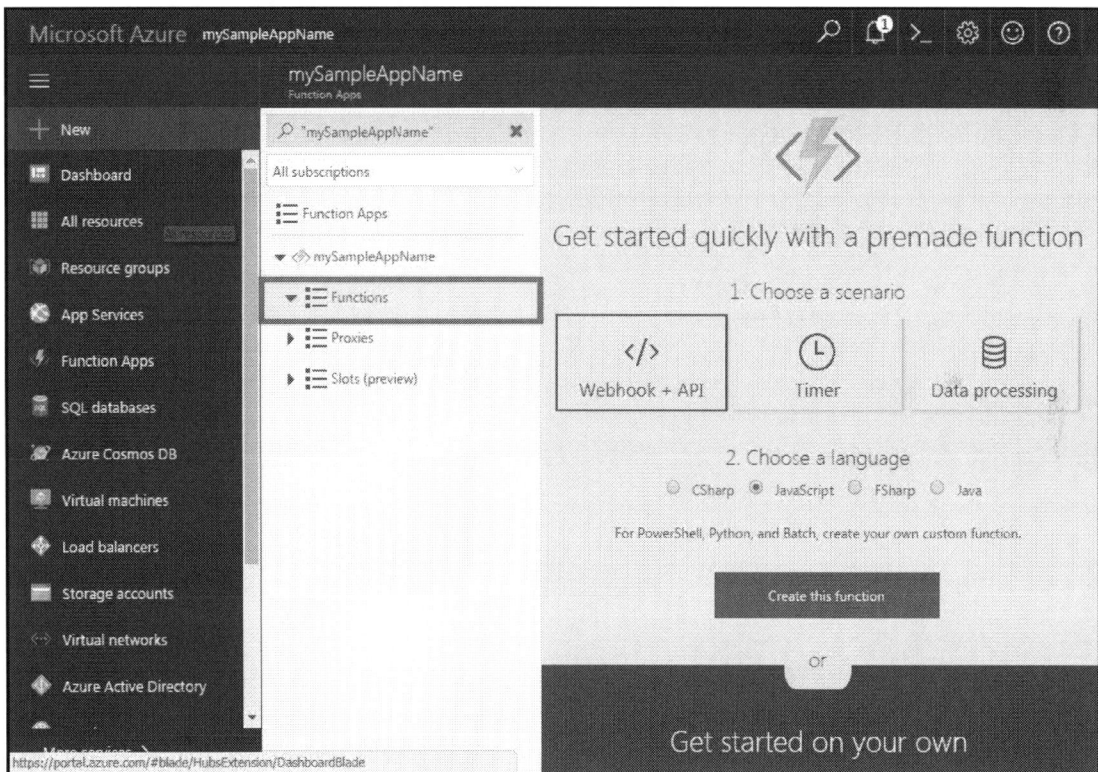

At the click of the button, a UI will open with an embedded sample Node.js function in it. We can run the same Azure Function to check how it performs.

We can run the function with two methods, one is the **POST** method and another is the **GET** method. By default, the function runs with the **POST** method. So let's click on the **Run** button. In the next window, replace **Request Body** with the JSON value and click on **Run again**.

In the **POST** method, let's add the following JSON details:

```
{
    "name": "My Azure Function"
}
```

Run will trigger the function and display the output in the request body, as displayed in the following screenshot:

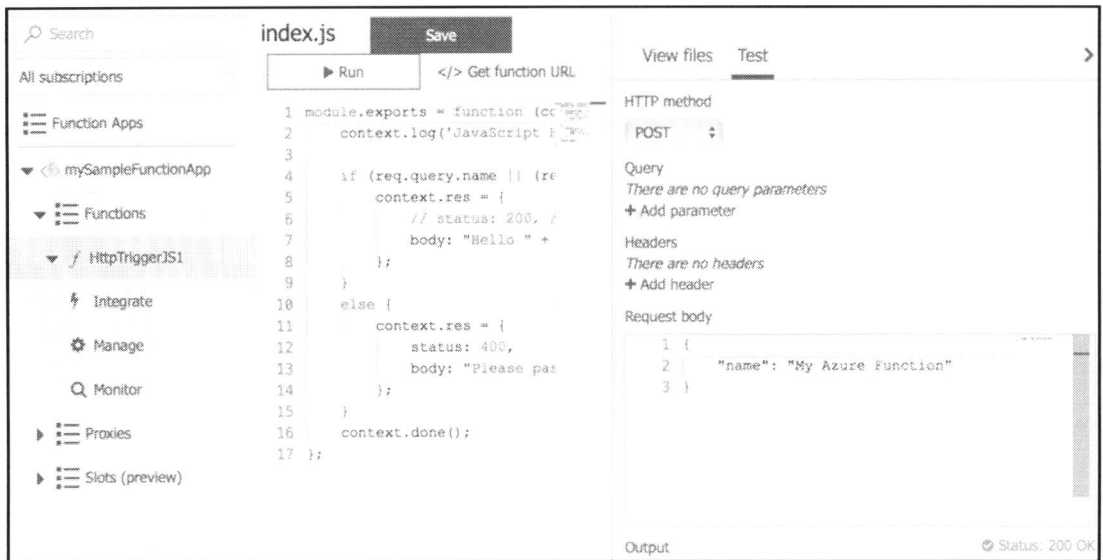

And, as we change the **HTTP method** to GET, we need to feed in a query parameter. To do this, click on **+ Add Parameter** in Query and fill in the key as **name** and value as **DevOps** and then click on **Run**. After the successful execution of this, we can see the output log in the log window as **Hello DevOps.**

So, in the previous tutorial, we learned how to create a simple hello world azure function and execute the same with the POST and GET methods. In further chapters, we will looking at how to automate the deployment.

Implementing continuous integration and continuous delivery with Azure Functions

Now that we have created a simple application through the Azure portal, the next question is how do we add a multiple number of functions, source code them and set up automated build and deployment. We do this, of course, through DevOps and automation. Let's start with continuous integration. As we know, continuous integration is an integral part of DevOps, where an application is integrated to work as one unit. We have to achieve the continuous integration, automated testing and continuous deployment for Azure Functions through automation.

To start, we will first create an assembly line. The assembly line starts with a code repository like GitHub or SVN and concludes with production deployment. Everything within this has to be automated with almost minimal manual intervention through a pipeline. We will be covering pipelines in detail in the next chapter.

To achieve continuous integration, we need to start with pushing the code into the GitHub repository. The developer should start building the application by creating a featured branch for building each piece of a functions module, then all the featured branches should be reviewed and merged to develop branch and finally to master branch for clean code building. All the featured branches should go through a continuous integration process , that is, a functions code will go through unit testing , state code analysis and various other testing in an automated way. Then code from the featured branch should be merged into the master. The master branch is used to build and deploy to a UAT or OAT environment, where performance testing should be performed and further deployed into production.

The continuous delivery process kicks in at the moment the developer checks in code into the local or featured branch. The automated build will be triggered, which is followed by unit testing and integration testing. Even though the code is very well tested, it still needs to be tested for usability and acceptance testing. So, a successful exit from the continuous integration process will trigger a continuous delivery process and delivery to QA staging. The QA environment normally resembles a production environment. This is where automated and manual acceptance testing kicks in. Having continuous delivery in place, we should be able to release the environment daily, weekly or fortnightly, or whatever suits the business requirement. But we should be able to deploy to production without much effort or manual deployment.

Let's look at an example which follows the continuous integration and delivery. In this example, we will be using open source DevOps tools to actually test and deploy the application on the Azure Cloud. We need tools like Jenkins, which is a popular open source orchestration tool, and the serverless framework which we used for AWS deployment, and the Node.js module for unit testing the code.

For my feasibility, I have used Docker for setting up the Jenkins instance with Node.js and npm installed on it. I have pushed the Dockerfile for this on the Git repository where all the example files reside on the GitHub link below, and also my tutorials are built on Linux:
`https://github.com/shzshi/azure-helloworld-ci.git`

If you are using the Dockerfile from the Git repository, then make sure Docker is installed on your laptop/PC. We will first clone the previous mentioned Git repository and build the Docker image with jenkins, serverless framework, and all the required dependencies for Azure Functions deployment, with the following command:

```
$ git clone https://github.com/shzshi/azure-helloworld-ci.git
$ cd azure-helloworld-ci
$ docker build -t chapter4jenkins:latest .
```

Then run the Docker container with the following command, this will create a container with Jenkins, Node.js 8.9, Serverless Framework 2.5 and npm 5.6:

```
$ docker run --rm -d -p 50000:50000 -p 8080:8080 chapter4jenkins:latest
```

> If you already have Jenkins set up, then make sure you have Node.js 8.9, npm 5.6, and serverless framework 2.5 installed on the server for the previous example to work.

Once Jenkins is up and running, we will create a job in Jenkins which will run the unit test and then deploy the Azure Function through a serverless framework to the Azure Cloud. Once successfully deployed, we will invoke the function through a serverless framework.

Use the following steps in order:

1. The following is the screenshot of the Jenkins homepage. We will create a new job, so click on the link **New Item** and create a new job:

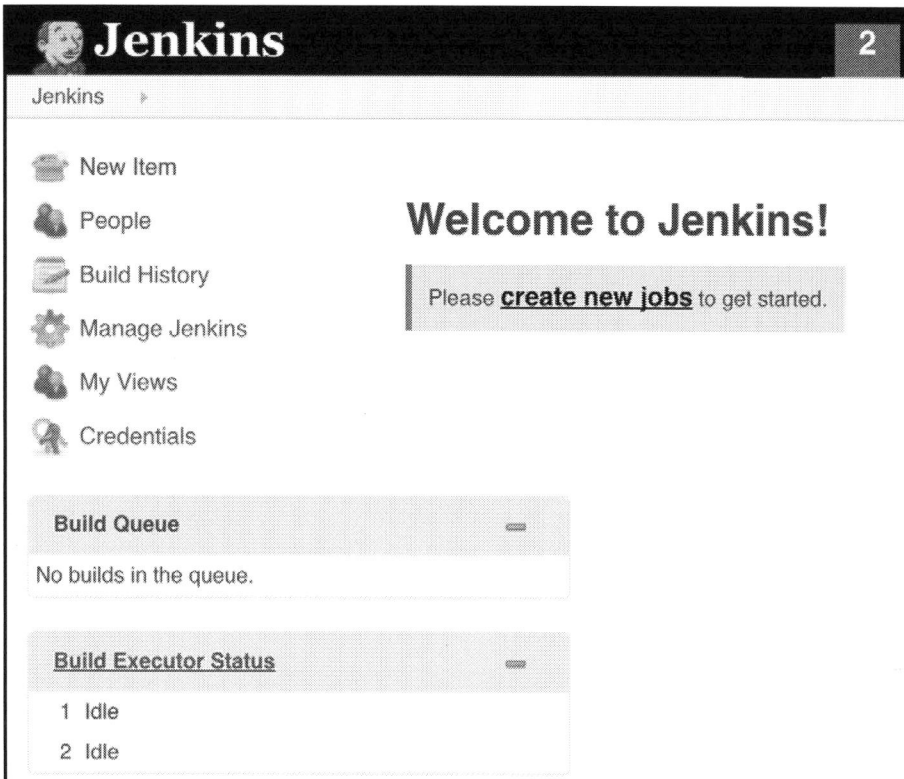

2. Create a job name, whatever suits, and select **Freestyle project** and submit **OK**:

3. Then we will redirect to the configure page for the job, where we will add the Git repository for cloning, click on the **Source Code Management** tab, and add details in the Git repository as shown here:

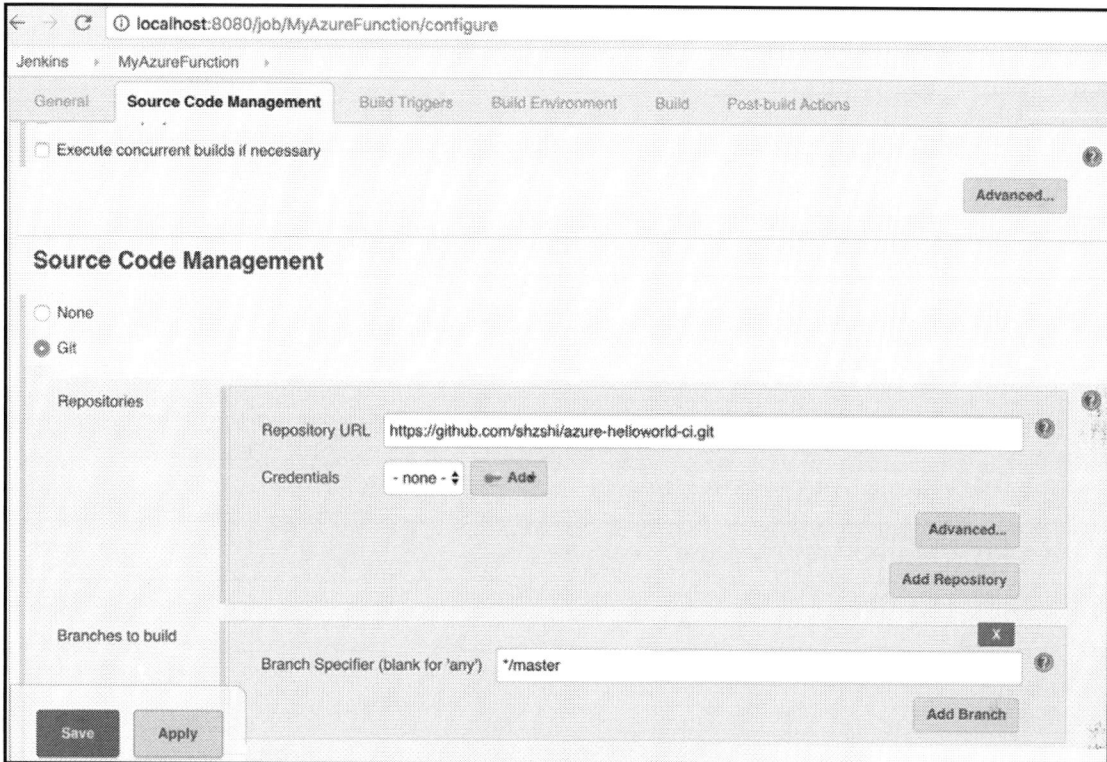

4. Then click the **Build** tab and create an execute shell, and, through the **Add build step** drop-down menu, we add `npm install` to install the required Node.js modules from the internet, and then run the Node.js test, which will unit test the Azure library function and give us the result.

We can add many unit tests to test our function, before deploying it to Azure Cloud, to make sure the app is unit tested before it goes on to the cloud:

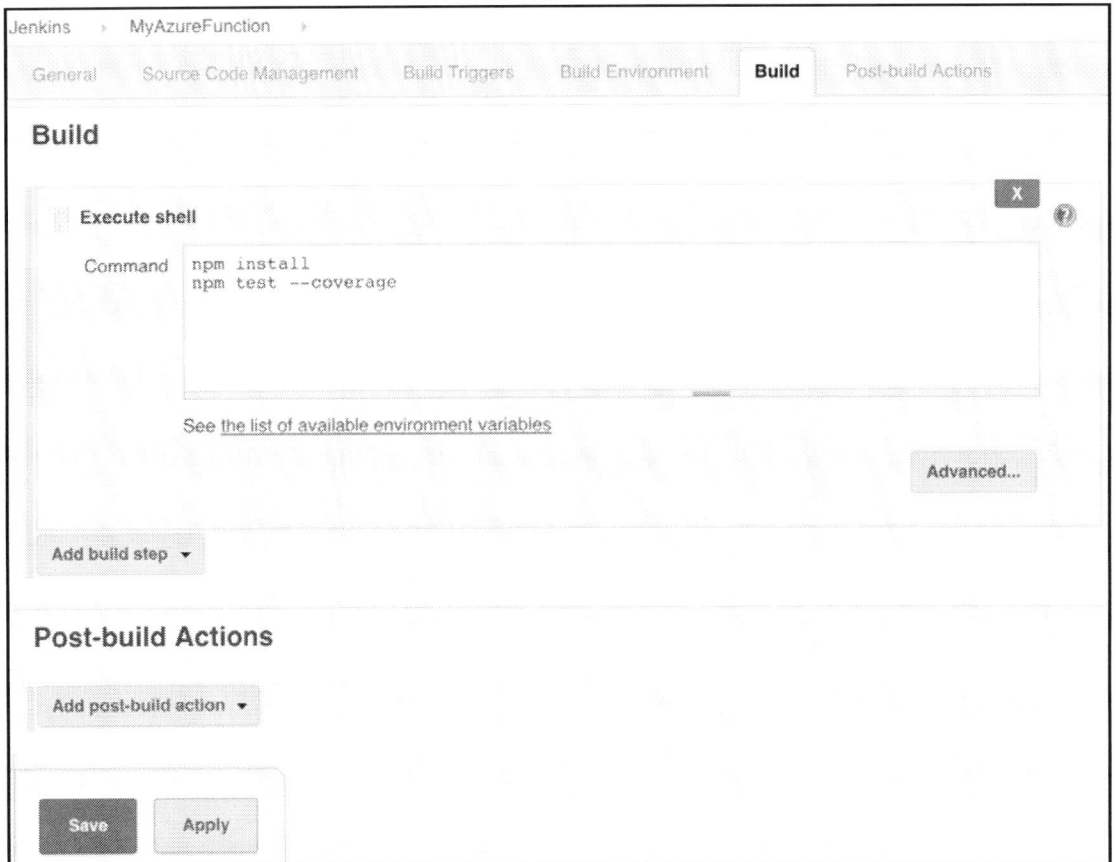

Make sure you have the **Publish HTML report** plugin already installed through steps **Jenkins Home** | **Manage Jenkins** | **Manage Plugins**.

5. Once we run the preceding job, then a unit test is performed and the report is generated for the unit test, which we can view by configuring post-build action. So, let's click on the **Post-build Actions** tab, then click on the dropdown **Add post-build action** and select **Publish HTML reports**, click on **Add** and then configure it as per the following screenshot:

6. **Save** the job and run the build. Once the job has built successfully, we should be able to view the code coverage HTML view, from the job's homepage. The coverage will look like the following screenshot, which should give us a good view of how our unit test has performed:

In the previous section, we unit tested our function and looked at coverage of the function. Next we will configure deployment onto the cloud.

Continuous integration with Azure Functions

Now, moving on to deploying to Azure Cloud Functions, we will be using a serverless framework. The framework will be doing all the heavy lifting, but it needs a few pre-requisites to make it work. They are: **serverless-azure-functions** and **cli az login** to get the required credentials and account details. Please use the following steps to do this in the pre-requisites section:

Prerequisites

We can install `serverless-azure-functions` through the npm. The following command will install the latest version of the plugin, but if you are using the docker image which is created above, it already has the plugin added to it:

```
$ npm i --save serverless-azure-functions
```

But, to interface with the Azure platform, we need to set up Azure subscription credentials locally. For the `serverless-azure-functions` plugin to work we need to set up a service principal, which can done through the Azure portal URL as seen in the following:

```
https://docs.microsoft.com/en-us/azure/azure-resource-manager/resource-group-create-service-principal-portal
```

However, if you are using PowerShell cmdlets, then use the following:

```
https://docs.microsoft.com/en-us/azure/azure-resource-manager/resource-group-authenticate-service-principal
```

I will be using CLI for our tutorial , but you are free to use whichever fits best. or through Azure CLI , Please follow the given steps to get the Azure CLI locally:

```
https://docs.microsoft.com/en-us/cli/azure/install-azure-cli?view=azure-cli-latest
```

Alternatively, you can use the Azure Cloud Shell, as follows:

```
https://docs.microsoft.com/en-us/azure/cloud-shell/overview
```

Once the Azure CLI is successfully installed we should be able to access `login` by using the following command:

```
$ az login
```

The previous command will prompt us to visit `https://aka.ms/devicelogin` and provide us with a code and with Azure identity. We will then be able to access our account through the CLI. We will be provided with account details like the following one on the command line:

```
{
  "cloudName": "AzureCloud",
  "id": "c6e5c9a2-a4dd-4c81b4-6bed04f913ea",
  "isDefault": true,
  "name": "My Azure Subscription",
  "state": "Enabled",
   "tenantId": "5bc108159c-4cbe-a7c9-bce05cb065c1",
   "user": {
     "name": "hello@example.com",
       "type": "user"
   }
}
```

We also need to get subscription details through the following command:

```
$ az account list
```

Next, we need to create a service principal. We can do this by running the following command. It will provide us with a JSON object that we will need to authenticate with Azure Cloud:

```
$ az ad sp create-for-rbac
 Retrying role assignment creation: 1/36
 {
   "appId": "e28115c2-ba87-4ddb-b3fb-62c91ade4a2e",
   "displayName": "azure-cli-2018-01-30-01-28-48",
   "name": "http://azure-cli-2018-01-30-01-28-48",
   "password": "e87a0489-63a7-41a1-b0ef-9054eda5b8c8",
   "tenant": "0a76ffdc-0cda-4d93-850f-025f940889dc"
 }
```

And the last pre-requisite we need is for an **EnvInject** plugin to be installed in Jenkins to mask the Azure credentials. So please make sure that it is added.

Setting up environment variables

Finally, we create environment variables with subscription ID, tenant, name, and password. We need to export this on the Jenkins node and set up a deployment. So let's do that:

1. Open the Jenkins in browser and add a new job with a click on **New Item**. Enter the item name **myAzureFunctionDeploy** and select **Freestyle project**, and click **OK**.

2. On the job configuration page, tick **This project is parameterised** and add **Password Parameter** below the name and default values retrieved from the Azure commands as follows:

   ```
   azureServicePrincipalTenantId
   azureServicePrincipalClientId
   azureServicePrincipalPassword
   azureSubId
   ```

3. Let's click on the **Source Code Management** tab and add the repository URL as https://github.com/shzshi/azure-helloworld-ci.git, the repository has the required files.

4. In **Build Environment** select **Inject passwords to the build as environment variables**. We are doing this to mask the Azure credentials and other details.

5. Next, click on the **Build** tab and, in the execute shell, add the steps mentioned in the following example, and then click on **Save**.

   ```
   export azureSubId=${azureSubId}
   export
   azureServicePrincipalTenantId=${azureServicePrincipalTenantId}
   export
   azureServicePrincipalClientId=${azureServicePrincipalClientId}
   export
   azureServicePrincipalPassword=${azureServicePrincipalPassword}
   serverless deploy
   ```

6. Let's click on **Build with parameters**. Then click on **Build** the job will build, create a package and deploy the functions onto the Azure portal. We can test the function on the cloud. Once the function is deployed we can invoke or run through a serverless command prompt. We can integrate this in smoke testing or functional testing, so we test the running of the function in actuality through command line or adding the same line into Jenkins job, as seen in the following:

```
$ serverless invoke -f hello --data {"name": "DevOps"}
```

We can also stream the logs of the function, to check how functions got deployed, or how it performed while it ran:

```
$ serverless logs -f <function_name>
```

We can change the code in the source code repository and run these commands individually, or through orchestrating tools like Jenkins to perform perfect continuous integration and continuous delivery.

We can integrate removal of the function from the Azure Function through the following command. This can be integrated within the Jenkins pipeline to undeploy or to rollback the function to a previous version:

```
$ serverless remove
```

Continuous deployment to Azure Functions

Continuous deployment means that every code we commit should go through an automated unit, integration, and performance testing, and also go through an automated source code analysis and be successfully deployed all the way to production without manual intervention. But, in some cases we should be able to roll back the deployment because of some bugs or issues in the production. Rollback can be automated, but usually rollback is done manually. We can set up a continuous delivery pipeline through the Azure portal. Let's set up a simple continuous delivery pipeline. Azure Cloud has an out-of-the-box feature to set up a pipeline for Azure Function. It integrates with a good number of source code managements, such as Git, GitHub, Bitbucket, Visual Studio team services, and a few others. The continuous deployment is set up on a per function app basis and also a function code can be maintained through a source repository, and the code within the portal becomes read only. So, the moment the code is updated and committed into the source code repository, the function code is automatically built and deployed on the portal.

Setting up a continuous deployment Azure deployment tool

Here we will demonstrate to how to set up continuous delivery with a GitHub repository through the Azure portal:

1. Log into the Azure portal (`https://portal.azure.com`). On successful login click on the **All resources** link. We should be able to see the **Function App** created:

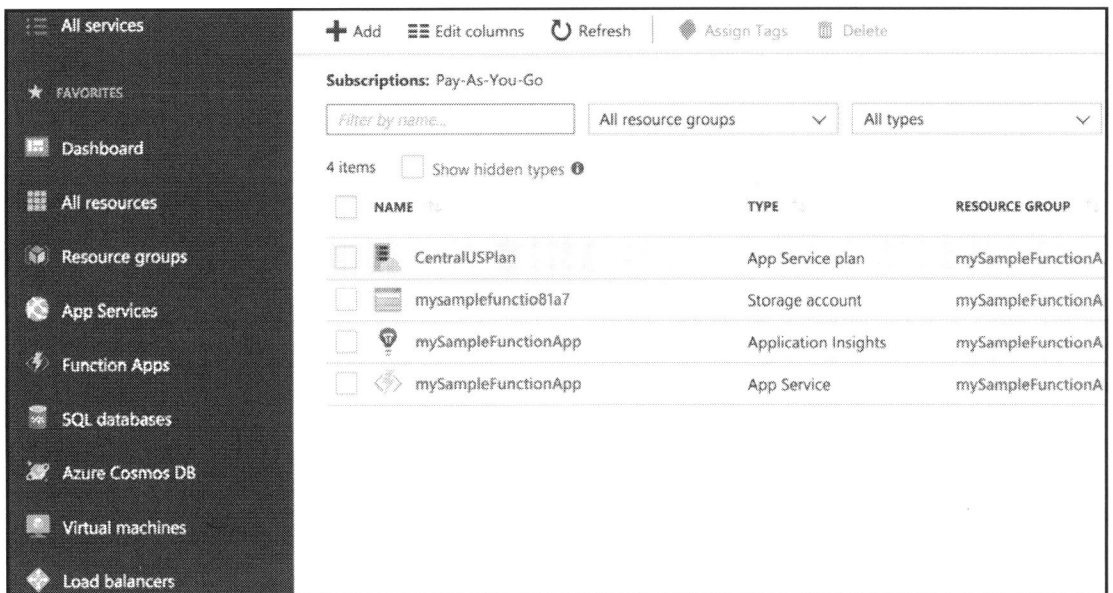

2. Select the app for which we need to set up the continuous deployment, as per my example. I will pick up **azure-helloword-ci** which takes me to the function apps windows. Then, on the function apps windows, we will select **Platform features** on the top right hand side tab and then click on **Deployment options**:

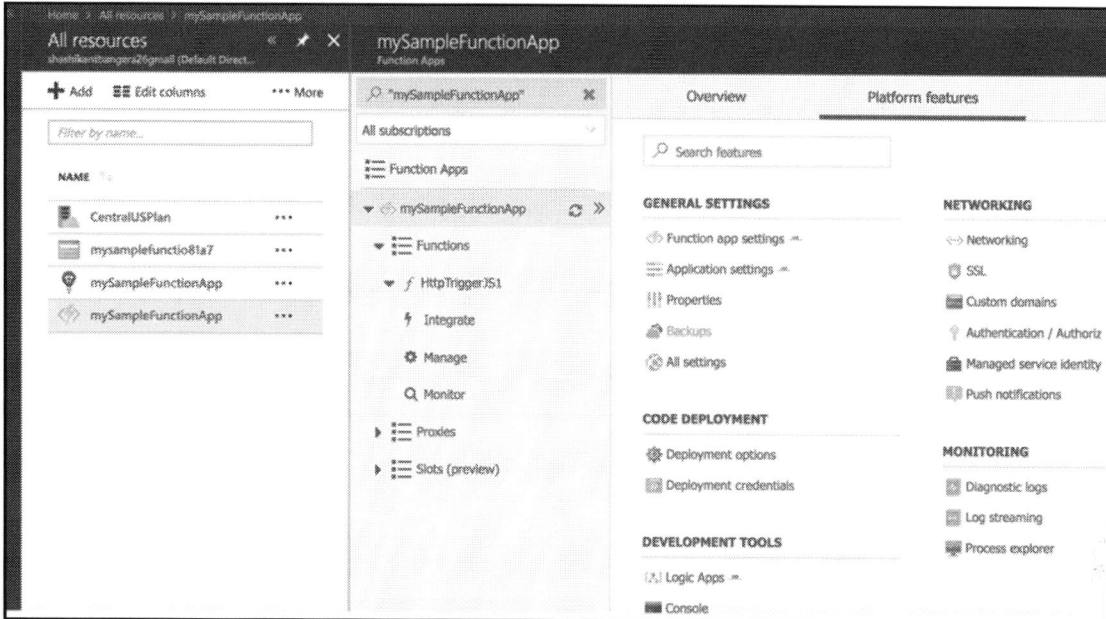

3. Then, in the deployment section, click on **setup**. Then another window will slide, with the heading **Deployment option**. Click on the link **Choose source**, then in the next window, we will see options to add the **Source control**. Let's select **GitHub**.

4. Then we will get options to configure GitHub repositories where we will be asked to authorize Azure Functions to access our private or public repositories. Please make sure you use your own account's public repository.

5. Once configured, we need to select the repository where we have to fill in choose source, authorization, choose your organization, choose project repository, branch and can configure performance test. We will be taken to the GitHub portal to put in our GitHub credentials to connect to the GitHub repository. After that, once we click **OK**, the repository will be configured with Azure Function and all the file changes in the GitHub are copied to the function app and a full site deployment is triggered.

6. We can set up performance testing with the button **Configure Performance Test**. We can create multiple environments by creating different branches, and by merging the code to the master branch for production deployment.

Blue-green deployment in Azure Functions

There are multiple deployment patterns in DevOps: canary deployment and blue green deployments. We will be talking about blue green deployment for Azure Functions in this book. Blue green deployment technique reduces the downtime and risk by having two identical production environments with the names blue and green. One environment will go live whilst the other is used for staging new changes. And there is workflow designed to switch between live and staging. Initially, a new version of the application is deployed to the blue environment with all the user traffic being redirected to the blue environment. After the next version of application has been developed, it is deployed to a staging environment (green) for testing. After the testing of the new version of the software is considered satisfactory, then all the traffic is redirected to the green environment and is considered as live.

The deployment dashboard

The development team always need to keep track of deployment and the health of the development pipeline. It also needs to know the track of deployment failure, the number of releases done, the number of check-ins, and many other metrics which are very important for the development cycle. There is one open source which can help to track all these details and it is Hygieia. Hygieia is an open source tool available for a holistic view on the single screen for tracking build, deployment, quality control, and application performance. It also helps to track deployment versions, and also the health of the application.

Hygieia is a DevOps dashboard tool, developed by Capital One, and the company has open-sourced the tool.

The Hygieia dashboard has two views, one is a widget and other is a pipeline. The widget view displays information about features in the current sprint, code contribution activities, continuous integration activities, code analysis, security analysis, unit and functional test results, deployment, and environment status. The pipeline view has components of the deployment life cycle which show progression through development, Int, QA, performance, and production. Hygieia also has product dashboard which displays a collaborative dashboard for multiple applications within each product.

Hygieia has lots of plugins which integrate or get the logs from many DevOps tools like Jira, Subversion, Jenkins, Sonar, IBM UrbanCode Deploy and, as Hygieia is an open source, we can build our own plugin and widget for the Hygieia.

Out of the box, the Hygieia dashboard application integrates with VersionOne, Jira, Subversion, GitHub, Hudson/Jenkins, Sonar, HP Fortify, Cucumber/Selenium and IBM Urbancode Deploy.

Hygieia is built on Java and plugins run through a Java command line. We can set up a whole Hygieia dashboard over the docker containers. Please follow the link for setup and integration: `https://github.com/capitalone/Hygieia`.

Monitoring and logging

Serverless applications help speed up development and independence and allow the execution which triggers events, but when these function do not work as expected, how do we verify that events are activating the right functions? With serverless applications, the root cause analysis becomes more complicated, because services are small and their functionality is very precise. While trying to track down the fault source, neither the services involved nor any of the integration points actually exist, and when there is more than one function which takes part in the operation, the investigation becomes very difficult.

That is where the logs plays a vital role, but there are some unique considerations which need to be taken into account when logging into a serverless architecture.
And it is normal for several functions to fail and not to deliver the requested functionality, or for the logs contain a unified identifier for the transaction, so when function logs are analysed, the transaction failure can be detected easily and the failure problem can be fixed.

In Azure Functions we can get logs in many ways. The easiest way is to log in to the Azure portal, go to the respective function and select the **Monitor** tab. Here we will see a list of function invocations, their status, and last run with duration. If we select the invocation that has failed, then, on the right-hand side, we can see the exact log and other required information.

Accessing logs through Kudu

We can access the logs through Kudu. Kudu was developed to access the Microsoft Azure web apps environment. As Azure Function runs on a web app, we can use Kudu to access the logs of the Azure Functions. Kudu can access environment information, and also details of the actual filesystem which is attached to the function while running.

Kudu can be accessed through a web browser. The link for the same would be `https://myAzureFunction.scm.azurewebsites.net`. We have to replace the `myAzureFunction` with our web app name. The best part of Kudu, is that it will give us the actual file system access of our function environment, either through shell or through browsing, which makes it easier to get to root cause of the failure.

Logging information via table storage

All logging and timing information of the function is stored in the storage account that we created earlier while creating our function app. We can access the log through Visual Studio if we have Azure SDK installed. We can also access the logs through Cloud Explorer Window. (If you have multiple Azure Function apps then it might be a bit tricky to remember which one belongs to which function app, but you can discover that by looking in your **Application Settings** at the contents of the `AzureWebJobsStorage` setting).

Monitoring the Azure Function

Monitoring the function is essential. It will give a good view of how our function or app is performing with traffic and also when it scales and descales. Azure Function has built-in integration with Azure application insight. Application insight is built in an APM (application performance management) service by Azure. We can configure application insight during the creation of a function app and send the telemetric data to **Application Insights**. Create a new function app and set the **Application Insights** switch **On** and the **Application Insights Location**:

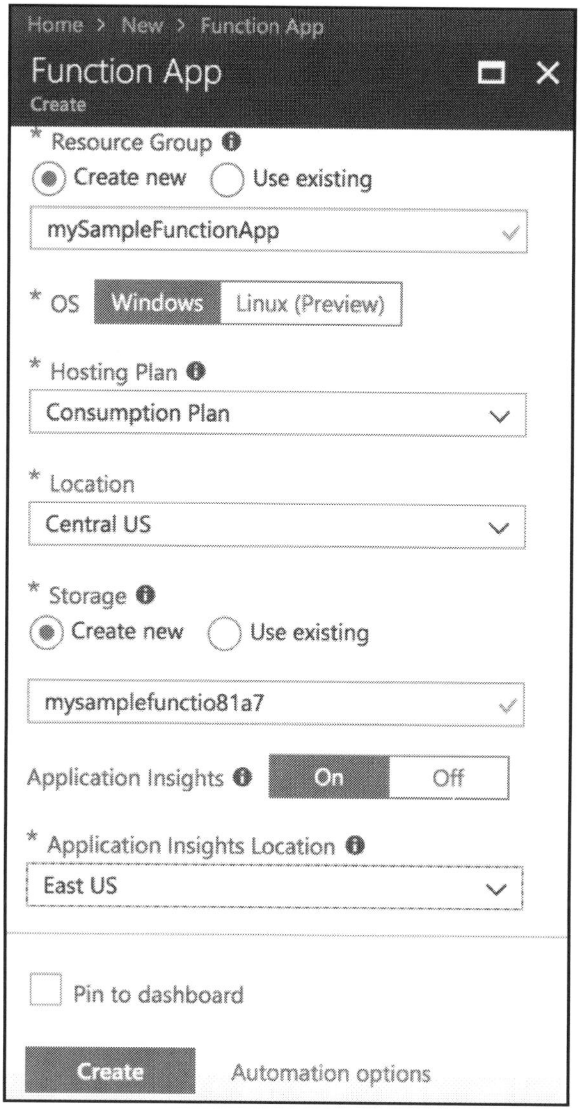
Home > New > Function App
Function App
Create
* Resource Group
Create new
Use existing
mySampleFunctionApp
* OS
Windows
Linux (Preview)
* Hosting Plan
Consumption Plan
* Location
Central US
* Storage
Create new
Use existing
mysamplefunctio81a7
Application Insights
On
Off
* Application Insights Location
East US
Pin to dashboard
Create
Automation options

We can see the performance graph in the **Metrics Explorer** of the Azure Cloud portal to monitor the function health:

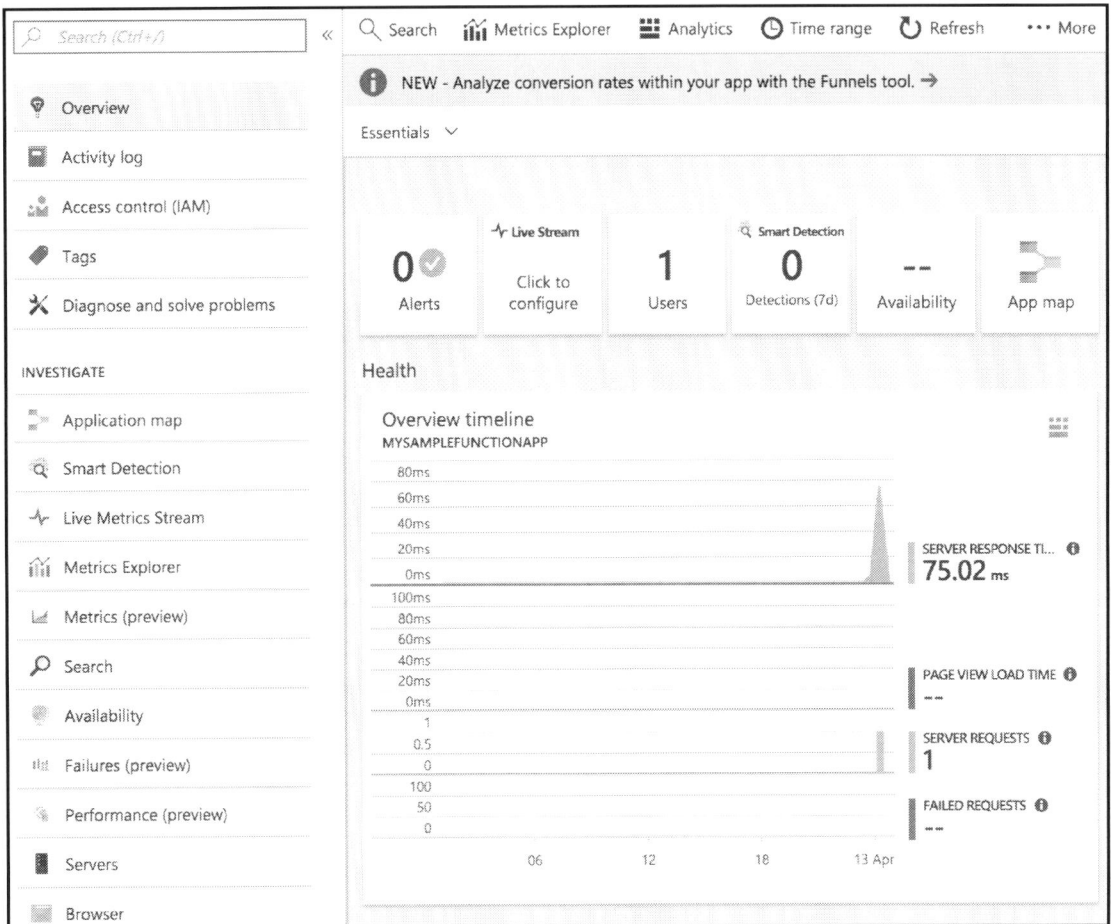

Integrating with New Relic

New Relic provides integration for Azure Function that does the following functions:

- Reports data from Azure Functions to New Relic products.
- Reports metric data, like the count of functions executed, bytes sent and received, and HTTP errors.
- Collects inventory data about the status and configuration of the service.

You can monitor and alert on your Azure Functions data from New Relic, and you can create custom queries and chart dashboards.

> To activate the Azure Functions integration, follow the Azure Integration Activation through the link: `https://docs.newrelic.com/docs/ integrations/microsoft-azure-integrations/getting-started/ activate-azure-integrations`.

Best practice

DevOps for serverless is pretty young and evolving. Serverless itself is emerging at a fast pace, and, within that framework, to automate deployment and integration with other DevOps, it is changing faster. Talking about best practice for smooth code deployment from development to production, we need to look at various tenants of DevOps for Azure Function and learn from the mistakes during implementation. But because serverless is still evolving, and DevOps with serverless is still niche, we would not be able to highlight every aspect of DevOps. However, we will look at some of the main tenants and talk about them in detail here. So the main tenant for DevOps with serverless are: source code management, build, deployment, release management, monitoring, and logging, which is almost the same as application. But because serverless are micro services, there is bit of a change when we apply DevOps to it. So let's look at each aspect of it and learn the best way of applying DevOps to the Azure Functions.

Source code management

Developers write the code and work together to perform a task, but developers keep adding to the new features, or they update the code to perform better, or to enhance the functionality. This is why we need source code management. Git is one of most popular source code management tools available. So we have to set up various strategies for efficient management of the code. But before that we need to set up a folder structure for Azure Function.

Folder structure

All the functions codes of a specific function app would be located in the root folder with one or many subfolders and a host configuration file. The `host.json` file will contain runtime specific configurations. And each function folder will have one or more code files, `function.json`, configurations, and other function dependencies:

```
wwwroot
| - host.json
| - myazurenodefunction
| | - function.json
| | - index.js
| | - node_modules|
| | - ... packages ...
| | - package.json
| - myazurecsharpfunction
| | - function.json
| | - run.csx
```

With the folder structure we need to apply the best method of branching strategy for robust development and smooth deployment. The best practice is to have multiple branches with a master, which is a default branch, for easy development, and future easy release into production. Those branches are feature, develop, release, and hot fixes branches.

The feature branch helps easy tracking of a feature, as well as aiding parallel development between team members. A feature branch might branch from a develop branch, but should always merge back to a develop branch. The next main branch would be a develop branch and this branch lives through the life cycle of project development and support. When the source code from a develop branch is stable, then it is merged back to the master branch, after successful release, and every merge to the master will trigger a production release.

A release branch may be from a develop branch, but they must merge back to the develop and master branches. The release branch is used for preparation of new production release. The release branch is used for next big release. It provides with us room for minor bug fixes, and for setting up meta data for release. When the release branch is ready to be a real release then we need to make sure it is merged with the master and the commit must be tagged for future historical versions. Finally, the release branch should be merged with the develop branch, so that we get all the changes of this release in future releases.

Last of all is the hotfix branch. This is almost the same as the release branch, as it helps us in production release. Hotfix is actually useful when production deployment fails and you need to hotfix production, so that we can get it back live. So to resolve the production failure, we branch hotfix branch off a production tag from the master branch, so that one team can fix the production failure and rest of the team can continue development on the develop branch. The rule of thumb is that the hotfix branch might branch from a master and then, once hotfix is successful, the changes are merged back to the master. They also need to merge to the develop branch, to make sure we have these hotfix changes in future releases.

Testing and static code analysis

Testing is an essential part of development, it is must when we develop any application. It helps to mitigate most of the bugs and performance issues before going to production. There are many types of testing involved in application development. These include, unit testing, integration testing and performance testing. They integrated into different stages of the environment deployment. Unit testing is integrated in the development stage.

The serverless handler should always be a thin layer that uses modules out of your code library. And modules should be well-covered with unit tests; then testing of the serverless application will be easy during the integration tests.

We should try to run unit tests and integration test the modules and function locally, this will help to run the tests faster, and find issues in code base easily, and without deploying to cloud. We should run them remotely as well, because remote infrastructure is a bit different from local infrastructure. We can achieve both by setting up a pipeline and staging them as different environments (development, stage, user acceptance testing, pre-production and production), where development and stage testing should be invoked locally, and same testing with better performance is tested remotely on the rest of the environment.

Static code analysis is the process of analyzing source code to flag programming errors, bugs, stylistic errors, and suspicious constructs. We have to make sure we have to integrate linting tool for serverless function in the pipeline stage. This helps to keep the code clean, less buggy and perfectly indented.

Deployment and release

There are various types of deployment pattern, but we should select one which fits our case, and which uses all the functions together in one go: blue-green and canaries, and also lots of complexities, such as redundancy, high availability, rollback, A/B testing and incremental roll outs. All these need to be considered during deployment, and deployment should be achieved with ease and flexibility. So it should always be better to decide on the pattern before starting the automation.

We have to make sure deployment is constantly monitored and deployment failures are analysed and improved with time. All the deployment should be triggered through automated pipelines with minimal manual intervention, attached to a GitHub repository, with strict branching strategy. We can also package the function app and upload into Nexus to set up easier roll back. All the deployment should have a feedback loop all the way to project tracking tools like JIRA/rally. This will make it easier to trace the failure.

Summary

To summarize, we covered continuous integration, continuous deployment, logging, and monitoring of Azure Functions and also fleshed out best practices around how to manage the Azure Functions in a source code repository, the importance of testing and automated deployment. Serverless or functions with Azure Cloud are still an early development but improving as each day passes. There is still lots to achieve in terms of adoption and improvement. But once adoption of serverless grows, DevOps practices around it will improve and become robust. In the next chapter, we will learn how to apply DevOps to OpenWhisk, another serverless provider.

5
Integrating DevOps with IBM OpenWhisk

In this chapter, we will be looking at OpenWhisk, which is an open source on-cloud serverless provider. We will also be learning how to build, test, and deploy OpenWhisk functions, as well as how to manage logs and monitor the functions. We will also look at the best practices for DevOps with OpenWhisk.

OpenWhisk

OpenWhisk is an incubator project of Apache and IBM. It offers an open source and on-cloud serverless platform through the IBM Bluemix portal. We can set this up on premises or directly use the cloud model. The commercial side of OpenWhisk is provided by IBM on Bluemix, and the open source version can be provisioned as on-premises **Infrastructure as a Service (IaaS)**, as well as on a cloud, such as Bluemix, Amazon EC2, Microsoft Azure, or GCP. The open source version is available on GitHub. It is been made public through the Apache license, and people can contribute to it.

> For the open source OpenWhisk version on GitHub, go to `https://`
> `github.com/apache/incubator-openwhisk/tree/master/docs#getting-`
> `started-with-openwhisk`.

Like any other serverless offering, OpenWhisk executes small chunks of codes that are called **actions** (that is, functions) at the triggering of events. Events can originate from Bluemix or external sources. It is also claimed by OpenWhisk that it allows the integration of a home-grown event provider, or any other event provider, rather than being limited to specific ones, as other serverless service providers do.

OpenWhisk provides many features, such as autoscaling and load balancing, out of the box without having to manually configure clusters, load balancers, and HTTP plugins. Let's look at the architecture diagram for OpenWhisk:

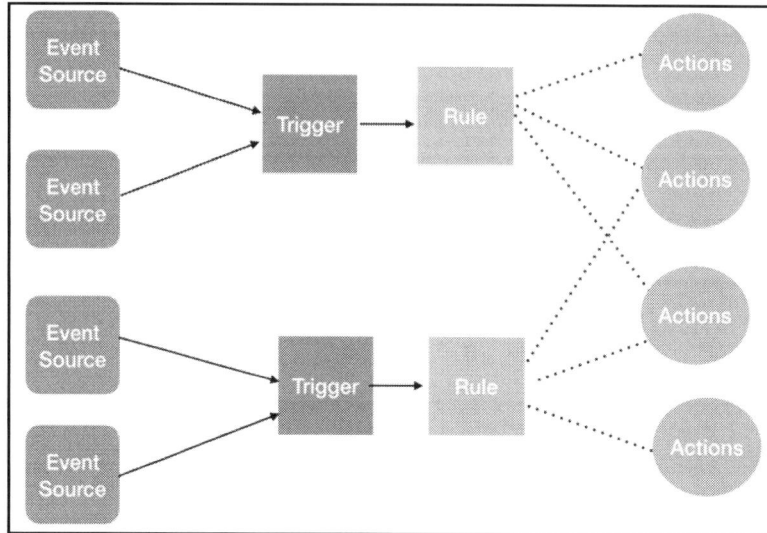

The actions/functions are performed at the triggering of events, which could be changes to database records, IoT sensor readings, code commits to a GitHub repository, or simple HTTP requests from web or mobile apps. Events from these sources are channelled through a trigger, and rules within the triggers allow actions to react to these events.

Action is an OpenWhisk term for functions. Actions could be small snippets of JavaScript or Swift code, or custom binary code embedded in a Docker container.

Actions are normally invoked in a sequence, and output from one action can be passed as input to the next action in the sequence. Actions can be invoked through multiple sources, such as the OpenWhisk API, CLI, and iOS SDK, in addition to triggers.

The languages supported by OpenShift are Node.js, Python, Swift, Java, and PHP, and it is claimed by OpenShift that one of their USPs supports the Swift language, which will come in handy while writing functions or actions for mobile apps.

Services and event provider integrations can be performed using packages. A **package** is a bundle of feeds and actions. A **feed** is a piece of code that configures an external event source to fire trigger events. For example, in a bank account transaction, a trigger is created when a debit or credit event takes place and a function/action will run to send the SMS to the user about the transaction that has taken place. The actions in the packages have reusable logic that service providers make available for the people to use the service. These service providers are event sources, and they can also be invoked through the API.

OpenWhisk is built on NGINX, Kafka, Docker, and CouchDB. All of these components work together to make a serverless service for OpenWhisk.

OpenWhisk setup and configuration

OpenWhisk operates four important concepts, which are listed as follows:

- Triggers
- Actions
- Rules
- Sequences

Triggers

Triggers are like events that are created by data sources. Some examples include changing database records, new code commits to your repository, and HTTP requests from a web/mobile app. The events from the sources are channeled through a trigger.

Actions

An **action** is a snippet of code written in Node.js or Swift, or embedded in Docker containers. The code is deployed and is executed at the firing of the trigger.

Rules

Rules form a part of the triggers when combined with an action. So every time the trigger fires, the respective action is invoked by the rule.

Sequences

The chains of actions are called **sequences**. We can chain the actions, and they will be invoked in order. The output of one action can become the input for the next action.

Building an OpenWhisk application

In this book, I will not be setting up an open source version of OpenWhisk. Instead, we will be using tutorials through the Bluemix portal, so to do this, we need to sign up to the Bluemix portal. They give new members the option of a free subscription for a month. So let's register with Bluemix at `https://bluemix.net`. As I mentioned earlier, IBM Bluemix comes with a free trial that doesn't need credit card details for the first 30 days. Following the trial, we do not have to enroll using a credit card. All the users get access to around 400,000 GB-seconds of serverless computing time per month. Additional execution time would be charged at $0.000017 per GB-second of execution, rounded to the nearest 100 ms.

Creating a hello world OpenWhisk action

The prerequisites for this tutorial is an IBM cloud account (free trial) and knowledge of Node.js (which we have used throughout the book). We will be starting with a simple example first and then move towards applying automation to the tutorial code as we go on with the chapter. So, let's create a simple hello world application with Node.js on the user interface of IBM Bluemix Cloud and then execute/invoke it.

To create an OpenWhisk action, go through the following steps:

1. Go to the OpenWhisk console at `https://console.bluemix.net/openwhisk/` in the IBM Cloud.
2. Log into the IBM Cloud and click **Start Creating** to use OpenWhisk from your browser and enter the editor.
3. Click **Create Action** from the multiple options.

4. Create a new action with the following parameters:

Field	Value
Action Name	HelloWorld
Enclosing Package	(Default Package)
Runtime	Node.js 6

5. Click **Create**. This will open an editor interface for Node.js.

6. By default, OpenWhisk actions are JavaScript. They receive an associative array in their input and return another as their output.

7. Replace the existing Nodejs code with the following:

```
/**
 *
 * main() will be invoked when you Run This Action.
 *
 */
function main(params) {
    var myName;
    myName = params.name;
    if (myName == undefined)
        myName = "";
    return {
        html: "<b>" + JSON.stringify(params) + "</b>",
        js: "alert('hello " + myName + "');"
    };
}
```

8. Click on the **Save** button. This will save the action and redirect you to the page to invoke the action.

9. Let's click on **Change Input** and add the following name input, and then click on the **Apply** button:

```
{
  "name": "Serverless"
}
```

10. Now let's click the **Invoke** button to execute the action/function. We should be able see the following output:

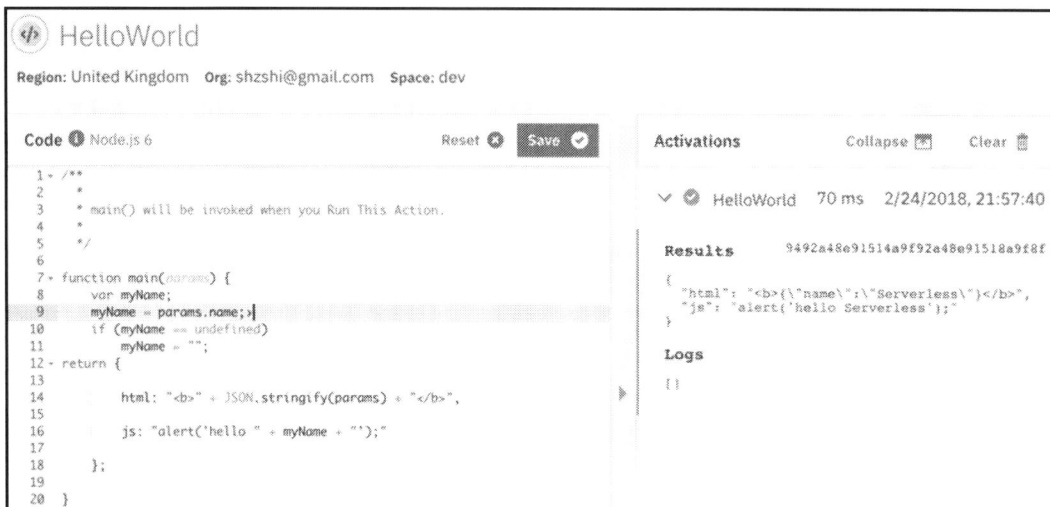

The output will be in the form of both JavaScript and HTML. In the preceding tutorial, we created an OpenWhisk action and deployed it through the Bluemix console. In the next section, we will use Serverless Framework to set up a deployment and automation.

OpenWhisk with Serverless Framework

To set up a deployment with Serverless Framework, we need to have a few things in place first. So, considering that you are already signed up, we need to retrieve the Bluemix endpoint and keys through the Bluemix CLI, and so first we need to set up and configure the Bluemix CLI, which can be done at `https://console.bluemix.net/openwhisk/learn/cli`.

Once the CLI is set up, we will then install the Cloud Function plugin through the Bluemix CLI, then log into Bluemix Cloud and deploy the action. Go through the following steps to do this:

1. First, we get the endpoint and authentication keys from the Bluemix portal using the following command:

```
$ bx wsk property get --auth whisk auth
00700a7f-2b1a-4831-
bf323a566263ed44:4TBcM7f8g0gj5UPgSVHXwNmMkfpbX36OdWximngOwqZYAJrDSk
ZwPjeSPjQ45Wm1
```

2. Once we get the authentication details through the preceding command, we can set `--apihost` and `--auth` through the `wsk` command line, as follows:

```
$ wsk property set --apihost OpenWhisk.ng.bluemix.net --auth
00700a7f-2b1a-4831-
bf32-3a566263ed44:4TBcM7f8g0gj5UPgSVHXwNmMkfpbX36OdWximngOwqZYAJrDS
kZwPjeSPjQ45Wm1

ok: whisk auth set. Run 'wsk property get --auth' to see the new
value.
ok: whisk API host set to OpenWhisk.ng.bluemix.net
```

Another way to get and set the keys would be through the portal. We can also configure the credentials through `bashrc` for the framework to use it. To do this, log into the Bluemix portal through the browser and go to the **API Key** section the retrieve and then export them. So, let's log into the Bluemix portal at `https://console.bluemix.net/openwhisk/`, then select the **API Key** menu on the left-hand side bar to get the authentication keys, as shown in the following screenshot:

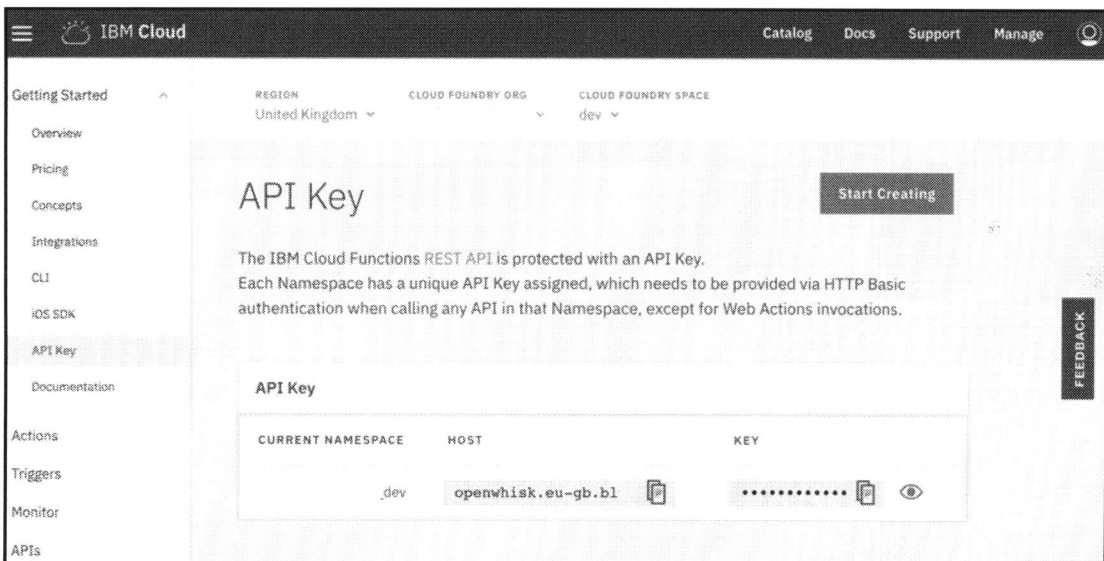

3. Let's go to the Linux or macOS Terminal and add the authentication details to the user profile using the following code:

```
$ vi ~/.bashrc
```

4. Copy the following export with the correct `auth` and `apihost` from the Bluemix portal:

```
export OW_AUTH=00700a7f-2b1a-4831-
bf32-3a566263ed44:4TBcM7f8g0gj5UPgSVHXwNmMkfpbX36OdWximngOwqZYAJrDS
kZwPjeSPjQ45Wm1
export OW_APIHOST=OpenWhisk.eu-gb.bluemix.net
```

5. The next step is to install Serverless Framework and the respective dependencies with the provider plugin, as shown in the following code:

```
$ npm install --global serverless serverless-openwhisk
```

The plugin has to be installed as a global module to work.

A simple OpenWhisk application

Now let's create a simple service through the serverless Node.js template by going through the following steps:

1. Create a new serverless service/project:

```
$ serverless create --template openwhisk-nodejs --path new-service
```

2. Change into the newly created directory:

```
$ cd new-service
```

3. Install the npm dependencies:

```
$ npm install
```

4. Once we finished, deploy the service and function to the Bluemix portal:

```
$ serverless deploy -v
```

5. Then we invoke the function to check whether the function is deployed properly. Invoke the serverless application using the following code:

```
$ serverless invoke --function hello
{
"payload": "Hello, World!"
}
```

In the preceding tutorial, we got the `auth` keys, created an action, and deployed the function through Serverless Framework. In the next section, we will look into setting up CI and CD through different methodologies.

Continuous integration and continuous delivery with OpenWhisk

For deployment, we will normally use the `wsk` command line. We will use it to do the following things:

- Git pull code from GitHub
- Set up Bluemix space for running an app
- Create the services for an application to run
- Configure the environment variables, such as service credentials
- Deploy OpenWhisk triggers and actions
- Push the Node.js application

We can do this with the IBM Bluemix toolchain or through open source tools, such as Jenkins and Serverless Framework. Let's look at both options, starting with the Bluemix toolchain.

Setting up the toolchain and repository integration

Let's create a new blank toolchain by going through the following steps. This is easily done from the Bluemix home page at `https://console.bluemix.net/devops/`:

1. Go to the preceding URL, and then click on **Create a toolchain**. Then you pick the **Build your own toolchain** template as shown in following screenshot, you give the toolchain a name, and you click **Create**. Done!

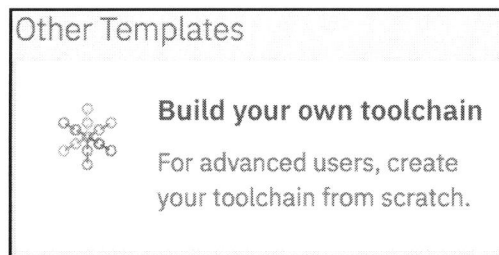

Other Templates

Build your own toolchain

For advanced users, create your toolchain from scratch.

2. You will redirected to the **Build your own toolchain** page; fill in the details and click on the **Create** button.

3. Once the toolchain is created, click on **Add a Tool**. Since the idea is to deploy it when the code is pushed to Git, the first thing to add is a GitHub integration. So let's select **GitHub** and then follow the steps. You will be prompted to authorize a GitHub account, and then give the URL of the repository you cloned earlier. Once this is done, an entry for your GitHub repository (and another for its issues, if you ticked that box) will appear in the toolchain, and we'll then add the deployment piece, which will respond to changes on our GitHub repository.

Configuring the deployment

Next, click **Add a Tool** again to put a new entry into the pipeline, and then click **Delivery Pipeline** for the tool to add, as shown in the following screenshot:

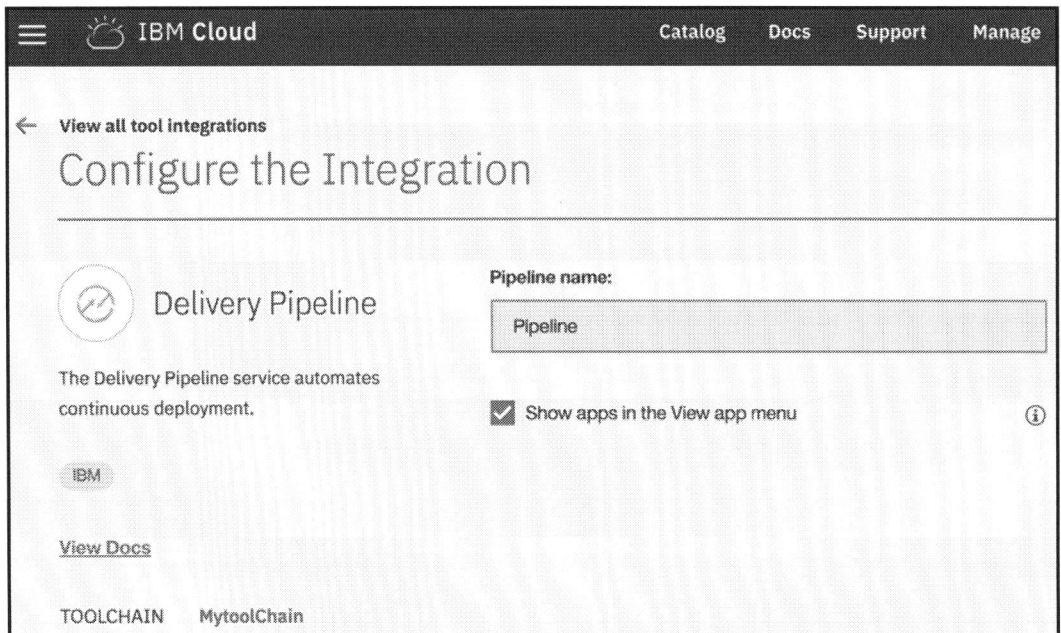

Once the delivery pipeline tool is in place, click on it and then go ahead and click **Add Stage**. There are three tabs at the top—**Input**, **Jobs**, and **Environment properties**. These govern how the deployment activity itself is set up. Here's a quick overview of these tabs:

- **Input**: This simply manages which repository and branch to use, and whether to run the deployment manually or change them as appropriate.

- **Environment properties**: This manages the variables that we can use in our setup scripts. It's possible to add both plain text and a secret field. We can set the values that we will need here, such as database credentials, access tokens, and so on. This must include a Bluemix API key, which can be generated by using `bx iam api-key-create keyname`. In our case, we need to create a variable name `APIKEY`, as shown in the following code:

```
$ bx iam api-key-create myFunction
Creating API key myFunction as user@email.com...
OK
API key myFunction was created
Please preserve the API key! It cannot be retrieved after it's
created.
Name myFunction
Description
Created At 2018-02-24T19:16+0000
API Key X4klgOXvNotJqN_haPWpPirPLhckCA9OFdZDufjcIxLY
```

- **Jobs**: This tab is where the real work gets done. We'll use a single job, so click on **ADD JOB**, type **Deploy,** and on the deployment page let's keep most of the details as their default settings, making sure that the account, organization, and space information looks correct.

The following deploy job shell script will grab the Cloud Functions plugin for the command (find out more about the Bluemix command-line tool in the documentation at `https://console.bluemix.net/docs/cli/reference/bluemix_cli/get_started. html#getting-started`), and then log in with the API key that we configured earlier and target the desired Bluemix organization and space. Add the following shell script to the **Deploy Script** column of **JOBS** and click on **Save**:

```
#!/bin/bash
bx plugin install Cloud-Functions -r Bluemix -f
#bx login -a https://api.ng.bluemix.net --apikey $APIKEY -o <email_address>
-s development
bx login -a api.eu-gb.bluemix.net --apikey $APIKEY -o <email_address> -s
dev
# handy for debugging
bx wsk action invoke /whisk.system/utils/echo -p message helloWorld --
blocking --result
# now set up your actions etc
zip helloWorld.zip index.js
bx wsk action update helloWorld --kind nodejs:6 helloWorld.zip
# check everything is as expected
bx wsk action list
```

After adding the Cloud Functions plugin to the Bluemix command-line tool, this script logs us in using the API key we created when configuring the deployment tool. Using the built in `/whisk.system/utils/echo` action will show us the output in the logs if everything is configured correctly to work with Cloud Functions, or cause a (hopefully helpful and informative) error if that's not the case. The `action update` command does the actual deployment, taking the newly zipped file and deploying it as an action. The final call to the action list simply shows us that the action is there as expected.

Check that everything works as expected by checking the green play button on this task, as depicted in the following screenshot. If it plays, you're all set!

Continuous integration and continuous delivery with Serverless Framework

Earlier, we set up continuous deployment using IBM Bluemix tools. Here, we will be using open source tools to set up continuous integration and continuous delivery for OpenWhisk functions. I will be setting up a Jenkins container with Serverless Framework installed on it. I have created a Dockerfile that does the heavy lifting for us by creating a Jenkins container with Node.js, Serverless Framework, and an OpenWhisk plugin installed. I have added this Dockerfile to the Git repository. We will be using the weather reporting OpenWhisk application, and we will code it, commit it on GitHub, and then deploy it on the Bluemix cloud through Serverless Framework. We will unit test the application and run a smoke test by invoking the function (see `https://github.com/shzshi/OpenWhisk-weather-report-serverless.git`). Let's look at these steps in more detail:

1. Git clone the repository:

   ```
   $ git clone
   https://github.com/shzshi/OpenWhisk-weather-report-serverless.git
   ```

2. Once it is successfully cloned, we need to build the OpenWhisk image using the following code:

   ```
   $ docker build --rm -f OpenWhisk-weather-report-
   serverless/Dockerfile -t OpenWhisk-weather-report-serverless:latest
   OpenWhisk-weather-report-serverless
   ```

3. Once the Docker image is built, we will create a container for the `OpenWhisk-weather-report-serverless:latest` image, using the following code:

   ```
   $ docker run --rm -it -p 50000:50000 -p 8080:8080 -v
   /Users/HOST_PATH/OpenWhisk-weather-report-
   serverless/jenkins:/var/jenkins_home OpenWhisk-weather-report-
   serverless:latest
   ```

4. Now we will go to the browser, navigate to the Jenkins application, and create a job. As my Docker container is running on the localhost, my URL would be `http://localhost:8080/`.

5. Open the Chrome/IE browser, paste the preceding localhost URL, and open Jenkins. At the first page, we will be asked for the administrator password. We can get this password from the logs of container run. It should look something like the following:

```
Jenkins initial setup is required. An admin user has been created
and a password generated.

Please use the following password to proceed to installation:
7d4a4a91efb24f369bac95122686bd45
```

6. Once we enter the password, we will be asked to install a suggested plugin. Go ahead and do this. It will be a one-time activity, as we are saving the plugin on the Docker host, and once the plugin is added, we will be asked to create an admin user. Go ahead and create the user, and make sure that you remember the password. Then, once the user is created, go ahead and start using Jenkins.

7. Now let's create a job called `Serverless-OpenWhisk`. Click on **New Item**; it will open a new page. Type in `Serverless-OpenWhisk` in the text box, select **Freestyle project**, and click **OK**.

8. Now select **Git** in the **Source Management** tab and add `https://github.com/shzshi/OpenWhisk-weather-report-serverless.git` in **Repositories URL**. We won't feed in the credentials as this is a public repository. If we use the private GitHub repository, then we add can credentials for Jenkins to clone the repository.

9. Next, in the **Build** tab in the **Add build step** dropdown, select **Execute shell**. A **Command** text box will open up. Let's add the following code in the **Execute shell** field. You need to replace the `OW_AUTH` and `OW_APIHOST` keys that are highlighted with one that we have created previously, or we can log into the OpenWhisk portal and get the details:

```
npm config set prefix '~/.npm-global'
export PATH=~/.npm-global/bin:$PATH
npm install
./node_modules/mocha/bin/mocha test/test.js
export OW_AUTH=00700a7f-2b1a-4831-
bf32-3a566263ed44:4TBcM7f8g0gj5UPgSVHXwNmMkfpbX36OdWximngOwqZYAJrDS
kZwPjeSPjQ45Wm1
export OW_APIHOST=OpenWhisk.eu-gb.bluemix.net
serverless deploy -v
serverless invoke --function main -d '{"location":"Paris"}'
```

10. Once that is done, save the job and then click on the **Build Now** link. The job will then run. It will download and install the npm dependencies mentioned in `package.json`, then run the mocha unit test, deploy the action to the OpenWhisk cloud, and then invoke the function/action with a parameter to make sure that the deployment was successful. The output will look something like the following:

```
Building in workspace /var/jenkins_home/workspace/Serverless-
OpenWhisk
Cloning the remote Git repository
Cloning repository
https://github.com/shzshi/OpenWhisk-weather-report-serverless.git
 > git init /var/jenkins_home/workspace/Serverless-OpenWhisk #
timeout=10
Fetching upstream changes from
https://github.com/shzshi/OpenWhisk-weather-report-serverless.git
 > git --version # timeout=10
 > git fetch --tags --progress
https://github.com/shzshi/OpenWhisk-weather-report-serverless.git
+refs/heads/*:refs/remotes/origin/*
 > git config remote.origin.url
https://github.com/shzshi/OpenWhisk-weather-report-serverless.git #
timeout=10
 > git config --add remote.origin.fetch
+refs/heads/*:refs/remotes/origin/* # timeout=10
 > git config remote.origin.url
https://github.com/shzshi/OpenWhisk-weather-report-serverless.git #
timeout=10
Fetching upstream changes from
https://github.com/shzshi/OpenWhisk-weather-report-serverless.git
 > git fetch --tags --progress
https://github.com/shzshi/OpenWhisk-weather-report-serverless.git
+refs/heads/*:refs/remotes/origin/*
 > git rev-parse refs/remotes/origin/master^{commit} # timeout=10
 > git rev-parse refs/remotes/origin/origin/master^{commit} #
timeout=10
Checking out Revision af9511727c7610915701372a7d617e73a03825f5
(refs/remotes/origin/master)
 > git config core.sparsecheckout # timeout=10
 > git checkout -f af9511727c7610915701372a7d617e73a03825f5
Commit message: "updated jenkin host"
First time build. Skipping changelog.
[Serverless-OpenWhisk] $ /bin/sh -xe
/tmp/jenkins660311873862513550.sh
+ npm config set prefix ~/.npm-global
+ export PATH=~/.npm-
global/bin:/usr/local/sbin:/usr/local/bin:/usr/sbin:/usr/bin:/sbin:
```

```
/bin
+ npm install
---
---
Finished: SUCCESS
```

This aim of this exercise was to show how we can set up continuous integration through Jenkins, Mocha, and Serverless Framework. In the next section, we will see how make it more robust, and learn how to set up a continuous delivery pipeline with the same set of tools. We will also set up automated deployment across the different environments using gates.

Continuous delivery pipeline to OpenWhisk

Continuous delivery is one of the essential features of DevOps. It not only helps in facilitating quicker deployment to production, but it also helps to create a bug-free application. We will be using Jenkins, Serverless Framework, and features of the OpenWhisk cloud to build a continuous delivery platform for OpenWhisk functions. We will be picking up the same weather system app that we built earlier with the freestyle job and enhance it to conform to the continuous delivery model. I have added the required files to the Git repository that I mentioned earlier in the chapter. By using Jenkinsfile at the root, we define a multistage pipeline for this project. Jenkinsfile is a groovy script that is used by Jenkins to run pipelines. We will use master branch to code for deploying and testing to various environments from the development stage all the way to production, provided that the deployment and tests passes within the pipeline. Integration tests run after each deployment (except production) and validate whether the deployed stack is functioning as expected. The pipeline we are creating here will be using Jenkinsfile and Serverless Framework, creating multiple Cloud Foundry spaces for different environments, unit-testing sessions, and building promotions. Let's start with Cloud Foundry spaces by going through the following steps:

1. Log into Bluemix at `https://bluemix.net`.
2. Navigate to **Manage** | **Account** | **Cloud Foundry Orgs**.
3. Click on the **View details** link and then on the link to add Cloud Foundry space. A popup should open.
4. Add four environments: development, SIT, preproduction, and production.

Once the space is created, we will create API keys for the environment and push them as parameters in Jenkins to use them for deploying to different environments:

1. Click on **Three Line** on the left-hand side of the Bluemix portal.
2. Then go to **Functions** and click on it, and then click on the **API Key** link.
3. We will copy the host and key for all environments. We can change and move to the environment from the **CLOUD FOUNDRY SPACE** dropdown, as shown in the following screenshot:

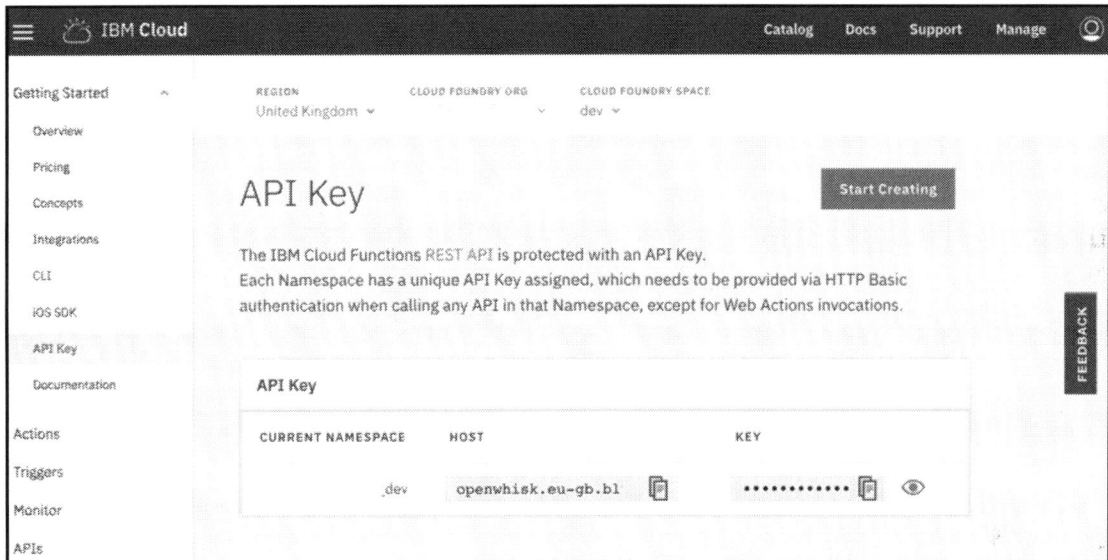

Now we will move to Jenkins, where we will create a pipeline job. I have added the Jenkinsfile to the Git repository at `https://github.com/shzshi/OpenWhisk-weather-report-serverless/blob/master/Jenkinsfile`, where we will use the same Git to set up the pipeline.

We will use the same Jenkins Docker container that we created earlier in the previous tutorials. We will create a new job and work on it. Go through the following steps:

1. Open Jenkins in the browser at `http://localhost:8080`.

2. Log into Jenkins and create a **New item**.

3. Enter the item name as `OpenWhisk_serverless_pipeline`, select **Pipeline**, and click **OK**.

4. We will be redirected to another page, where we need to parameterize the pipeline with OpenWhisk `auth`, OpenWhisk `host`, and a Git path for the pipeline. For this, we will tick the **This project is parameterised** checkbox.

5. Then, in the **Add Parameter** dropdown, we need to select **Credentials Parameter** as the parameter for the pipeline. The following screenshot shows the page for adding details into the credentials parameter. We have to add credentials parameters for all the environments that we created earlier in the chapter through the Azure portal. The **Credential type** should be **Secret text**, because this will help us to keep the authentication keys hidden, as they are passed as environment variables within the Jenkins pipeline. So, in total, we will create five credentials parameters: four for the different environments that are in development, SIT, preproduction, and production, and then the fifth for the OpenWhisk host. The secret text values should be populated from the Bluemix portal in the **API Key** section. The **Default Value** should be filled by clicking the **Add** button and then selecting **Jenkins**, which will help us to add `auth` keys into the Jenkins credentials provider. Look at the following screenshot for more information:

Credentials Parameter

Name OPENWHISK_DEV_AUTH

Credential type Secret text

Required

Default Value OPENWHISK_DEV_AUTH ⟵ Add

Description

Credentials Parameter

Name OPENWHISK_SIT_AUTH

Credential type Secret text

Required

Default Value OPENWHISK_SIT_AUTH ⟵ Add

Description

Credentials Parameter

Name OPENWHISK_PRE_PROD_AUTH

Credential type Secret text

Required

Default Value OPENWHISK_PRE_PROD_AUTH ⟵ Add

Description

Credentials Parameter

Name OPENWHISK_PROD_AUTH

Credential type Secret text

Required

Default Value OPENWHISK_PROD_AUTH ⟵ Add

Description

Credentials Parameter

Name OW_APIHOST

Credential type Secret text

Required

Default Value OW_APIHOST ⟵ Add

Description

Save   Apply

6. We will set the credentials as **Secret text**. Then the **Secret** text box will be filled with the **API Key** for each environment, which we can get from the Azure portal. Then the **ID** and **Description** fields would each be given a simple name, such as OpenWhisk_DEV_AUTH, as references, as shown in the following screenshot:

7. Once all the parameters for each environment are added, we need to move to the **Pipeline** tab and add the GitHub path. The following screenshot shows us adding the configuration for the Jenkins pipeline:

8. Once everything is set, then we need to run the job with the parameters. Once the job runs successfully, as shown in the following screenshot, Serverless Framework will package the functions files and they will be deployed on the different environments that we are testing through the serverless invoke:

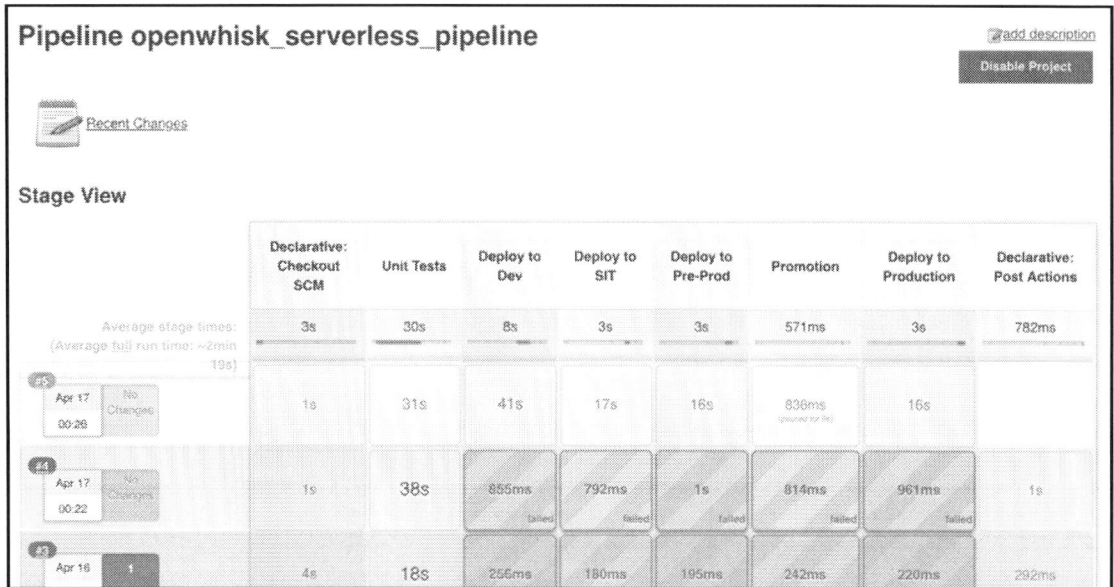

Deployment patterns with OpenWhisk

There are various deployment patterns available, but two patterns are quite popular in the DevOps world. One of them is canary and the other is blue–green. I tried my best to fit the serverless deployment to fit into this pattern, but there is always scope for improvement. Let's look at how we can fit OpenWhisk actions into these patterns.

Canary deployment

The canary deployment pattern involves rolling out a new release in small chunks to subsets of users or servers. We then test it, and if it performs well, then we roll it out to the rest of the users or servers. The advantage here is that the percentage of failure is quite low, and we can analyze and fix the issues of the actions without disrupting all of the traffic. So, with respect to OpenWhisk, we can set this up by using regions and routing a percentage of traffic to the newly released version into this region. If you do not want to create the region or organization, then you can set up a Cloud Foundry space as a **disaster recovery (DR)** environment on the Bluemix portal and shift the percentage of traffic into DR. The best part here is that if you discover that the released version is faulty, then you should be able to roll back to the previous version.

As of now, there is no provision to set up a percentage of the traffic to a specific action through the CLI or Serverless Framework. So we have to manually set this up through the action's code as we can do in Lambda. But once OpenWhisk matures further, we should see this feature added.

Blue–green deployment

Although blue–green deployment is similar to canary deployment, the difference is that instead of routinizing the percentage of traffic, two separate identical environments are used in parallel to mitigate the risks of introducing new versions of actions. To do this, we create a new environment named staging. The production environment is used for going live and the staging environment is used for new changes. We then switch the environments back and forth between staging and production.

With respect to OpenWhisk, we can achieve this by creating a new staging environment using Cloud Foundry spaces. Then we deploy the current release version of our actions into the blue (production) environment and redirect traffic using an alias to the blue environment. Then, after the new versions of the actions are developed, we deploy them to the green (staging) environment for testing. Once the results of the testing are satisfactory, we redirect all the traffic to the green (staging) environment, and it is made live. Then the new version is deployed to the blue version for testing.

In case where the performance degrades or the release is buggy, we roll back the blue (go live) version to the current version and redirect the traffic again to blue and green environment becomes staging.

Dynamic dashboard

IBM Cloud has an out-of-the-box monitoring dashboard, which provides a graphical summary of the function's invocation. It also helps to determine the performance and health of your Cloud Functions actions. The monitoring page is divided into three tabs—**Activity Summary**, **Activity Log**, and **Activity Timeline**. Let's look at each tab in more detail.

Activity Summary

The **Activity Summary** widget provides a high-level summary of the Cloud Functions environment. It helps us to understand and monitor the overall health and performance of the Cloud Functions-enabled service. The metrics provide us with the following details:

- The usage rate of the OpenWhisk actions, displaying the number of times they were invoked.
- The overall rate of failure across all actions. We can spot an error and isolate the services that have the errors; we can do this using activity log widgets.
- The performance of the actions, displaying the average completion time that is attached to each action.

Activity Timeline

The **Activity Timeline** widget shows a vertical bar graph that displays the activities of the **Actions**. Red indicates errors within specific **Actions**, and we can correlate this view with the **Activity Log** to understand the exact error in the action.

Activity Log

The **Activity Log** widget displays activation logs in a format that we can use to view the details of every activation, as shown in the following screenshot. If we click on the √ button to view the detailed log, then it will also display the time taken for each invocation as well as the date:

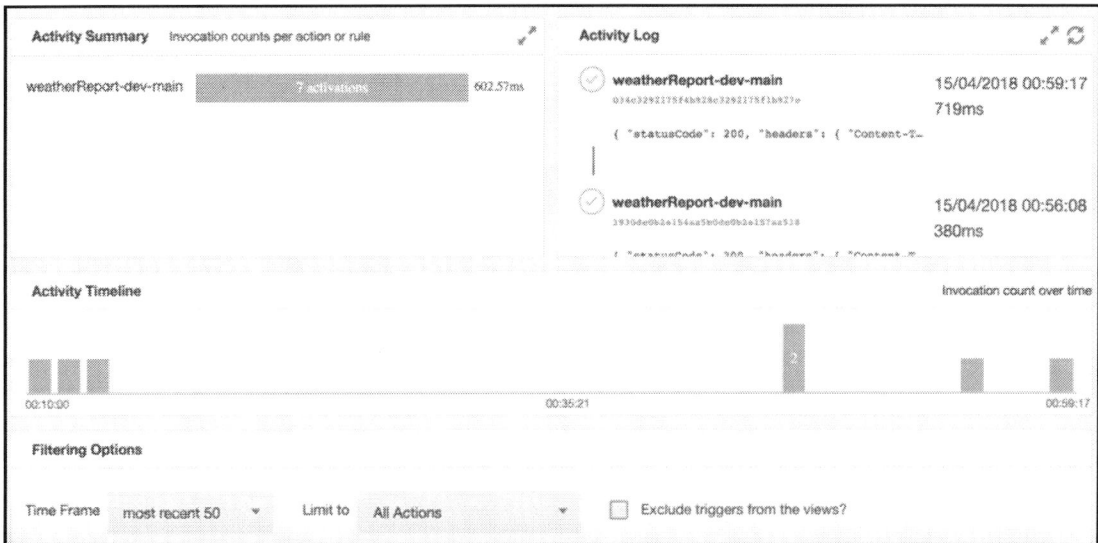

We can also set up Hygiea as we did in previous chapter, and monitor the build, development, and testing of the OpenWhisk actions. We can also set up the deployment dashboard with Hygiea to track the deployment across different environments. As mentioned earlier, Hygiea would be an ideal dashboard to monitor DevOps' progress and performance.

OpenWhisk action logging management

Logging is pretty limited with serverless applications as there are no VMs, no OS, and no middleware packages. But we have to make the best use of what logging functionalities we do have in order to efficiently debug and resolve any issues we might have with OpenWhisk actions. The bright side is that we still have access to output logging for actions. So the only thing we have to do is it to push the files into Elasticsearch and index them for better use. We will be look at how to do this in this section.

We will be setting up ELK with Docker locally and pushing the OpenWhisk action logs into ELK. The OpenWhisk cloud has out-of-the-box ELK configuration, so we can view the aggregated logs on the portal itself. To do this, we need to log into the Bluemix portal. Go through the following steps:

1. Log into the Bluemix portal at `https://console.bluemix.net/`.
2. Click on the **Functions** link; this will take you to the functions/actions portal.

3. In the portal, click on **Logs**. We will be taken to a page with a Kibana dashboard. There, we can search for the required logs. More details for viewing these logs can be followed at `https://console.bluemix.net/docs/openwhisk/openwhisk_logs.html#viewing-activation-logs-in-the-ibm-cloud`.

However, it is quite expensive to maintain logs on the portal, and it is more difficult and costly to retain them for longer periods, so to save some infrastructure cost, we can pull the logs locally and retain them for a long period, and at much cheaper cost. Next, we will see how we can set up ELK locally and pull the logs.

Setting up ELK

We will be setting up ELK locally using Docker. We have used Docker in many chapters, so it should be easy for us to set up ELK using it. We will be using the official Docker image that available on Docker Hub. We will be using Elasticsearch 2.4.1, Logstash 2.4.0, and Kibana 4.6.1 for our setup. Enter the following command:

```
$ docker run -p 5601:5601 -p 5000:5000 -it --name elk
sebp/elk:es241_l240_k461
```

The moment you run the preceding command, Docker will connect to Docker Hub, download the image, and then the container for the ELK stack will be created. Once the Docker container is loaded successfully, we should be able to access the Kibana dashboard through the browser using `localhost:5601`.

Now we need to create a public hostname and port from the localhost port `5000`, for which we need to tunnel our localhost. For our example, we will use `https://burrow.io`.

OpenWhisk actions

We will be using the existing OpenWhisk action that we created earlier in the chapter. Let's log into the Bluemix portal. Go to **Functions** |**Actions** | **On monitor**. We should be able to see the logs of the OpenWhisk functions/actions on the **Activity Log** widget. We need to pull these logs on our local ELK. We will use the logs of the weatherReport app for our example.

OpenWhisk log forwarder

J Thomas has written an OpenWhisk forwarder, which is another OpenWhisk function. This function will push the OpenWhisk actions log to the local ELK stack. Let's see how this is done. First, we need to clone the public repository that he has created, make a few changes, and then deploy the function to the Bluemix portal for the particular space. This function will push the logs into the local ELK using burrow tunneled host and port:

1. Git clone the `j thomas` repository using the following code:

   ```
   $ git clone https://github.com/jthomas/OpenWhisk-logstash-
   forwarder.git
   ```

2. Export the OpenWhisk `auth` and `api` host for deploying to the Bluemix portal. You need to log into the portal to get the latest details using the following code:

   ```
   $ export OW_AUTH=00700a7f-2b1a-4831-
   bf32-3a566263ed44:4TBcM7f8g0gj5UPgSVHXwNmMkfpbX36OdWximngOwqZYAJrDS
   kZwPjeSPjQ45Wm1
   $ export OW_APIHOST=OpenWhisk.eu-gb.bluemix.net
   ```

3. Install the serverless OpenWhisk plugin and the latest version of Serverless Framework (if it is not already installed) using the following code:

   ```
   $ npm install --global serverless serverless-openwhisk

   /usr/local/bin/serverless ->
   /usr/local/lib/node_modules/serverless/bin/serverless
   /usr/local/bin/slss ->
   /usr/local/lib/node_modules/serverless/bin/serverless
   /usr/local/bin/sls ->
   /usr/local/lib/node_modules/serverless/bin/serverless
   > serverless@1.26.1 postinstall
   /usr/local/lib/node_modules/serverless
   > node ./scripts/postinstall.js
   serverless@1.26.1
    + serverless-OpenWhisk@0.12.0
    added 5 packages, removed 2 packages and updated 38 packages in
   13.232s
   ```

4. Install the dependencies, as shown in the following code:

   ```
   $ npm install
    WARN registry Unexpected warning for https://registry.npmjs.org/:
   Miscellaneous Warning EINTEGRITY: sha512-
   1R3gD69osqm6EYLk9wB/G1W/laGWjzH90t1vEa2xuxHD5KUrSzp9pUSfTm+YC5Nxt2T
   8nMPEvKlhbQayU7bgFw== integrity checksum failed when using sha512:
   ```

```
wanted sha512-
lR3gD69osqm6EYLk9wB/G1W/laGWjzH90t1vEa2xuxHD5KUrSzp9pUSfTm+YC5Nxt2T
8nMPEvKlhbQayU7bgFw== but got sha1-ygtl2gLtYpNYh4COb1EDgQNOM1Y=.
(57090 bytes)
 ---
 ---
> fsevents@1.1.2 install
/Users/shashi/Documents/packt/chapter5/ELK/OpenWhisk-logstash-
forwarder/node_modules/fsevents
 > node install
[fsevents] Success:
"/Users/shashi/Documents/packt/chapter5/ELK/OpenWhisk-logstash-
forwarder/node_modules/fsevents/lib/binding/Release/node-v57-
darwin-x64/fse.node" already installed
 Pass --update-binary to reinstall or --build-from-source to
recompile
> OpenWhisk-logstash-forwarder@0.1.0 postinstall
/Users/shashi/Documents/packt/chapter5/ELK/OpenWhisk-logstash-
forwarder
 > npm link serverless-OpenWhisk
/Users/shashi/Documents/packt/chapter5/ELK/OpenWhisk-logstash-
forwarder/node_modules/serverless-OpenWhisk ->
/usr/local/lib/node_modules/serverless-OpenWhisk
 added 606 packages in 9.933s

Update available 5.5.1 → 5.8.0
Run npm i -g npm to update
```

5. Deploy the action with serverless, as shown in the following code:

```
$ serverless deploy
Serverless: Packaging service...
Serverless: Excluding development dependencies...
Serverless: Compiling Functions...
Serverless: Compiling Packages...
Serverless: Compiling API Gateway definitions...
Serverless: Compiling Rules...
Serverless: Compiling Triggers & Feeds...
Serverless: Deploying Functions...
Serverless: Deploying Triggers...
Serverless: Binding Feeds To Triggers...
Serverless: Deploying Rules...
Serverless: Deployment successful!

Service Information
platform: OpenWhisk.eu-gb.bluemix.net
namespace: _
service: logging
```

```
packages:
 no packages deployed
actions:
 logging-dev-logstash-forwarder myTEST weatherReport-dev-main
triggers:
 logging_logstash-forwarder_schedule_trigger
rules:
 logging_logstash-forwarder_schedule_rule
endpoints (api-gw):
 **failed to fetch routes**
 api gateway key is wrong or has expired! if it has expired, please
refresh with wsk bluemix login
endpoints (web actions):
 no web actions deployed
```

Once the action or function is successfully deployed, we will see the logs following your local ELK stack, and we should be able to view them.

Summary

In this chapter, we learned about what OpenWhisk is and looked into the various ways to simplify build, deploy, monitor, and log OpenWhisk functions. We also learned how to set up continuous delivery and created a pipeline to do this.

In the next chapter, we will learn about Google functions, look at what they are and how to start using simple functions to set up an automated pipeline with the Serverless Framework and other open source tools.

DevOps with Google Functions 6

Google decided to launch its serverless platform as Cloud Functions, but it is still in its maturing stage. At the time of writing this book, we can only write Google Cloud Functions with Node.js. The functions can be triggered through Google's internal event bus—Pub/Sub and through HTTP as mobile events from Firebase. I am not going to delve much into what Google Functions does, because we have already covered that in earlier chapters. So, in this chapter, we will be covering how we apply DevOps to Google Functions and what are the best practices of deployment, release management, monitoring, and logging. We will look into various examples and a demo with a `gcloud` command line, Serverless Framework, and Jenkins. So, let's jump in to DevOps.

CI and CD pipelines with Google Functions

As Google currently allows coding only with JavaScript, we will be using Node.js throughout this book, with examples and demos. Google terms its serverless functions as Cloud Functions, so we will be using this term throughout this chapter. So, Cloud Functions are to be written in JavaScript and executed in Node.js v6.11.5 (at the time of writing this book) and the cloud function source must be exported in a Node.js module. The module will be loaded using a `require()` call. So, functions are contained within an `index.js` file. We can invoke the function from HTTP request methods such as GET, POST, PUT, OPTIONS, and DELETE. The deployment can be done through a command-line tool provided by Google Cloud CLI, through the cloud function UI on a GCP console, and can also be done through a serverless framework. We will be looking into each way throughout this chapter. The deployable is a ZIP file, which has functions packaged into it, and it is deployed on the Google Cloud storage bucket. Functions source code can be directly put into Cloud Functions as well, or we can reference it by uploading to the Google Cloud storage bucket. Let's look at various way to deploy function and further automate it through the Jenkins pipeline.

Prerequisites for Cloud Functions

Let's look at how to create and deploy a Cloud Function using the GCP console. But before that prerequisite, we need to have access to the Google Function platform. At the time of writing, Google provides a free GCP account with $300 credit for a year to use for any product on the GCP. So let's create one. Please follow the given steps:

1. Go to the following link: `https://cloud.google.com/free/`.
2. Click on the **TRY IT FREE** button, which will be redirected to the Google account page. If you already have a Google account, you can then use it or create a new Google account.
3. Feed in the credentials and you will be redirected to the GCP home page.
4. As the account is already created, let's create a GCP project. So go to the **MANAGE RESOURCES PAGE** (`https://console.cloud.google.com/cloud-resource-manager`).
5. We will now create a project, so let's click on **Create Project**, enter the project name as `My Serverless Project` and click on **Create**. You will see that the project is getting created in the notification bell image on the top right-hand side of the page. Once it has stopped, refresh the page and you will see the project in the list.
6. Now enable the cloud API for the project by opening the link: `https://console.cloud.google.com/flows/enableapiapiid=cloudfunctionsredirect=https://cloud.google.com/functions/quickstart`. The page will have a drop-down list for projects. Select **My Serverless Project** and click on **Continue**; then API will be enabled for the project.
7. We will now install and configure the Google Cloud SDK. The following link will guide you through this: `https://cloud.google.com/sdk/docs/`. While doing the `gcloud init`, you will be prompted to select the project. Select the project **My Serverless Project** which we created, and we will be authenticated with GCP as well.
8. Set up the Node.js environment.

Cloud Functions through the GCP console

We will now create a cloud function through the GCP console:

1. Go to the Cloud Functions overview page in the GCP console, select the project from the drop-down list for which the function is attached.
2. Click on **Create Function**.

3. Name the function as `my-serverless-function`.
4. Select the trigger as an **HTTP trigger**.
5. Let's use the default code, so it should be checked by an inline editor. The text area will have two scripts, one is `index.js` and the other is `package.json`. This is a simple `helloworld` function provided by Google Functions. The function logs a message which you provide in a later step. When you finish the steps you will see something similar to the following screenshot:

6. Click on the **Create** button. Now the function will be deployed and the GCP console redirects to the **Overview** page. While the function is being deployed, the icon next to it is a small spinner. After deployment is complete, the spinner turns to a green check mark.

7. We will test the function. Click on the three vertical dots on the right-hand side of the page for the particular function and click on the **Test function**:

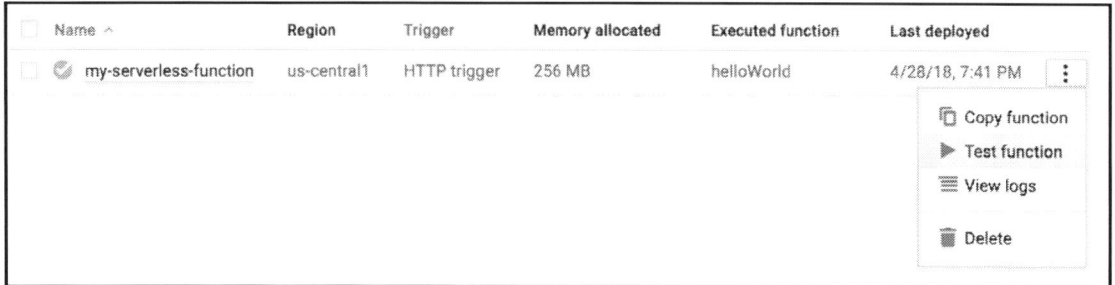

Name ^	Region	Trigger	Memory allocated	Executed function	Last deployed	
my-serverless-function	us-central1	HTTP trigger	256 MB	helloWorld	4/28/18, 7:41 PM	⋮

Copy function
Test function
View logs
Delete

8. We will be redirected to a function test page. In the **Triggered Event** field, replace the text with `{"message":"Hello World!"}` and click on **Test function**. In the **Output** field we should see the **Success: Hello World!**. and in the **Logs** field the status code 200 will indicate that the function ran successfully. We can see detailed logs by clicking on the arrow for each log.

9. We can see the logs history by click on **VIEW LOGS** on top right. So, this is how we create and deploy the function through the GCP console and also view the function logs and their history:

Cloud Function using a gcloud command line

In this part of this chapter, we will be deploying the `helloworld` application through the `gcloud` command line. First, we need to have created a GCP project through the **Manage resources** page, enabled the Cloud Function API as a prerequisite, and, most importantly, to have installed the `gcloud` SDK locally:

1. Let's update the `gcloud` components. Go to your Command Prompt and add the following command. You will be prompted to install components using the `gcloud beta` commands. Go ahead and install them. The `gcloud` selected components will be installed and configured locally:

```
$ gcloud components update && gcloud components install beta
```

We can follow the deployment steps with Google Cloud Shell (https:// console.cloud.google.com/?cloudshell=true) as well. Google Cloud Shell is a command-line environment with `gcloud` SDK on the GCP console.

2. Let's create a function for this. We need to create a directory where our function will reside:

```
$ mkdir helloServerless
$ cd helloServerless
```

3. Let's create a file `index.js` in the `helloServerless` directory with the following content:

```
/**
 * HTTP Cloud Function.
 * @param {Object} req Cloud Function request context.
 * @param {Object} res Cloud Function response context.
 */
exports.helloServerless = (req, res) => {
  res.send('Hello My Serverless World!');
};
```

4. We will deploy the function using the following command. It will deploy the function into the GCP. The `--trigger-http` is the trigger we need to be specified. While deploying with the trigger, the function will be assigned an endpoint which can viewed by using the `describe` command. There are various different triggers which can be used for deployment:

```
$ gcloud beta functions deploy helloServerless --trigger-http

Deploying function (may take a while - up to 2 minutes)...done.
 availableMemoryMb: 256
 entryPoint: helloServerless
 httpsTrigger:
 url:
https://[GCP_REGION]-[PROJECT_ID].cloudfunctions.net/helloServerles
s
 labels:
 deployment-tool: cli-gcloud
 name: projects/my-serverless-project-201920/locations/us-
central1/functions/helloServerless
 serviceAccountEmail: my-serverless-
project-201920@appspot.gserviceaccount.com
 sourceUploadUrl:
https://storage.googleapis.com/gcf-upload-us-central1-39234144-2d9a
-4a19-
bf5f-82ef8d19a71b/d2611724-50d0-4339-9ee5-9d140aa674ae.zip?GoogleAc
cessId=37314512027@cloudservices.gserviceaccount.com&Expires=152494
7393&Signature=WCwiJ8E%2B8a6EMMZiz5cWG%2FE%2F7pt8V%2FbqIDyW68utF%2F
QXMJR0Pt94e0fC8DcqHbWBAEqHaE9%2B71fOYoWVcXg%2FWos38q%2FIfl%2BTNfaav
Rr9WyIi6V3M5our8aNI%2FGcntOrHm%2FpMK2LdiBzN6QI%2FiDjPDaA5%2FXohjLD%
```

```
2BLaGGDHEoHp97%2BqCA7Mzifs%2B%2BhNcYknZ0vjLdpegUqfTUVjDF1h%2BQqg68s
IurtT14Bay3uXryeMqYB%2FZv0lTjZIsd7svnUZtXZTNi72HOzP2J7vo1qo%2B74hO7
Yy7WJOj2yvDKiFJ4ZXyk8cXvPu3ooNV%2BGy2dc758CF13u87M%2FuKJV%2Bl0VkDwn
Q%3D%3D
```

```
 status: ACTIVE
 timeout: 60s
 updateTime: '2018-04-28T19:59:54Z'
 versionId: '1'
```

5. Once the function has successfully deployed, we can execute the function through the URL property from the deployment output, or we can get the URL through the following command:

```
$ gcloud beta functions describe helloServerless
```

6. Copy, paste, and run the URL on any browser and then we should be able to see the following message:

```
Hello My Serverless World!
```

So, you can see how easy it is to deploy the function through `gcloud` on the GCP. But how do we make sure we unit test it, integrate test, and finally automate the deployment? That is what we are going to cover further on in the chapter. But we can do most of this locally by setting up a development environment.

Building and testing locally

As the Cloud Functions run on a `Node.js` environment, we can build and test our application locally just using a `Node.js` emulator with development tools. The emulator is an open source and code is hosted on the GitHub. Let's look at how to use it:

1. Install the emulator through npm or Yarn; you need to make sure you have `Node.js` installed on your machine:

```
$ npm install -g @google-cloud/functions-emulator

/usr/local/bin/functions-emulator ->
/usr/local/lib/node_modules/@google-cloud/functions-
emulator/bin/functions
 /usr/local/bin/functions -> /usr/local/lib/node_modules/@google-
cloud/functions-emulator/bin/functions

> @google-cloud/functions-emulator@1.0.0-beta.4 postinstall
/usr/local/lib/node_modules/@google-cloud/functions-emulator
 > node scripts/upgrade-warning
```

```
If you're using the Emulator via the Firebase CLI, you can
disregard this message.

If you're upgrading @google-cloud/functions-emulator, these
 are the recommended upgrade steps:
1. Stop the currently running emulator, if any:
functions stop
2. Uninstall the current emulator, if any:
npm uninstall -g @google-cloud/functions-emulator
3. Install the new version of the emulator:
npm install -g @google-cloud/functions-emulator

If you have trouble after upgrading, try deleting the config
 directory found in:

~/.config/configstore/@google-cloud/functions-emulator

Then restart the emulator. You can also check for any renegade
 Node.js emulator processes that may need to be killed:

ps aux | grep node
+ @google-cloud/functions-emulator@1.0.0-beta.4
 added 314 packages in 21.252s
```

2. Let's start the emulator. This command will start the emulator and wait for the prompt:

```
$ functions start
 Warning: You're using Node.js v8.9.2 but Google Cloud Functions
only supports v6.11.5.
 Starting Google Cloud Functions Emulator...
 Google Cloud Functions Emulator STARTED
 No functions deployed "_". Run functions deploy --help for how to
deploy a function.
```

3. Deploy the function locally; so go into a folder before the function folder and run the following command:

```
$ functions deploy helloServerless --trigger-http
 Warning: You're using Node.js v8.9.2 but Google Cloud Functions
only supports v6.11.5.
 Copying
file:///var/folders/mj/74rcnfp94ll_sj3s95z4nnx00000gn/T/tmp-6681yxq
JsPl2WsYI.zip...
 Waiting for operation to finish...done.
 Deploying function......done.
 Function helloServerless deployed.
```

```
| Property | Value |
├─────────────────┤

| Name | helloServerless |
├─────────────────┤

| Trigger | HTTP |
├─────────────────┤

| Resource |
http://localhost:8010/my-serverless-project-201920/us-central1/hell
oServerless |
├─────────────────┤

| Timeout |· 60 seconds |
├─────────────────┤

| Local path |
/Users/<username>/Documents/packt/chapter6/googlefunction_hello_wor
ld |
├─────────────────┤

| Archive |
file:///var/folders/mj/74rcnfp9411_sj3s95z4nnx00000gn/T/tmp-6681yxq
JsPl2WsYI.zip |
└─────────────────┘
```

4. Open the URL mentioned in the output in the browser. You should see the message Hello My Serverless World! ; or execute it through the command line:

```
$ functions call helloServerless
 Warning: You're using Node.js v8.9.2 but Google Cloud Functions
only supports v6.11.5.
 ExecutionId: 4b32f8b9-2452-45ee-a0c9-57f2fd3f9d8a
 Result: Hello My Serverless World!
```

5. Also, you can see the following logs:

```
$ functions call helloServerless
Warning: You're using Node.js v8.9.2 but Google Cloud Functions
only supports v6.11.5.
ExecutionId: 4b32f8b9-2452-45ee-a0c9-57f2fd3f9d8a
Result: Hello My Serverless World!
<username>s-MacBook-Pro:googlefunction_hello_world <username>$
functions logs read
Warning: You're using Node.js v8.9.2 but Google Cloud Functions
only supports v6.11.5.
2018-04-28T20:54:55.907Z - info: User function triggered, starting
execution
2018-04-28T20:54:55.914Z - info: Execution took 11 ms, user
function completed successfully
2018-04-28T20:56:10.393Z - info: User function triggered, starting
execution
2018-04-28T20:56:10.394Z - info: Execution took 1 ms, user
function completed successfully
2018-04-28T21:07:14.853Z - info: User function triggered, starting
execution
2018-04-28T21:07:14.859Z - info: Execution took 6 ms, user
function completed successfully
2018-04-28T21:12:13.228Z - info: User function triggered, starting
execution
2018-04-28T21:12:13.229Z - info: Execution took 0 ms, user
function completed successfully
```

More details for the emulator can be found in the link below. We can integrate the emulator with the our favorite development tools and debug the Google Functions: `https://github.com/GoogleCloudPlatform/ cloud-functions-emulator`. For debugging Cloud Functions: `https:// github.com/GoogleCloudPlatform/cloud-functions-emulator/wiki/ Debugging-functions`.

CI and CD with testing

Until now, we have just created a function and come up with a couple of ways to build and deploy. We have also learned how to run the function locally through emulator. But we cannot manually build and deploy every function each time, and we should also be versioning the code. We will looking into all those aspects within this part of the chapter.

Source code management

Source code management is a very important part of software development. It is always best to version and tag the code. Git is the most popular source code management tool, and we have been using it throughout this chapter. So, for a perfect deployment cycle, we should always create different branches. These are feature branch, develop branch, release branch, and then we have the default master branch. I have already covered best practice around this in earlier chapters, so I won't talk here about the structuring of branches and how code flow across branches is managed. However, it is important to about the folder structure to be followed for Cloud Functions. In earlier chapters, we wrote function in `index.js`. If functions are limited then they can easily be managed within `index.js`. But if we have hundreds of functions then managing them within one file becomes really tedious and painful. So, one simple way to structure the functions would be as follows:

```
├──── /build/                    # Compiled output for Node.js 6.x
├──── /src/                       # Application source files
│     ├──── someFuncA.js          # Function A
│     ├──── someFuncA.test.js     # Function A unit tests
│     ├──── someFuncB.js          # Function B
│     ├──── someFuncB.test.js     # Function B unit tests
├──── index.js                    # Main export(s)
└──── package.json                # List of project dependencies and NPM
scripts
```

There are many ways to structure it, but I have kept it simple. However, I would let the developer decide over the structure.

Continuous integration and testing

Continuous integration and testing are other important aspects of the development cycle. Continuous integration clubs the codes together, and testing will make sure that the code which goes into production is bug free, and that most of the issues are mitigated in a lower environment. There are many different way of testing: unit testing, integration testing and system testing. We will be integrating this testing in an automated pipeline in the example. I will be using the examples provided by Google Cloud with a simple `hello world` function, and running them in an automated way, and then putting them into a pipeline for single-touch deployment.

I have created a `HelloWorld` function referencing from Google's existing example repository. I have put them on my local repository, which we will be using for setting continuous integration and testing. I have also created a Dockerfile, which will help us to create a docker container for Jenkins, pre-installed `gcloud`, Node.js and the functions emulator which we will be using to set up our DevOps automation:

1. Git clone the Git repository mentioned as follows. We are cloning this locally to get the Dockerfile, and you can play around with it by making changes to the script and testing the deployment:

   ```
   $ git clone
   https://github.com/shzshi/google-functions-helloworld.git
   ```

2. We will build a Docker image locally and then start a Jenkins portal to enable us to set up the automation. You need to make sure Docker is installed on your local machine for this example.

3. We move to the Dockerfile directory:

   ```
   $ cd google-functions-helloworld
   ```

4. We create a Docker image with Jenkins, `gcloud`, a function emulator, Node.js and all other required libraries:

   ```
   $ docker image build -t google-functions .
   ```

5. Here, run the Docker container with the image created in the previous line. The Docker container will be hosted locally with port 8080 and 50000 exposed. We will also map the volume with a local host directory:

   ```
   $ docker run --rm -it -p 50000:50000 -p 8080:8080 -v
   /My/Local/Host/PATH/chapter6/google-
   functions/jenkins:/var/jenkins_home google-functions:latest
   ```

6. Once the container is running, we will browse the Jenkins portal through `http://localhost:8080`. If you are creating this container for the first time without mapped volume, you will be asked to copy and paste the password and install a default plugin.

7. Log in to the Jenkins portal using the credentials you had created earlier, or you already had. Then click on **New Item**.

8. Enter the item name as `my-serverless-google-functions`, select the freestyle project and then click on **OK**.

9. Go to the tab **Source Code Management** and select **Git**, then copy and paste the repository mentioned below into the **Repository URL** textbox and leave the rest as default: `https://github.com/shzshi/google-functions-helloworld.git`.

10. We need to create a Google service account for `gcloud` within Jenkins to authenticate with GCP:
    - Go to the **OPEN THE LIST OF CREDENTIALS** (`https://console.cloud.google.com/apis/credentials?_ga=2.77044693.-1734735492.1524930885`) page
    - Click on **Create Credentials**
    - Select the **Service Account Key**
    - Click on the drop-down for **Service account** and select **New Service Account**
    - Enter a name for the service account in **Name**
    - Use the default **Service account ID** or generate a different one
    - Select the **Key type: JSON**
    - Click **Create**, the **Service account created** window is displayed, and the private key for the **Key type** you selected is downloaded automatically to our local machine which we will be using further.
    - Click **Close**

11. You need to fork your repository and copy the content of the `gcloud` service account key JSON file into the file `My-Serverless-Project-1d8bacd4886d.json`, because we will be using this JSON file in Jenkins to authenticate: `https://github.com/shzshi/google-functions-helloworld.git`.

12. Go to the **Build** tab, and from the drop-down menu's **Add build step** select **Execute Shell** and then add the following steps into the **Command** text area:

```
gcloud auth activate-service-account --key-file=${WORKSPACE}/My-
Serverless-Project-1d8bacd4886d.json
 gcloud config set project ${YOUR_GCP_PROJECT_ID}
 npm install

export NODE_PATH=${WORKSPACE}/node_modules


# executing unit test
 ${WORKSPACE}/node_modules/.bin/ava test/unit.http.test.js

 # executing integration test
 export
BASE_URL=http://localhost:8010/${YOUR_GCP_PROJECT_ID}/${YOUR_GCF_RE
```

```
GION}
${WORKSPACE}/node_modules/.bin/functions start
${WORKSPACE}/node_modules/.bin/functions deploy helloHttp --
trigger-http
${WORKSPACE}/node_modules/.bin/ava test/integration.http.test.js
 # deploying to GCP project and executing system test
 gcloud beta functions deploy helloHttp --trigger-http
export
BASE_URL=https://${YOUR_GCF_REGION}-${YOUR_GCP_PROJECT_ID}.cloudfun
ctions.net/helloHttp
${WORKSPACE}/node_modules/.bin/ava test/system.http.test.js
```

13. We need to parameterize the job, which means that we need to add two text parameters, one for the gcloud project id and another for the gcloud region. Add the parameters as mentioned in the following screenshot. The **Default Value** needs to be changed with your project name and region:

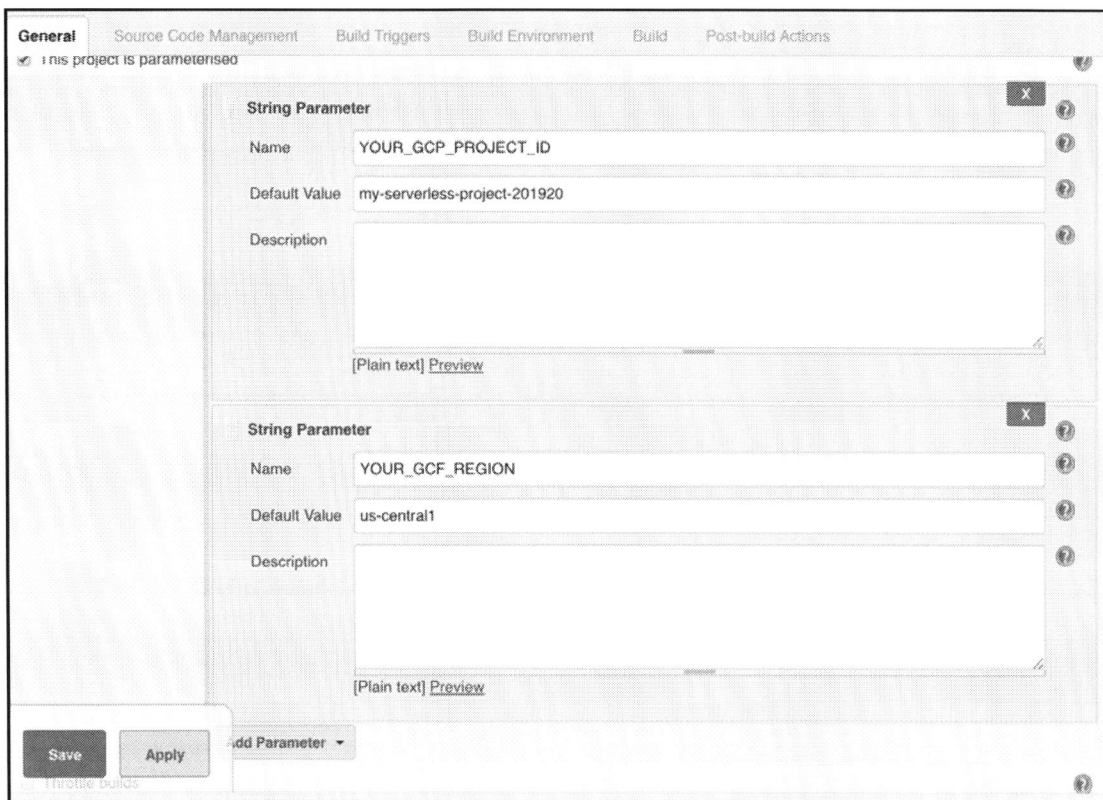

14. Once everything looks fine, as mentioned in the previous 13 steps, click **SAVE**, and save the project.

15. To run the job, click **Build with Parameters** and run the job with a default parameter.

16. If the job runs successfully, we should see the following output and therefore Google Function has successfully passed the unit, integration and system tests:

```
Building in workspace /var/jenkins_home/workspace/my-serverless-
google-functions
 > git rev-parse --is-inside-work-tree # timeout=10
Fetching changes from the remote Git repository
 > git config remote.origin.url
https://github.com/shzshi/google-functions-helloworld.git #
timeout=10
Fetching upstream changes from
https://github.com/shzshi/google-functions-helloworld.git
 > git --version # timeout=10
 > git fetch --tags --progress
https://github.com/shzshi/google-functions-helloworld.git
+refs/heads/*:refs/remotes/origin/*
 > git rev-parse refs/remotes/origin/master^{commit} # timeout=10
 > git rev-parse refs/remotes/origin/origin/master^{commit} #
timeout=10
Checking out Revision bbfb5c17a65dab7f0a8e0b3dc3de82e5792fe21d
(refs/remotes/origin/master)
 > git config core.sparsecheckout # timeout=10
 > git checkout -f bbfb5c17a65dab7f0a8e0b3dc3de82e5792fe21d
Commit message: "added function emulator"
 > git rev-list --no-walk bbfb5c17a65dab7f0a8e0b3dc3de82e5792fe21d
# timeout=10
[my-serverless-google-functions] $ /bin/sh -xe
/tmp/jenkins2470859504083131546.sh
+ gcloud auth activate-service-account --key-
file=/var/jenkins_home/workspace/my-serverless-google-functions/My-
Serverless-Project-1d8bacd4886d.json
Activated service account credentials for: [jenkins@my-serverless-
project-201920.iam.gserviceaccount.com]
+ gcloud config set project my-serverless-project-201920
Updated property [core/project].
+ npm install
npm WARN optional SKIPPING OPTIONAL DEPENDENCY: fsevents@1.2.3
(node_modules/fsevents):
npm WARN notsup SKIPPING OPTIONAL DEPENDENCY: Unsupported platform
for fsevents@1.2.3: wanted {"os":"darwin","arch":"any"} (current:
{"os":"linux","arch":"x64"})

up to date in 30.041s
```

```
+ export NODE_PATH=/var/jenkins_home/workspace/my-serverless-
google-functions/node_modules
+ /var/jenkins_home/workspace/my-serverless-google-
functions/node_modules/.bin/ava test/unit.http.test.js

  helloHttp: should print a name
  helloHttp: should print hello world

  2 tests passed

+ export
BASE_URL=http://localhost:8010/my-serverless-project-201920/us-cent
ral1
+ /var/jenkins_home/workspace/my-serverless-google-
functions/node_modules/.bin/functions start
Warning: You're using Node.js v8.11.1 but Google Cloud Functions
only supports v6.11.5.
Starting Google Cloud Functions Emulator...
Google Cloud Functions Emulator STARTED
```

Status	Name	Trigger	Resource
READY	helloHttp	HTTP	http://localhost:8010/my-serverless-project-201920/us-central1/helloHttp

```
+ /var/jenkins_home/workspace/my-serverless-google-
functions/node_modules/.bin/functions deploy helloHttp --trigger-
http
Warning: You're using Node.js v8.11.1 but Google Cloud Functions
only supports v6.11.5.
Copying file:///tmp/tmp-1653qKGF3wXgKZdC.zip...
Waiting for operation to finish...done.
Deploying function..........done.
Function helloHttp deployed.
```

Property	Value

Name	helloHttp

Trigger	HTTP

Resource	

http://localhost:8010/my-serverless-project-201920/us-central1/hell
oHttp |

Timeout	60 seconds

Local path	/var/jenkins_home/workspace/my-serverless-google-

functions |

Archive	file:///tmp/tmp-1653qKGF3wXgKZdC.zip

```
+ /var/jenkins_home/workspace/my-serverless-google-
functions/node_modules/.bin/ava test/integration.http.test.js

   helloHttp: should print a name (110ms)
   helloHttp: should print hello world (104ms)

  2 tests passed

+ gcloud beta functions deploy helloHttp --trigger-http
Deploying function (may take a while - up to 2 minutes)...
.............done.
availableMemoryMb: 256
entryPoint: helloHttp
httpsTrigger:
  url:
```

```
https://us-central1-my-serverless-project-201920.cloudfunctions.net
/helloHttp
labels:
  deployment-tool: cli-gcloud
name: projects/my-serverless-project-201920/locations/us-
central1/functions/helloHttp
serviceAccountEmail: my-serverless-
project-201920@appspot.gserviceaccount.com
sourceUploadUrl:
https://storage.googleapis.com/gcf-upload-us-central1-39234144-2d9a
-4a19-bf5f-82ef8d19a71b/5433a10a-52ed-4330-b68a-
f3c3be016035.zip?GoogleAccessId=37314512027@cloudservices.gservicea
ccount.com&Expires=1525049193&Signature=C3H2oyjrieTuykum%2BH09BqZO6
3bCXE4vlrWVzOhEMTBAoPAUFTHU96JVqTk7ZiGdl2iv34a7FlR70vE9oo4jnnZApVtC
YHVSY9JA3X%2BAn4VR4Aw510UUC7ilZbGGJ5U3eyk1bVlzQxTkx20Mq6yx8JUQqRMj%
2FTisHqs0MCHC9k83NJj6JQdF%2BBbgVLzPg%2Bfrm06kZzhKqKmLQ7XOMXwSHlm%2F7
4N6%2B5JyByPvtPlHqgGoIdW8X7eyys4%2B22X3zU0Z3MjXG7emlA9t4Hrpa3oQ0AUi
SD78b1Mnfbz%2FYXdj%2BKDY4fjv5JQcOBZLj8DEw8sbcSdJcIvvAKrPwcKy7Y1eiMg
%3D%3D
status: ACTIVE
timeout: 60s
updateTime: '2018-04-30T00:16:35Z'
versionId: '2'
+ export
BASE_URL=https://us-central1-my-serverless-project-201920.cloudfunc
tions.net/helloHttp
+ /var/jenkins_home/workspace/my-serverless-google-
functions/node_modules/.bin/ava test/system.http.test.js

  helloHttp: should print hello world (371ms)
  helloHttp: should print a name (1.3s)

 2 tests passed

Finished: SUCCESS
```

So, through the previous example, we were able to build, test and deploy the function locally and on `gcloud`. But we did this just randomly on a project. Imagine that we need to have multiple environments, and performance systems, and performance testing with very minimal manual intervention. We need to set up a pipeline with approval gates which deploys to multiple environments, mitigating most of the problems before the function is actually in production. This is where continuous delivery comes in handy.

Continuous delivery with Google Functions

Continuous delivery is about removing risk, delivering frequently and getting fast feedback, and it helps speed up the time to get the product to market. So, how do we do that for Cloud Functions? There are many ways of doing it, but I would like to use a serverless framework to achieve this. There are couple of reason for this. One reason for this is that a serverless framework is a very mature framework for serverless functions deployment. It supports many different vendors, as we have seen, and also has good community support. We can achieve continuous delivery even through `gcloud` and the Jenkins pipeline. We will be reusing most of the setup which we used in previous sections of this chapter.

Google environments

It is essential to have multiple environments for setting up continuous delivery for any type of application. But for a serverless world, there is no clear demarcation for the environment. So we always have to come up with alternatives. We have to do the same for Cloud Functions. We set up environment separation in two ways—first, we could separate the functions for the environment with separate names, for example, `my-serverless-dev`, `my-serverless-sit` or `my-serverless-prod`, but this will add unnecessary complications. So, the ideal way would be to separate the environment by creating a different project, as follows:

1. Log on to the GCP console, go to the **Manage Resource Page** (`https://console.cloud.google.com/cloud-resource-manager?_ga=2.108039562.-900655901.1524348645`), click on **CREATE PROJECT**, enter the project name as `Serverless-SIT` in the **Project Name** and click on **Create**. You will see that the project is being created in the notification bell image on the top right-hand side of the page. Once it has stopped, refresh the page and you will see the project in the list. Likewise, let's create `Serverless-UAT` and `Serverless-PROD` projects. I am not creating `dev` as we are using a local emulator for `dev` environment.

2. Let's enable the cloud API for the project by opening the link: `https://console.cloud.google.com/flows/enableapi?apiid=cloudfunctionsredirect=https://cloud.google.com/functions/quickstart`. The page will have a drop-down list for projects. Select **My Serverless Project** and click on **Continue**, then API will be enabled for the project.

3. Log in to the Jenkins portal (`http://localhost:8080`), which we created in a previous section of the chapter. Then click on **New Item**.

4. Enter the item name in the textbox as `my-serverless-google-function-pipeline` and then select **Pipeline** from the list and then click **OK**.

5. Click on the checkbox **This project is parameterized** and, in the **Add Parameter** drop-down, select **String Parameter**. Then let's add `DEV_PROJECT_ID` in the **Name** textbox and the **Default Value** textbox should have `project id` for the `dev` which we created in Step 1. Likewise, let's create a text parameter for each environment until PROD, and then the last text parameter should be `YOUR_GCF_REGION`.

6. Click on the **Pipeline** tab, in the definition dropdown **Pipeline script from SCM**, and in the **SCM** dropdown select **Git**. Now, in the repository URL textbox add `https://github.com/shzshi/google-functions-helloworld.git` and then keep everything as default and click on **Save**.

7. Once the job is saved, we will build the pipeline, for which we need to click on **Build with Parameters**, so we will see default values for each parameter. In case you want to change the environment or add a different project id, we can feed it through the textbox.

8. Now click on **Build**, the job should first init, which is setting up pre-requisites, then it will run a unit test, then the function is deployed on the local dev environment, then integrate test run. In the next stage, functions are deployed into the UAT environment and the same will happen to other environments. The gated approval is been setup for production deployment. This pipeline can be done in many ways.

Monitoring and logging

Google has provided a dashboard to view the invocation and also view the logs of the invocation through the console. So, once you log in to the console and select the specific function, we should be able to see the invocation graph and also should be able to see the execution time and also the memory used. We can view the source code and also test the function. If we click on **View Logs**, as per the following screenshot, we should be able to see the logs of the invocation and also be able to drill down to a detailed log:

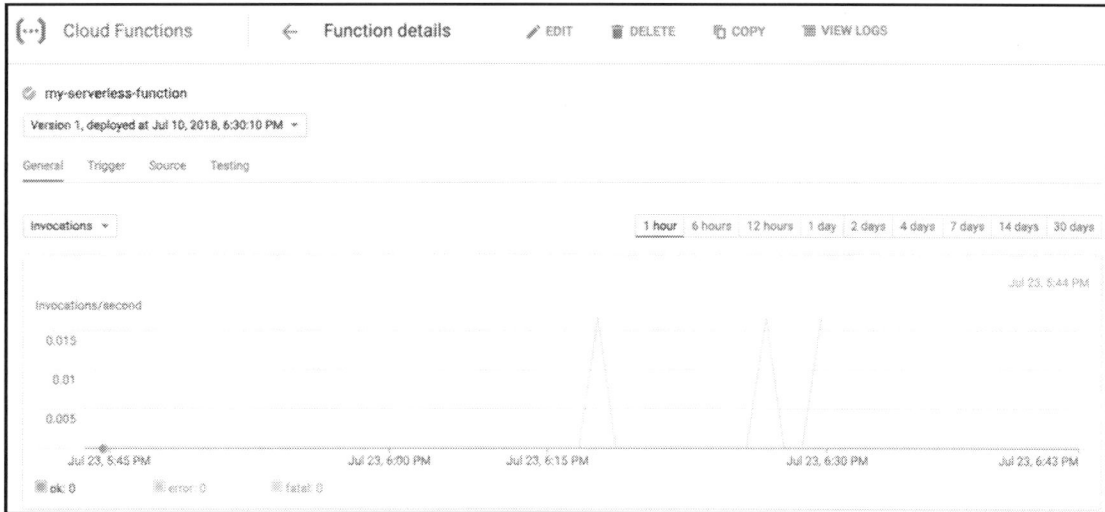

With the dashboard, Google Cloud also has a monitoring and logging platform called **stackdriver**. It show us insights into the health, performance, and availability of Cloud Function. It is natively integrated with the Google Cloud platform. Stackdriver provides a wide variety of metrics, dashboards, alerting, log management, reporting, and tracing capabilities.

It has advanced alerting to help you identify issues quickly. Integrated logging, tracing, and error reporting enable rapid drill-down and root-cause analysis.

Stackdriver gives you access to logs, metrics, traces, and other signals from your infrastructure platform(s), virtual machines, containers, middleware, and application tier, so that you can track issues all the way from your end user to your backend services and infrastructure. Native support for distributed systems, auto-scaling, and ephemeral resources means that your monitoring works seamlessly with your modern architecture.

Best practice

Google Function is still in beta and it is being evaluated and getting better day by day. In terms of best practice for DevOps, it would be pretty similar to what I suggested in the previous chapter, in that I would recommend using a serverless framework for automating deployment in Google Functions. A serverless framework also supplies a template for creating a basic function setup for Node.js.

Developing a DevOps culture across the organisation and moving from monolithic application to micro-services will have a huge impact. But we should be able to guide the team to follow the right path. This would call for some mentoring and educating the team with new processes and terms.

We must extend security to the DevOps tools and organization as well. Security should be part of every aspects of DevOps, right from the automated testing, continuous integration and continuous deployment processes on the cloud platform. It is good to look into monitor security within DevOps in the cloud, and you should have a dedicated person doing this.

Vendor lock-in is really is painful when we develop functions or projects on AWS and then want to move to Google Cloud. The code has to be modified as per the vendor requirements. But, in terms of deployment, I recommend using a serverless framework for DevOps as it mitigates vendor locking of the DevOps tools and framework.

Summary

In this chapter, we learned how to set up CI and CD with Google Functions and set up a dynamic dashboard for Google Functions. In the next chapter, we will talk about how to set up our own private serverless form. We will also will talk about setting up CI and CD for this serverless architecture, as well as monitoring and logging, and unit and integration testing.

7

Adding DevOps Flavor to Kubeless

In the previous chapter, we learned about Google Functions and how to automate deployment of Google Functions using various different tools and process. We also looked at how to monitor and log the service. This chapter will look at yet another open source serverless framework—Kubeless. We will learn how to set up the Kubeless framework over the minikube, create, deploy, and invoke Kubeless functions, and how to build, deploy, log, and monitor the Kubeless functions.

What is Kubeless?

Kubeless is an open source serverless framework based on Kubernetes. It allows us to deploy and execute a piece of code without worrying about the underlying infrastructure. It uses the resources of Kubernetes to provide autoscaling, routing, and monitoring. Post-deployment functions can be triggered with pub–sub, HTTP, and scheduling. The pub–sub events are managed through a Kafka cluster, an out-of-the-box component within Kubeless, which consists of a basic Kafka cluster with a broker and a zookeeper. HTTP triggers are available through the Kubernetes services, and schedule functions translate to a cron job. The languages/runtime supported by Kubeless are `python2.7`, `python3.4`, `python3.6`, `nodejs6`, `nodejs8`, `nodejs_distroless8`, `ruby2.4`, `php7.2`, `go1.10`, `dotnetcore2.0`, `java1.8`, `ballerina0.980.0`, and `jvm1.8`. Kubeless also supports HTTP, NATS, Kafka, cron, and stream triggers.

Kubeless architecture

Kubeless uses custom resource definition, which means that when you create a custom resource definition, then the Kubernetes API server creates a resource path for each version specified. Custom resource definition can be namespaced or cluster-scope, so CRD is called a function, which means that Kubeless functions can be created as normal Kubernetes resources in the background, and a controller is created. The controller will watch these custom resources, and will launch upon runtime demand. The following diagram shows how this architecture works:

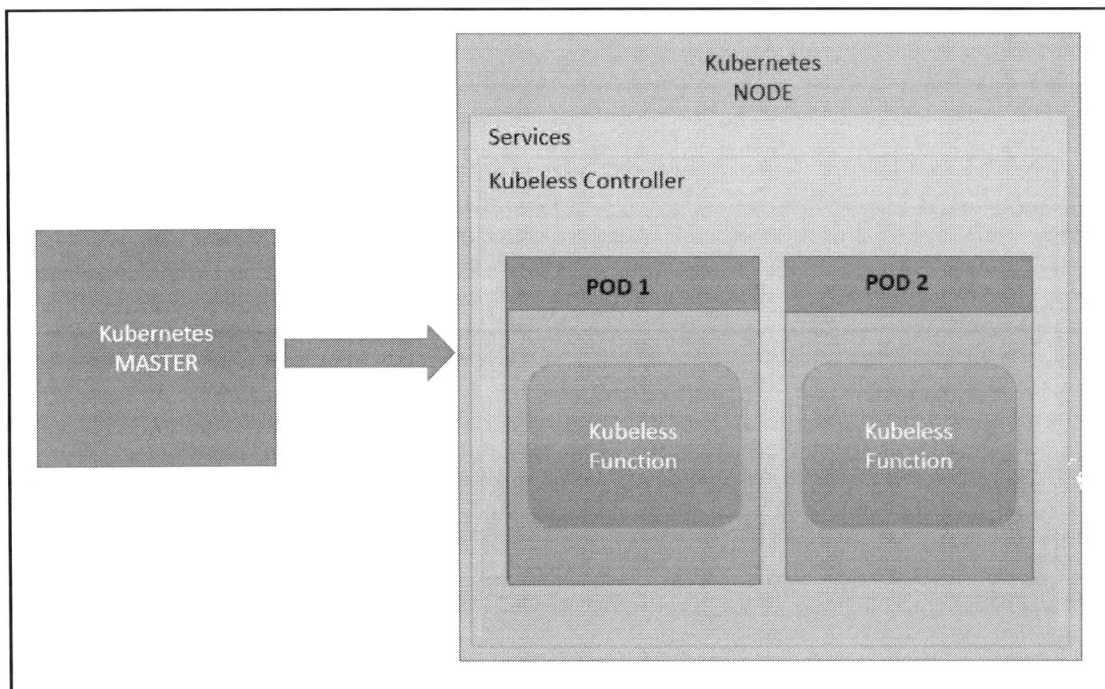

How to set up Kubeless

It is pretty easy to set up Kubeless. First, we download Kubeless from the release page, create a namespace, and then, through the YAML manifest found on the release page, we create the functions' custom resource definition and launch a controller. If you are setting up Kubeless on your personal laptop, then we have to use minikube to do this. So, let's see how to set up minikube, as we will be using it for our tutorials.

First, let's set up minikube by going to `https://github.com/kubernetes/minikube`. Once minikube is installed, we should be able to have a single node Kubernetes cluster inside a virtual machine. We should also be able to execute minikube commands through the Command Prompt. Let's create a cluster and then create Kubeless resources within this cluster. Then, we will create a simple Kubeless function and then deploy and invoke it. We will also set up a dashboard for minikube and see how the controller and function are created and deployed, respectively. Let's look at the how to implement this:

1. Let's create a minikube local Kubernetes cluster, as shown in the following code:

```
$ minikube start
Starting local Kubernetes v1.9.0 cluster...
Starting VM...
Getting VM IP address...
Moving files into cluster...
Setting up certs...
Connecting to cluster...
Setting up kubeconfig...
Starting cluster components...
Kubectl is now configured to use the cluster.
Loading cached images from config file.
```

2. Next, create a minikube dashboard with the following command. The command trigger will open up a browser with the dashboard. The dashboard will show us the services, pods, and manager:

```
$ minikube dashboard
```

3. Now that we have a cluster, let's deploy Kubeless to it, as shown in the following code. There are several Kubeless manifests available for multiple Kubernetes environments (non-RBAC, RBAC, and OpenShift). We will be using the manifest for non-RBAC (nonrole-based access control):

```
$ export RELEASE=$(curl -sk
https://api.github.com/repos/kubeless/kubeless/releases/latest |
grep tag_name | cut -d '"' -f 4)
$ kubectl create ns kubeless
$ echo $RELEASE
$ kubectl create -f
https://github.com/kubeless/kubeless/releases/download/v1.0.0-alpha
.8/kubeless-non-rbac-v1.0.0-alpha.8.yaml
serviceaccount "controller-acct" created
customresourcedefinition "functions.kubeless.io" created
customresourcedefinition "httptriggers.kubeless.io" created
customresourcedefinition "cronjobtriggers.kubeless.io" created
configmap "kubeless-config" created
```

```
deployment "kubeless-controller-manager" created
```

4. Now that we have deployed Kubeless, let's check whether it has deployed properly:

```
$ kubectl get pods -n kubeless
NAME READY STATUS RESTARTS AGE
kubeless-controller-manager-c6b69df76-65gsh 1/1 Running 0 2m
$ kubectl get deployment -n kubeless
NAME DESIRED CURRENT UP-TO-DATE AVAILABLE AGE
kubeless-controller-manager 1 1 1 1 3m
$ kubectl get customresourcedefinition
NAME AGE
cronjobtriggers.kubeless.io 3m
functions.kubeless.io 3m
httptriggers.kubeless.io 3m
```

5. Next, we need to install the Kubeless CLI locally for deploying, invoking, and deleting the Kubeless functions, as shown in the following code:

```
$ export OS=$(uname -s| tr '[:upper:]' '[:lower:]')
$ curl -OL
https://github.com/kubeless/kubeless/releases/download/$RELEASE/kub
eless_$OS-amd64.zip
$ unzip kubeless_$OS-amd64.zip
$ sudo mv bundles/kubeless_$OS-amd64/kubeless /usr/local/bin/
```

6. Let's create a function and deploy it. The following is a simple Python function that we will deploy and invoke. Create a function named `test.py` with the following content:

```
def hello(event, context):
 print event
 return event['data']
```

Functions in Kubeless have the same format, regardless of the language of the function or the event source. In general, every function will do the following:

*   Receive an object **event** as its first parameter. This parameter includes all the information regarding the event source. In particular, the `data` key should contain the body of the function request.
*   Receive a second object **context** with general information about the function.
*   Return a string/object that will be used as a response for the caller.

7. Now, let's deploy the function, and when we refresh the minikube dashboard, we should be able to see the `hello` function deployed there, as shown in the following code:

```
$ kubeless function deploy hello --runtime python2.7 --from-file
test.py --handler test.hello --namespace kubeless
INFO[0000] Deploying function...
INFO[0000] Function hello submitted for deployment
INFO[0000] Check the deployment status executing 'kubeless function
ls hello'
```

The following list explains the various elements of the preceding code:

- `kubeless function deploy hello` tells Kubeless to register a new function named `hello`. The function will be accessible over the web using this name. Note that this doesn't need to be the same as the function name used inside the code (we'll specify that a little further along using the `--handler` option).
- `--trigger-http` tells Kubeless that the function will be invoked over HTTP. It's also possible to trigger the function in other ways, but that is not covered here.
- `--runtime python2.7` tells Kubeless to use Python 2.7 to execute the code. Node is also supported as a runtime, with more to come in the future.
- `--handler test.hello` tells Kubeless the name of the function to call inside the code module. You can see in the preceding Python code that the function is called `hello`.
- `--from-file /tmp/hello.py` tells Kubeless to upload and use the `/tmp/hello.py` file as the source for the function. It is possible to pass a function in other ways as well.

  We will see the function custom resource being created through the following commands:

  ```
  $ kubectl get functions
  NAME AGE
  hello 2m

  $ kubeless function ls --namespace kubeless
  NAME NAMESPACE HANDLER RUNTIME DEPENDENCIES STATUS
  hello kubeless test.hello python2.7 1/1 READY
  ```

8. Now, let's invoke the function, as follows:

```
$ kubeless function call hello --data 'Hello Serverless!' --
namespace kubeless
Hello Serverless!
```

9. We can also `delete` the function, as follows:

```
$ kubeless function delete hello --namespace kubeless
$ kubeless function ls --namespace kubeless
NAME NAMESPACE HANDLER RUNTIME DEPENDENCIES STATUS
```

So far, we have installed Kubeless locally, created a simple function, deployed it, invoked it, and undeployed it. In the next section, we will learn how to automate deployment using the Serverless Framework.

Setting up continuous integration and deployment

We will be using the Serverless Framework to kick-start the development and deployment of the Kubeless functions. The Serverless Framework has provided lots of feature to adopt Kubeless without much effort. Let's look at the various functionalities provided by Serverless.

Creation of the service

We will use the `create` command to create basic services using the passing of runtime and `path` to create a directory. Currently, two runtimes are provided—one is Python and the other is Node.js. So, if we run the following command with the `path` parameter, it will create a folder with a simple serverless function. The runtimes currently available are `kubeless-python` and `kubeless-nodejs`:

```
$ serverless create --template kubeless-python --path myKubelessFunc
```

The `create` command will create a service, and each service configuration will have the following three files:

- `serverless.yml`: The main responsibility of this file is to declare the service, define the provider, custom plugin (in our case, the serverless-kubeless plugin), and events or triggers that the function will execute, and configure files using serverless variables.
- `handler.py`: This file will contain function code. The function definition with `serverless.yml` will point to the `handler.py`.
- `package.json`: This is the file for the npm package definition of our functions, containing all the dependencies and the `kubeless-serverless` plugin.

Let's update these files with our function and configuration, as shown in the following code. We are updating a function to search a bike station from the station feed exposed through JSON. I have also put the code on the GitHub repository at `https://github.com/shzshi/kubeless-serverless.git`:

```python
#handler.py
import urllib2
import json
def find(event, context):
    term = event['data']['term']
    url = "https://feeds.capitalbikeshare.com/stations/stations.json"
response = urllib2.urlopen(url)
    stations = json.loads(response.read())
    hits = []
    for station in stations["stationBeanList"]:
        if station["stAddress1"].find(term) > -1:
hits.append(station)
    return json.dumps(hits)
```

Replace the `serverless.yaml` with the following content:

```yaml
# serverless.yml
service: bikesearch
provider:
    name: kubeless
    runtime: python2.7
plugins:
    - serverless-kubeless
functions:
    bikesearch:
        handler: handler.find
```

Deploying the function

As the required files were created through a template, we can modify them as per our needs and then simply deploy and invoke them when we need them. Let's go ahead and deploy them using serverless, then `npm install` will get the required dependencies for serverless, such as the `kubeless-serverless` plugin, and then we can deploy the function, as shown in the following code:

```
$ npm install
$ serverless deploy -v
Serverless: Packaging service...
Serverless: Excluding development dependencies...
Serverless: Deploying function bikesearch...
Serverless: Pods status: {"waiting":{"reason":"PodInitializing"}}
Serverless: Function bikesearch successfully deployed
Serverless: Skipping ingress rule generation
```

Invoking the function

The Kubeless function can be invoked through the command line or through a UI provided by Kubeless. The Kubeless UI can be provisioned by downloading the file locally and running it, or by using a Docker image and Dockerfile, or through the Kubernetes manifest that's available with the repository. For our tutorials, I will be using the Kubernetes manifest, as shown in the following code:

> Currently, the UI works perfectly fine with minikube, but it might need a few tweaks if you have an RBAC cluster, or it could just work without any tweaks.

```
$ kubectl create -f
https://raw.githubusercontent.com/kubeless/kubeless-ui/master/k8s.yaml
serviceaccount "ui-acct" created
clusterrole "kubeless-ui" created
clusterrolebinding "kubeless-ui" created
deployment "ui" created
service "ui" created
$ minikube service ui -n kubeless
```

The `minikube` command will pop a browser up and open a UI. The UI has the ability to create, edit, invoke, and delete the function, so invoke the function that we deployed. Let's add `{"term":"New York"}` in the `textarea` request, select the **Request** as **POST**, and click on **Run Function**. The function will be executed successfully, with the station data response output displayed, as shown in the following screenshot:

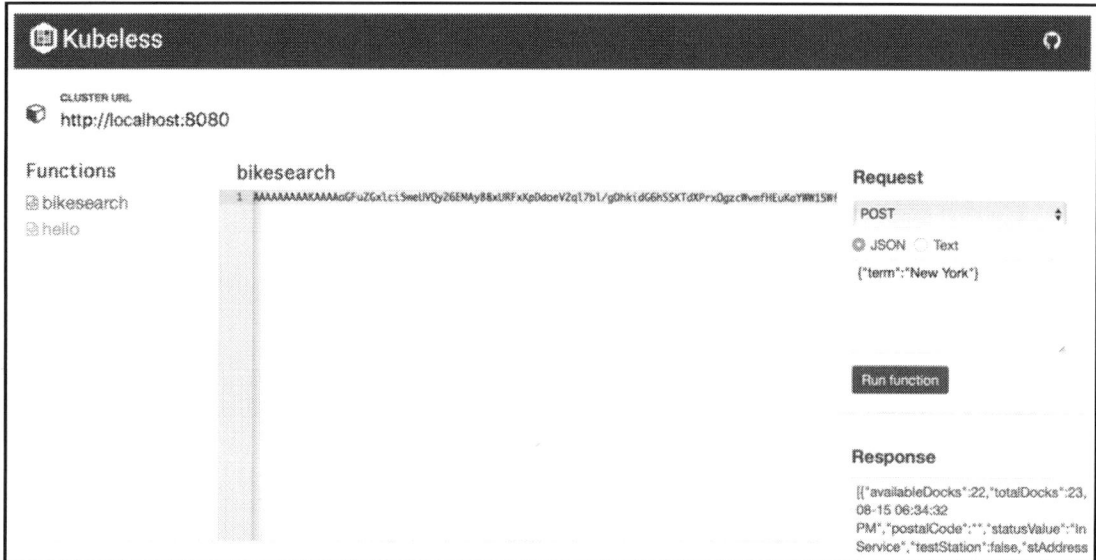

We can invoke the same function through the Serverless Framework as well, and the function will execute and get the required data, as shown in the following code:

```
$ serverless invoke --function bikesearch --data '{"term":"Albemarle"}' -l
Serverless: Calling function: bikesearch...
--------------------------------------------------------------
[ { availableDocks: 12,
 totalDocks: 15,
 city: '',
 altitude: '',
 stAddress2: '',
 longitude: -77.079382,
 lastCommunicationTime: '2018-08-15 04:16:15 PM',
 postalCode: '',
 statusValue: 'In Service',
 testStation: false,
 stAddress1: 'Tenleytown / Wisconsin Ave & Albemarle St NW',
 stationName: 'Tenleytown / Wisconsin Ave & Albemarle St NW',
 landMark: '',
 latitude: 38.947607,
 statusKey: 1,
 availableBikes: 1,
 id: 80,
 location: '' } ]
```

The Kubeless UI repository is listed at `https://github.com/kubeless/` `kubeless-ui`.

Serverless logs

What happens if something goes wrong? We do not have error handling in place, but we can test the logging just by feeding the error while invoking the function. So, let's invoke the function with an error in the data, as shown in the following code:

```
$serverless invoke --function bikesearch --data '{"trm":"Albemarle"}' -l
Serverless: Calling function: bikesearch...

  Error --------------------------------------------------

  Internal Server Error

     For debugging logs, run again after setting the "SLS_DEBUG=*"
  environment variable.

  Get Support --------------------------------------------
     Docs: docs.serverless.com
     Bugs: github.com/serverless/serverless/issues
     Forums: forum.serverless.com
     Chat: gitter.im/serverless/serverless

  Your Environment Information ---------------------------
     OS: darwin
     Node Version: 6.10.3
     Serverless Version: 1.26.1
```

Serverless returned an error message with a 500 server code, which is what you would expect from a web framework. However, it would be useful to see the Python stack trace in order to better debug the source of the error. So, let's get the logs to see what the error was:

```
$ serverless logs -f bikesearch
Hit Ctrl-C to quit.
172.17.0.1 - - [15/Aug/2018:20:17:18 +0000] "POST / HTTP/1.1" 200 460 "" ""
0/934928
172.17.0.1 - - [15/Aug/2018:20:17:18 +0000] "GET /healthz HTTP/1.1" 200 2
"" "kube-probe/." 0/133
172.17.0.1 - - [15/Aug/2018:20:17:48 +0000] "GET /healthz HTTP/1.1" 200 2
"" "kube-probe/." 0/72
172.17.0.1 - - [15/Aug/2018:20:18:18 +0000] "GET /healthz HTTP/1.1" 200 2
"" "kube-probe/." 0/108
```

```
172.17.0.1 - - [15/Aug/2018:20:18:48 +0000] "GET /healthz HTTP/1.1" 200 2
"" "kube-probe/." 0/123
172.17.0.1 - - [15/Aug/2018:20:19:18 +0000] "GET /healthz HTTP/1.1" 200 2
"" "kube-probe/." 0/74
172.17.0.1 - - [15/Aug/2018:20:19:48 +0000] "GET /healthz HTTP/1.1" 200 2
"" "kube-probe/." 0/138
172.17.0.1 - - [15/Aug/2018:20:20:18 +0000] "GET /healthz HTTP/1.1" 200 2
"" "kube-probe/." 0/75
172.17.0.1 - - [15/Aug/2018:20:20:48 +0000] "GET /healthz HTTP/1.1" 200 2
"" "kube-probe/." 0/149
172.17.0.1 - - [15/Aug/2018:20:21:18 +0000] "GET /healthz HTTP/1.1" 200 2
"" "kube-probe/." 0/187
172.17.0.1 - - [15/Aug/2018:20:21:48 +0000] "GET /healthz HTTP/1.1" 200 2
"" "kube-probe/." 0/147
172.17.0.1 - - [15/Aug/2018:20:22:18 +0000] "GET /healthz HTTP/1.1" 200 2
"" "kube-probe/." 0/71
172.17.0.1 - - [15/Aug/2018:20:22:47 +0000] "POST / HTTP/1.1" 200 2131 ""
"" 1/232988
Traceback (most recent call last):
 File "/usr/local/lib/python2.7/dist-packages/bottle.py", line 862, in
_handle return route.call(**args)
 File "/usr/local/lib/python2.7/dist-packages/bottle.py", line 1740, in
wrapper
 rv = callback(*a, **ka)
 File "/kubeless.py", line 76, in handler
 raise res
KeyError: 'term'
```

It is clear from the `KeyError` phrase that the function failed because of the wrong key name, so this gives us a view of what is going wrong. But in a production-like environment, we need to have more sophisticated error-handling methods.

Continuous integration with Jenkins

Throughout this book, we have looked at continuous integration and continuous deployment for different serverless providers, but with respect to Kubeless (as it is still developing) there is still a lot that needs to be improved. While writing this book, I found that, using the Serverless Framework, we can only set up deployment if our Kubernetes cluster (minikube), Serverless Framework, and Jenkins are set up locally. There is no provision to set up a remote deployment with the Serverless Framework. But as the Serverless Framework and Kubeless mature over time, these features will be added. In the following tutorials, I have created files to set up deployment locally.

> You can find out how to set up remote deployment by reading the following article at `https://aws.amazon.com/blogs/opensource/running-faas-on-kubernetes-cluster-on-aws-using-kubeless/`.

If you clone the repository at `https://github.com/shzshi/kubeless-continuous-integration.git`, then you should be able to use this template to set up continuous integration locally.

However, we can run the files locally on the laptop, provided we have the Serverless Framework installed and configured. Let's look how do this:

```
$ git clone https://github.com/shzshi/kubeless-continuous-integration.git
$ cd kubeless-continuous-integration
```

We should see six files and one directory in this folder, but we won't be using Dockerfiles and Jenkinsfiles in this tutorial. They can be used once remote deployment is possible with the Serverless Framework for Kubeless, as shown in the following code:

```
$ npm install
$ npm test

> kubeless-nodejs@1.0.0 test
/Users/shashi/Documents/packt/chapter7/kubeless-continuous-integration
> mocha ./test/*.js
kubelesshello
✓ should return 0 when "Hello Kubeless" is present
1 passing (8ms)
```

We ran `npm install` to get the required dependencies for the Serverless Framework and Node.js application and test. Post that we ran the npm test, for which I created a simple unit test to check the sanity of our function before we deployed them to the cluster, as shown in the following code:

```
$ serverless deploy -v
Serverless: Packaging service...
Serverless: Excluding development dependencies...
Serverless: Deploying function kubelesshello...
Serverless: Pods status: {"waiting":{"reason":"PodInitializing"}}
Serverless: Pods status: {"waiting":{"reason":"PodInitializing"}}
Serverless: Function kubelesshello successfully deployed
Serverless: Skipping ingress rule generation
```

So, our Node.js function will be deployed successfully, and we can invoke it locally or through the Kubeless UI and test it. Post-invocation, we should get the output of `Hello Kubeless`, as shown in the following code:

```
$ serverless invoke -f kubelesshello -l
Serverless: Calling function: kubelesshello...
--------------------------------------------------------------------
Hello Kubeless
```

Monitoring Kubeless

We can monitor the `kubeless` function using Prometheus. There is in-built runtime support for Prometheus; the runtime will automatically collect metrics for each function. Prometheus will show those metrics on the default dashboard.

The Prometheus metrics can be visualized through Grafana. The Grafana dashboard can be configured through the sample dashboard JSON file provided by Kubeless at `https://github.com/kubeless/kubeless/blob/master/docs/misc/kubeless-grafana-dashboard.json`.

Kubeless pros and cons

In the world of serverless, Kubeless has just started its journey; it has as a long way to go to be a biggie, like AWS Lambda, Azure Function, or Google Functions. However, it still has a good number of brownie points, and it will definitely grow to be one of the leading Serverless Frameworks. Let's look at some of its pros:

- No provisioning of servers
- Can run the code in parallel and scale easily
- Not vendor-agnostic, like other service providers, such as AWS Lambda, Azure Function, or Google Functions
- Integration with the serverless deployment framework
- UI to create, update, delete, and invoke the functions

The following are some of its cons:

- The testing and integration of functions still needs improvement
- Remote deployment is not in place
- Requests that use a lot of memory state, cache, queue, and persistence storage are provided by other systems
- Environment management (dev, QA, UAT, or PROD) is not documented or not in place

So, in terms of applying automation, the framework still needs lots of improvement and features to be added in order to have adequate functionality.

Summary

In this chapter, we learned about the Kubeless serverless framework. We learned how to set up Kubeless, deploy, remove, and invoke Python and Node.js functions. We also learned how to monitor or log the functions. In the next chapter, we will learn the best practices for using serverless and for setting up automation and DevOps.

8
Best Practices and the Future of DevOps with Serverless

In the previous chapters, we learned what serverless is and the multiple different service providers for serverless features. We also looked at how to build, test, and deploy a serverless application, as well as how to monitor and log the execution. But this chapter is pretty interesting, because in this chapter, we will go one step further to learn some best practices for serverless. We will also learn the best practices for building, deploying, monitoring, logging, and securing our serverless application. We will also examine how DevOps works with serverless.

Important aspects of DevOps

The two important tenets of DevOps are automation and process. We have to automate every bit of development from the nonproduction environment to production, and at the same time we have to maintain continuous feedback, with information moving back and forth, while also logging everything. Let's look at some best practices of how to do this.

Collaboration and tools strategy

The DevOps team needs to come up with a common tool strategy across the organization, and they should collaborate with different teams—such as development, testing, and infrastructure—and agree upon the business objectives of DevOps. There should be seamless collaboration and integration between the teams. The objective is to automate everything, so the ideal goal should be one-click deployment from development to production, with very minimal human intervention.

Agile development

There are many Agile methodologies available. Scrum, XP, and Kanban are a few of the more popular ones. You can use one of these development methodologies to give you a more flexible option to plan, create a faster output, and give you clear focus and transparency throughout the development of your project. Agile methodologies help to limit the work in progress, which in turn helps maintain a balanced flow so that we don't attempt to do too much at once.

Version control everything

When we talk about version control, the first thing that comes to our mind is application source code versioning, which is a practice that we are well accustomed to. But with source code versioning, we should version control the database, the build artifacts, the dependencies, and everything that is involved in the application. This ensures that every aspect of the application can be historically tracked through the single origin that is the repository.

Capture every request

We should make sure that no ad hoc work or changes happen outside of DevOps, and that there should be a change request raised and maintained for every functional and nonfunctional requirement. These change requests should be captured and maintained within the tool.

Automate test and source code analysis

When we talk about automating the test, this does not mean just automating the testing. The test automation should include provisioning test data and running the standard test to ensure that the standard of the code meets the enterprise service level agreement. The testing must be continuous and should run 100 or 1,000 times, and then, upon successful completion, should automatically be promoted to a higher environment. The quality of the code should be checked regularly and returned back to the developer to be reworked if the code coverage, source code analysis, and performance of the code are not up to the baseline.

Continuous feedback

The feedback loop is very a important aspect of DevOps. It plays a very important role for the success of DevOps. The feedback loop consists of automated communication between an issue registered during development and the human element of the DevOps process. It should be managed by a tool, through which issues must be registered manually or via an automated mechanism. The issue should also be tagged with an artifact that developers can use to trace what occurred, why it occurred, and where in the process it occurred. The tool should help to define the chain of communication with all automated and human elements in the loop.

Time to market and the cycle time

During the DevOps process, we will get a rich array of metrics and real-time reports about our process, and we will want to measure the time to market and the cycle time of the application, because these two metrics play a very important role in how fast and efficiently we make new features available to customers. Time to market measures end-to-end efficiency in bringing valuable new features to market, and the cycle time is the measurement of the engineering team's process, which, once the feature is defined, indicates when it becomes available to move to production. It helps in understanding the efficiency of the team and improving it.

Log metrics

We should always track the productivity of DevOps processes, both automated and manual, and determine whether they working in favor of the organization. We need to define which metrics are relevant for the DevOps process, such as the deployment speed, the testing errors found, or the build time. With this definition, automated processes can correct these issues without manual intervention.

We skimmed through general DevOps practices that can be applied to application development, but when it comes to serverless applications, we need to add more specific best practices in terms of tools and process. We will look into each service provider and funnel the best practices for the serverless applications, as well for DevOps with serverless.

Best practices for Serverless

As we know, the serverless architecture consists of a small piece of code called a function, which runs in a stateless container. One major purpose of this architecture is to scale and descale as and when required. So, bearing this in mind, our best practices are more or less focused on this aspect of serverless. So let's look at a few of the best practices involved with the serverless concept.

One function, one task

When we start building functions, we might end up with monolithic functions behind the proxy route and use a `switch` statement. So, if we have one or a few functions to run our whole app, then we are actually scaling the whole application instead of scaling a specific element of the application. This should be avoided, as scaling would be a problem in this instance, and we also might end up with large and complex functions.

Functions call other functions

We should avoid calling a function within another function because we will end up paying more for this, and debugging would be a headache. We lose the value of isolating the functions. If required, it would be ideal to trigger another function if more work has to be done.

Minimize libraries

When we write a function, we might need libraries to make it run. But adding a huge set of libraries to the function would make it really slow. There are two types of starts when using functions—one is the cold start, which is function that is started for the first time, and the other is the warm start, which is function that has already been started and is ready to be executed from the pool. So in theory, a larger number of libraries will be slower during the cold start and will also impact the scaling of the application. With each increase in scale, the function has to perform a cold start, and so, as the cold start is slower, the scaling is slower.

Also, as the number of libraries rises, the less secure our code will be, so security testing has to be performed for each set of libraries added. They also need to be trusted before you actually start using them.

With HTTP – one function per route

We should avoid using single-function proxy if possible while using http route, as this hinders in scaling of the function, and also makes debugging tedious. There are occasions where we can avoid it, where a functionality of a series of routes is tied to a single table, and it's very much decoupled from the rest of the application.

Database connection to RDBMS

The concept of a serverless application is designed to work very well with services, so establishing the connection to RDMBS within the function could be troublesome, as the parts of the services are still relied upon to provide the fast responses.

As function scales with RDBMS connections, the number of connections grows with the scale, and we might end up introducing a bottleneck and an I/O wait into the cold start of the function.

So Serverless architecture makes us rethink the data layer, so if we try using serverless with the existing data layer (RDBMS), then you will see a performance lag in your overall application performance. This might also be the reason why DynamoDB works so well with Serverless.

Use messages and queues

A serverless application works efficiently when the application is asynchronous, but with web applications, this is not that simple, because web applications require lots of request–response interactions and lots of querying. Going back to functions not calling other functions, it's important to point out that this is how you chain functions together. Queues act as circuit breakers in the chaining scenario, so if the function fails, we can easily drill down to the failed queue and investigate the failure, which could be the result of pushing messages that failed to a dead-letter queue.

With applications that have serverless as the backend, it would be ideal to use CQRS, which separates out the conceptual model of input and output in a single model into separate models for the purposes of updates and displaying changes to the user.

Data in motion

In a serverless system, the data is in motion. It flows through the system, but it might end up in a datalake. Nevertheless, while in a serverless system it should in flow, so make sure that you keep all the data in motion instead of a datalake. Avoid querying from the datalake while using the serverless environment. It is not always possible to keep data in motion, but it is best to try.

Measure the scale

The main feature of serverless is efficient scaling, but we should code it so that it scales efficiently. We could avoid calling a direct data connection within the function, or avoid adding huge numbers of dependency libraries. So, in short, the lighter the function, the faster the cold start is, and eventually it will scale much faster. Also make sure that functions are load tested before they reach production for efficient scaling.

In this section, we looked into the various best practices that make serverless functions perform and scale very efficiently. Although this is not the complete list, these are a few of the very important ones. In the next section, we will learn the best practices for each cloud provider and also understand how best practices with DevOps will help make serverless development and deployment faster and more efficient.

DevOps best practices and troubleshooting for AWS Lambda

So far, we have learned the best practices for using DevOps and designing the architecture of a serverless application. We also looked at the best ways of writing functions to make them scalable and have a faster cold start. Going forward, we will learn how to apply the best practices for a specific cloud provider.

AWS Lambda is a very popular and mature serverless platform. Because of this, most serverless best practices are aligned with Lambda, and there are a number of tools and processes that align functions perfectly well with AWS Lambda. In this section, when we talk about DevOps, we will look at the source code versioning, building, testing, the package itself, releasing, monitoring, security, and controlling the cost aspects of DevOps. All of these aspects of DevOps are stitched together to perform as a single platform. This needs a lot of hard work and patience from us if we are to reach the nirvana of DevOps.

Source code versioning

Source code versioning is a very important part of development. If the code is not versioned, then it might as well not exist. There are many tools available for source code versioning, but these days, Git and Apache Subversion are the most popular ones. It is always good to have one repository for each application and then create multiple branches for development. With respect to Git, when we create a repository, there is already a master branch. The master holds the golden copy of the code, which is usually used as a benchmark and can also be used as a production copy. We can also create many other branches for the feature, release, and development versions of the code for efficient development and deployment.

So the best practices concerning the source code management is to commit often and also make sure that you raise the pull request every time you start your day. This allows us to avoid wasting time on merging the code and also prevents us from breaking the build. Usually, we have a huge team of developers in various parts of the globe building different modules for the application. If we forgot to commit one day, then the next morning we would have to waste lots of time merging our code before we actually started development. We should also make sure that we always inspect before we commit, because otherwise we might commit a whole bunch of junk, unwanted libraries, or JAR or debug files into the repository, which will clog the repository, as well as make our function bigger, eventually degrading the performance.

We should also make sure that we add the commit message while we commit the code. The comment should explain why we committed the code because this will help us to easily trace whether something failed, and also makes it easier for us to roll back if we committed buggy code, or if some functionality changes. When we add the commit message, we should make sure that it is not too generic or lacking in information. We should also ensure that it is fixed, that it works, and that it has no typos, because this won't help us to trace it back if we have introduced a bug or an issue. In addition, it is not good practice to have the same commit message appear after a previous commit, as we usually commit because something has changed in the code compared to the previous commit.

We should avoid committing a build artifact or compiled dependencies like `.dll` or `.jar` into the source control as this could well irritate your coworkers, as they will have to check out a huge list of files or have his on local environment corrupted by downloading these dependencies. Another way to avoid commit issues would be to write precommit hooks, which can mitigate most of the commit issues.

We have talked about versioning, but we should also talk about the version database component. Like the UI, application, and testing code, the database component should be versioned for stable deployment and application. If we don't version the database, then we might run the application with old data or an old configuration. It is also easier to track what DDL and DML statement were used in a particular release version.

So, in short, we should always remember to commit regularly, know what are we committing, add a valid commit message, and ensure that sure we do it ourselves.

AWS also supports the versioning of the functions. The Lambda function is versioned through publishing. One of the AWS Lambda consoles is specifically dedicated to publishing the new version of the Lambda function, and we can create multiple versions of the same function. Each Lambda function version is provided with a unique ARN, and becomes immutable postpublishing. Lambda also allows us to create aliases (as shown in the following screenshot), which are pointers to specific Lambda function versions. Each alias will have a unique ARN and can only point to one function version, and not to another alias:

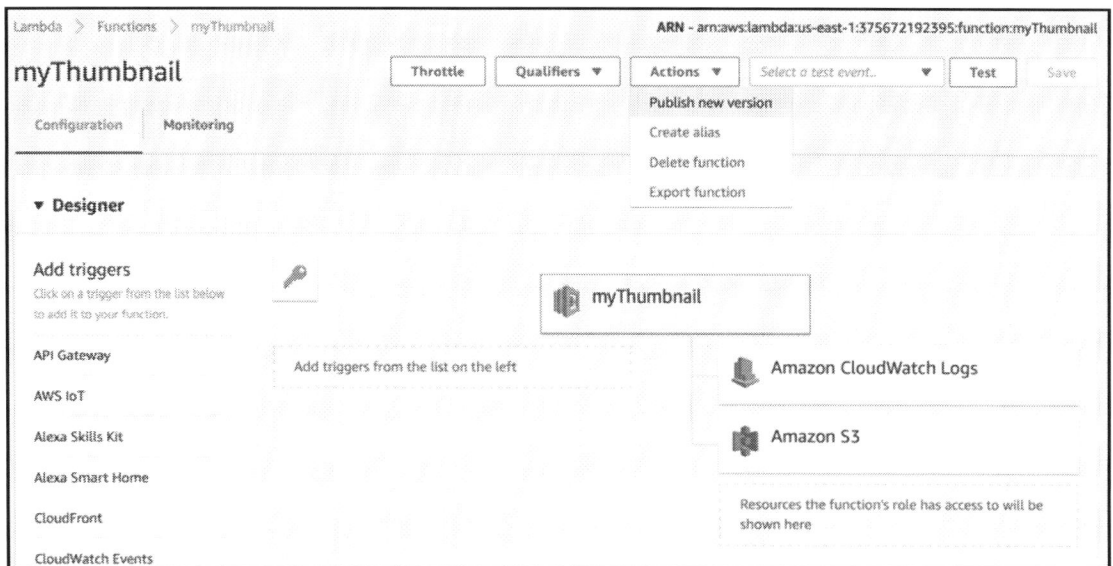

Let's look at an example of AWS Lambda versioning. Say that we have an AWS S3 bucket that is an event source for a Lambda function, so whenever any new item is added to the bucket, the Lambda function is triggered and executed. The event source mapping information is stored in the bucket notification configuration, and in that configuration, we can identify the Lambda function ARN that S3 can invoke. But the newly published version is not automatically updated, so we have to make sure that this is updated every time a new version of the function is created.

If we are using the Serverless Framework, the new version is created through the deployment. There is also the provision to roll back to a previous version through the following command line:

```
$ serverless rollback function -f my-function -v 23
```

Build

In programming terms, the build is the version of the program or product, but the term is also used to refer to the continuous integration of DevOps. So we should be sure of the build of the code is built each time code is committed into the Git repository. The reason for this is because there are many developers involved in such projects, working individually on their own machines, which might work fine. But until the code is committed and built on the continuous integration server, which will trigger source code analysis and unit testing on the committed code, we won't know if we have pushed broken code. So it is essential to trigger a build with every commit.

The artifact of a successful build should always be versioned. The best practice is to version them on the Nexus repository, so that all the nonproduction builds should be pushed into snapshot repositories of the nexus and the release candidate should be pushed into the release repository of the nexus. This process will help us to keep the release build separate from the snapshot build, which is temporary and should be regularly purged, as it is created for each build and will not be needed later.

The build should also trigger source code analysis, which could be linting for a Node.js and Python application, and if you are using Java or C#, then there are lots of tools available for source code analysis. The source code analysis will make sure that the proper coding standards are followed by developers. It also performs security checks and checks for cyclomatic complexity within the code. The tools will generate reports as well, and we can also set a threshold for the source code analysis pass parameters that will eventually pass the build. So if the source code analysis checks are below the baseline set, then the build will fail and then the developer will have to fix the issue.

If we are using Java as a language for serverless, then there are many open source tools available for us to use, such as PMD, Checkmarx, Checkstyle, FindBugs, and SonarQube. **SonarQube** is a popular tool for source code analysis. It supports lots of languages, such as Java, C# , Node.js, and Python. It also has a lovely dashboard and is pretty easy to install and configure. The SonarQube official image is there on Docker Hub. You can set it up and give it a try.

> You can find the SonarQube image on Docker Hub at `https://hub.docker.com/_/sonarqube/`.

Test

Testing is one of the essential parts of the development cycle. Testing ensures that bug-free and secure code is deployed to the higher environment, and we should make sure that the testing should be automated as much as possible. Testing should be combined with the continuous integration process and eventually with continuous deployment. The benefit of testing is that it saves lots time and money for organizations because it mitigates most of the bugs and errors at the initial stage of development. There are many different levels of testing, such as unit testing, integration testing, functional testing, and performance testing. Let's look at the best practices around these levels.

Unit testing

Unit testing is the foundation level of testing when testing software. It basically means testing the units of your code to check the correctness of its functioning. During unit testing, the code is tested in a test environment using simulated input. The output of the execution is then compared with the expected output, and if the output matches the expected output, then the test passes.

With respect to the serverless concept, we do not have to worry about Lambda functions or handlers or events; we just need to organize our code base for easy integration of unit testing. If you look at the following code, you can see that we are separating our core logic into separate modules instead of within the handler so that they can be unit tested individually:

```
const createUser = (event, context, callback) => {
    const user = utils.RegisterUser(event.user)
    const photoUrl = utils.updatePhoto(user)
    callback(null,
```

```
{
    statusCode: 200,
    body: 'User Created!'
})
}
```

So, it always better to separate your business logic so that it is independent of the service provider, reusable, and more easily testable. With this separation of business logic, the unit testing would be easier to write and run, and it would also take less effort to move to a different provider.

There are many unit-testing frameworks available for Node.js and Python, but the ones we will look at are **Mocha** and **Jest**. There are serverless framework plugins available for these two frameworks.

The following code shows the Mocha serverless plugin installation and usage. It can be installed locally as a service or included within the serverless.yml, as follows:

```
# serverless.yaml
plugins:
  - serverless-mocha-plugin
```

Likewise, we can add the Jest serverless plugin into the serverless.yml, as shown in the following code:

```
plugins:
  - serverless-jest-plugin
custom:
  jest:
    # You can pass jest options here
    # See details here:
https://facebook.github.io/jest/docs/configuration.html
    # For instance, uncomment next line to enable code coverage
    # collectCoverage: true
```

Similarly, **Nose** is a popular framework for Python serverless applications.

In addition to this, we can use **LocalStack** for mocking an AWS environment. LocalStack helps us to create a local testing environment that is similar to AWS. It spins up a core Cloud API for us to test our functions locally.

Integration testing

Integration testing is basically when tests cover more than one unit. Our Lambda function must be integrated with third-party code dependencies, which have to be tested thoroughly. That's where integration testing comes into play. Integration testing plays a very important role in the serverless world, but it is also expensive if you are always doing it over the cloud. But we can reduce the cost by mocking, as we talked about when looking at the LocalStack framework. Using this method, we can put it to use mocking a large number of AWS resources.

Similarly, we can invoke the Lambda function locally using the `serverless invoke local`, and if our functions need to read/ write from DynamoDB, then this can also be mocked using `dynamodb-local` Node.js libraries.

While these methods don't emulate Lambda 100%, we'll still be able to find issues in our code base quickly without having to wait for a deployment.

Performance testing

Performance testing is a type of testing where we check how our application is performing with an expected workload. This is a very essential type of testing for our type of application because performance testing will provide us with an opportunity to improve the performance of our functions, and will also help to improve the speed of scaling. Scaling is a very important feature of functions, but it is our responsibility to code it in a fashion that will help it scale faster. This is where performance testing will help.

One of the very popular tools for performance testing is **Jmeter**. It is widely used across the industry. The Jmeter stress test will examine load-testing KPIs, such as the response time, error rate, memory leaks, slowness, security issues, and data corruption. Jmeter requires a performance parameter script. We can start creating the script with the BlazeMeter Chrome extension.

Another popular tool is **Artillery**, which can be used for performance testing, load testing, and functional testing. It is an open source tool, and is built over Node.js. It can generate a load for an application and can simulate virtual users. You can run through this simple installation using the following code:

```
$ npm install -g artillery

$ artillery quick --count 10 -n 20 https://artillery.io/
Started phase 0, duration: 1s @ 21:13:07(+0100) 2018-08-28
Report @ 21:13:10(+0100) 2018-08-28
  Scenarios launched: 10
```

```
Scenarios completed: 10
Requests completed: 200
RPS sent: 69.44
Request latency:
min: 28.3
max: 248.4
median: 41.9
p95: 127.1
p99: 191.7
Codes:
200: 200

All virtual users finished
Summary report @ 21:13:10(+0100) 2018-08-28
 Scenarios launched: 10
 Scenarios completed: 10
 Requests completed: 200
 RPS sent: 69.44
 Request latency:
 min: 28.3
 max: 248.4
 median: 41.9
 p95: 127.1
 p99: 191.7
 Scenario counts:
 0: 10 (100%)
 Codes:
 200: 200
```

There is also a combination of Serverless Framework and Artillery, called `serverless-artillery`. This package will help us to deploy the function and run the performance test through a single Node.js package, and makes it easier to integrate it into our CI/CD pipeline. More information can be found at: `//github.com/Nordstrom/serverless-artillery`.

Testing is very important in order to weed out defects and errors in the early stages of development, but we have to make sure that it is introduced very early in the development cycle, and should be performed until production. But it is equally important to automate it, and it should be integrated with the continuous integration and continuous delivery cycle. But serverless testing has its challenges, as follows:

- Serverless architecture is actually an integration of separate, distributed services that need to be tested both together and independently.

- We can test the serverless functions locally, but it is hard to emulate them completely locally, and it is equally important to test them over the cloud. This process should be automated.
- The serverless architecture can feature event-driven, asynchronous workflows, and testing them thoroughly is not that easy.

Monitoring

When we think of monitoring, the first thing that comes into our mind is observing and tracking the operations and activities of the software application regularly and setting up an alarm to trigger upon a system or application failure. Monitoring should begin right from the start of the development, in such instances as the monitoring of the speed of the application or monitoring how many resources a developed piece of code is using. This monitoring system should be coupled with a notification system, triggering a notification such as an email when memory is used beyond a defined threshold.

But monitoring serverless functions is more tricky. In server monitoring, we monitor the performance of the server, network latency, and CPU, but these details are irrelevant with respect to serverless as the infrastructure is completely managed by the service provider. But then what should we monitor with respect to serverless? We can still monitor memory and concurrency rate. Although the service provider handles the provisioning and execution of Lambda functions, there is still a limit to the amount of memory that can be used and the concurrent executions allocated to the function.

To perform serverless monitoring, there are number of tools available. There are a few out-of-the-box tools from AWS, such as **AWS CloudWatch**, which involves all the AWS resources feeding into AWS CloudWatch. CloudWatch will be our first tool to monitor the Lambda functions. CloudWatch tracks metrics such as the latency of execution, number of functions executed, and errors made during the execution. But we can go beyond this by setting up custom metrics within CloudWatch. We also looked at the CloudWatch dashboard for use with the Lambda function.

AWS provides another powerful tool for the application performance of the lambda function, and that tool is X-ray. X-ray is a tracing tool that is integrated with AWS Lambda out of the box. It provides an end-to-end view of requests as they move. With X-ray, we can analyse how lambda functions and their connected services are performing. We can identify and troubleshoot the root causes of performance issues and errors, and with the map view of the application, we can see all of its components.

Thundra is another monitoring tool that can be used as an application performance monitoring tool for AWS Lambda. It asynchronously publishes the data from CloudWatch into Thundra using functions and agents to send the monitoring data into the application. It has some really good charts that cover many metrics, such as the invocation counts, cold-start invocation counts and durations, error counts by error types and function names, and many more.

Deployment

To get the latest version of the Lambda function for execution, they should be deployed on the cloud. In this way, if our deployment package is heavier, then deployment will be slower. This will eventually degrade the performance of the function as it unpacks when it is invoked. The packing of our function also affects our execution. For example, if we are using Java, then packaging the function with all the dependencies grouped together as one function is slower compared to putting the dependencies within the lib folder.

There are many tools that are available for deployment, but Serverless Framework is one of the main candidates for this job. Of course, there is lot that we still have to achieve, but this is still a far more mature solution than any other open source option available on the market.

Also with respect to deployment , it should be orchestrated and should go through lots of approval and change request process with respect to UAT and prod environment. Deployment in production should be managed through service-now change request and CAB approvals.

Logging

The runtime language for Lambda provides a mechanism for your function to deliver logged statements to CloudWatch logs. We need any type of application to make the best use of its logs, not just serverless applications. With other applications, we can retrieve the logs from the server in which the application is deployed. However, with serverless applications that is not possible, as there is no server, and present, we don't have the ability to "step through" the code of a live, running lambda function. As a result, we are heavily dependent on the logs that we create to inform our investigation of our functions' behavior. Because of this, we have to make sure that any logs generated should have the right balance of verbosity to triage the issues without demanding too much computing time. It is recommended that we use an environment variable to create a loglevel variable.

The appropriate use of log levels can ensure that we have the ability to selectively incur the additional compute and storage cost only during an operational triage that our function can refer to so that it can determine which log statements to create during runtime.

Security

Security should be first in our list of priorities while designing and implementing functions. One of the major differences between serverless applications and server-based applications is that with a serverless application, we do not have control over the servers, so we must bake in most of the securities within our code. So while coding the serverless application, we should make sure that we write a secure code so that all the third-parties' security configuration is validated. Let's look at some of the best practices that are essential for implementing this secure code.

An IAM role per function

It is advisable that you create a role for each function, because this would decouple the IAM roles. This would also enable least privilege to be provided to individual functions. Say, for example, that a function is using a KMS key within its code. If we have a common role for the KMS key, then all the other functions would have access to the KMS key.

No long-lived credentials

Using temporary AWS credentials with lambda function code is always secure. This is where static analysis configuration plays an important role. It best to create an AWS service client within the function code through AWS SDK without providing any credentials. The SDK should automatically manage the retrieval and rotation of the credentials for the alloted role.

Do not persist secrets

 It is best practice to not persist the secrets. However, our function might need some secrets to be long lived, such as database credentials and dependency service access keys. Because of this requirement, it is recommended that you encrypt these secrets. There are a few options available to us, such as using the lambda environment variable with encryption and the Amazon EC2 systems manager's parameter store.

Secrets should not be saved or persisted on memory. Instead, the function should retrieve temporary credentials and keep rotating them, revoking them from time to time. API interaction with the lambda function should be authenticated and authorized.

Lambda in VPC

When using Lambda functions in VPC, we should follow the best practices of using network security by using least-privilege security groups, lambda-function-specific subnets, and route tables to allow traffic specific to our lambda function, if we have used resources from the VPC.

AWS Lambda best practices

So far we learned about the best practice for DevOps with respect to AWS Lambda, but I feel that this chapter cannot end without knowing the best practices for the lambda function. These best practices will eventually help us to develop efficient lambda functions, and will also help us to achieve faster deployment. Let's look at these best practices individually.

Keep the handler independent of business logic

It is always advisable to keep business logic outside the handler because this will decouple our business logic from the lambda function runtime environment, reuse the business logic functions, and make it easier to test our written unit test, as we discussed earlier in the chapter.

Keep warm containers alive

When we code, we have to make sure that our code is be written in such a way that it uses the resources of a warm container instead of doing a cold start. This means that we have to scope our variables in such a way that they can be reused multiple times on subsequent invocations wherever possible. We should reuse our connection (such as an HTTP or a database connection) that was established in a previous invocation.

Dependency control

Lambda needs many libraries during invocation. Lambda will always look for the latest libraries and security updates, but this will also bring changes in the behavior of the lambda function. As a result, it is best to package the dependencies along with the functions and deploy them. They should also be controlled and managed for the sake of performance within the lower environments.

Shorter timeout for dependencies

We need to configure a shorter timeout for all external dependencies. We cannot allow them to run while they are continuously looking for dependencies because Lambda is billed based on the duration of the execution of the function. The larger the execution time, the higher the are charges.

Exception handling

We should evaluate what the failure behavior of our functions should be, and accordingly, our functions should throw the correct exceptions back for faster resolution.

Recursive coding

We should avoid recursive code within our lambda function because the function will call itself recursively until a criteria is met. But this will lead to multiple volumes of invocation and increased cost. If we still accidentally do it, then we should set the function's concurrent execution limit to 0 to immediately throttle all invocations to the function while you update the code.

High availability

When we go into production, high availability becomes essential, and with respect to serverless applications, high availability depends on the number of zones in which the lambda functions can be executed. If our function uses the default network, then it is automatically able to execute within all available zones in that region. Nothing else is required to configure the high availability for the function in the default network environment. Therefore, while designing the VPC, it is important to include the subnets from multiple availability zones.

Runtime language

Choosing a runtime language is quite tricky when we start designing a serverless application. But we can always seek comfort in our skills sets when we decide on the runtime language. But the runtime language also determines the performance of our application. For example, if we use Java or .NET (the compiled language) as our runtime language, then this incurs the largest initial startup cost for a container's first invocation, but the performance will improve for subsequent invocations. Interpreted languages, such as Node.js or Python, have very fast initial invocation times compared to compiled languages, but they cannot output the maximum performance compared to complied languages. So if the application is latency sensitive or very spiky, then it is recommended that you use an interpreted language, and if the application does not experience large peaks or valleys within its traffic, or if user experience is not blocked with the lambda functions response time, then we can choose any language as the runtime language.

Code for cold and warm containers

The performance of the lambda function is dictated by the logic that we code within it and the dependencies we call. So the best practice to code the lambda function would be to consider the cold and warm start of the containers.

For improved performance for warm starting the container, make sure that you store and reference any externalized configurations or dependencies that your code retrieves locally. Limit the reinitialization of the variables/objects on every invocation that uses global and static variables. Keep the HTTP and database connections alive.

For better performance for cold starting the container, it is always better to use the default network environment, unless connectivity to a resource within a VPC via a private IP is required. Choose an interpreted runtime language over a complied language. Keep the function code package as small as possible, as this will reduce the time to download, unpack the code from the S3 bucket, and invoke it.

Cost optimizing

It's an antipattern to assume that the smallest resource size available to your function will provide the lowest total cost. If your function's resource size is too small, you could pay more because of a longer execution time than if more resources were available that allowed your function to complete more quickly.

You don't need to implement all use cases through a series of blocking/synchronous API requests and responses. If you are able to design your application to be asynchronous, you might find that each decoupled component of your architecture takes less compute time to conduct its work than tightly coupled components that spend CPU cycles awaiting responses to synchronous requests. Many of the Lambda event sources fit well with distributed systems, and can be used to integrate your modular and decoupled functions in a more cost-effective manner.

Some Lambda event sources allow you to define the batch size for the number of records that are delivered on each function invocation (for example, Kinesis and DynamoDB). You should run tests to find the optimal number of records for each batch size so that the polling frequency of each event source is tuned to how quickly your function can complete its task.

The variety of event sources available to integrate with Lambda means that you often have a variety of solutions available to meet your requirements. Depending on your use case and requirements (request scale, volume of data, latency required, and so on), there might be a nontrivial difference in the total cost of your architecture based on which AWS services you choose as the components that surround your Lambda function.

Best practices for Azure functions

With respect to other cloud providers, such as Azure, the best practices should align with the Lambda function. In this section, we will look at a few of these best practices for Azure that are closely related to Lambda functions.

Avoid large and long-running functions

Large and long-running functions can cause unexpected timeout issues and A function can become large because of many Node.js dependencies. Specially Importing dependencies can also cause increased load times that result in unexpected timeouts.

Whenever possible, we should refactor large functions into smaller function sets that work together and return responses fast.

Cross-function communication

If we are not using durable functions or logic apps to integrate multiple functions, it is generally a best practice to use storage queues for cross-function communication. The storage queues are cheaper and much easier to provision.

Individual messages in a storage queue are limited in size to 64 KB. If we need to pass larger messages between functions, an Azure Service Bus queue could be used to support message

functions should be be stateless

It is recommended that functions are stateless and idempotent where ever possible. Associate any required state information with your data. For example, an order that is being processed will likely have an associated state member. A function could process an order based on that state while the function itself remains stateless.

and very importantly it is recommended that idempotent functions have timer triggers. For example, if you have something that absolutely must run once a day, we should write it so that it can run at any time during the day with the same results. The function can skip when there is no work for a particular day. Also, if a previous run failed to complete, then the next run should pick up where it left off.

functions is defensive

It is always good to design our functions with the ability to continue from a previous fail point during the next execution. It is recommended to write the function with proper error handling considering networking outages, reached quota limits, or made any other kind of mistake. All of these issues can affect our function at any time. we need to design our functions to be prepared for such things.

Let assume our code fails after inserting 2000 items into the a queue for processing, we should be able to track the items in a set that is been completed or else we might end up inserting them again.

How does your code react if a failure occurs after inserting 5,000 of these items into a queue for processing? You should track items in a set that you've completed. Otherwise, you might insert them again next time. This can have a serious impact on your work flow.

The same function app should not have code for test and production

We should not mix, test and production functions or resources within the same function app, the performance might be degraded because functions within the function app shares resources, for example memory is shared. So we should be careful what we load in our production function apps as memory is averaged across each function in the function app

Use asynchronous code, but avoid blocking calls

Asynchronous programming is a recommended best practice. However, always avoid referencing the `Result` property, or calling the `Wait` method on a `Task` instance. This approach can lead to thread exhaustion.

Configure host behaviors to better handle concurrency

The `host.json` file in the function app allows for the configuration of the host runtime and trigger behaviors. In addition to batching behaviors, you can manage concurrency for a number of triggers. Often, adjusting the values in these options can help each instance scale appropriately for the demands of the invoked functions.

The settings in the `hosts` file apply across all functions within the app, within a *single instance* of the function. For example, if you had a function app with 2 HTTP functions and concurrent requests set to 25, a request to either HTTP trigger would count towards the shared 25 concurrent requests. If that function app scaled to 10 instances, the 2 functions would effectively allow 250 concurrent requests (10 instances X 25 concurrent requests per instance).

Best practices for Google Functions

Most of the best practices are same across the Serverless functions even though the service providers are different , but I would still like to list some of them here.

Code idempotent functions

The functions should produce the same result even after calling them multiple times. This helps in retrying an invocation if the previous invocation fails partway through our code.

Signal the completion of function calls

Signal the completion of your function, failing to do so can result in your function executing until a timeout is hit. If a timeout occurs, you will be charged for the entire timeout time. Timeouts may also cause subsequent invocations to require a cold start, which results in additional latency.

Do not start background activities

A function invocation finishes once termination is signaled. Any code run after graceful termination cannot access the CPU, and will not make any progress. In addition, when a subsequent invocation is executed in the same environment, your background activity resumes, interfering with the new invocation. This may lead to unexpected behavior and errors that are hard to diagnose. Accessing the network after a function finishes usually leads to connections being reset (and the ECONNRESET error code).

Background activity is anything that happens after your function has terminated. It can often be detected in logs from individual invocations by finding anything that is logged after the line saying that the invocation finished. Background activity can sometimes be buried deeper in the code, especially when asynchronous operations such as callbacks or timers are present. Review your code to make sure that all asynchronous operations finish before you terminate the function.

Always delete temporary files

Local disk storage in the temporary directory is an in-memory filesystem. Files that you write consume memory available to your function, and sometimes persist between invocations. Failing to explicitly delete these files may eventually lead to an out-of-memory error and a subsequent cold start.

You can see the memory used by an individual function by selecting it in the list of functions (`https://console.cloud.google.com/getting-started`) in the GCP console and choosing the **Memory usage** plot.

Do not attempt to write outside of the temporary directory, and be sure to use platform/OS-independent methods to construct file paths.

You can bypass the size restrictions on temporary files by using `pipelining`. For example, you can process a file on Cloud Storage by creating a read stream, passing it through a stream-based process, and writing the output stream directly to Cloud Storage.

Local development

Function deployment takes a bit of time, so it is often faster to test the code of your function locally using a **shim**.

Error reporting

Do not throw uncaught exceptions, because they force cold starts in future invocations. See the **Error Reporting guide** (`https://cloud.google.com/functions/docs/monitoring/error-reporting`) for information on how to properly report errors.

Use SendGrid to send emails

Cloud Functions does not allow outbound connections on port 25, so you cannot make nonsecure connections to an SMTP server. Instead, you should use `SendGrid` to send emails.

Use dependencies wisely

Because functions are stateless, the execution environment is often initialized from scratch (during a cold start). When a cold start occurs, the global context of the function is evaluated.

If your functions import modules, the load time for those modules can add to the invocation latency during a cold start. You can reduce this latency, as well as the time needed to deploy your function, by loading the dependencies correctly and not loading dependencies that your function doesn't use.

Use global variables to reuse objects in future invocations

There is no guarantee that the state of a Cloud function will be preserved for future invocations. However, Cloud Functions often recycles the execution environment of a previous invocation. If you declare a variable with a global scope, its value can be reused in subsequent invocations without having to be recomputed.

This way, you can cache objects that may be expensive to recreate on each function invocation. Moving such objects from the function body to a global scope may result in significant performance improvements.

Do lazy initialization of global variables

If you initialize variables with a global scope, the initialization code will always be executed via a cold start invocation, increasing your function's latency. If some objects are not used in all code paths, consider initializing them lazily on demand.

Summary

As its name implies, this chapter was all about learning the troubleshooting techniques and best practices to apply when using DevOps to construct serverless architecture. In the next chapter, we will talk about the various use cases of AWS Lambda, Azure Functions, and open source versions, and how DevOps fits in to it all.

9
Use Cases and Add-Ons

In the previous chapter, we learned how to apply some best practices in relation to serverless functions and DevOps. We understood how important it is to build light and secure serverless functions. We also learned about some best practices for monitoring and logging a serverless application. So, moving forward, let's look at the big picture of how serverless can be used in the real world and also learn how we can implement end-to-end DevOps around it.

As developers are moving from monolithic application toward the serverless architecture more and more use cases are coming into existence. But it is getting equally more difficult to build, test and deploy them. So, in this chapter, we will learn few serverless use cases and also learn how to set up end-to-end deployment pipeline.

This chapter will cover the following topics:

- AWS Lambda use cases and add-ons
- Azure Functions add-ons
- Google Functions add-ons

AWS Lambda use cases and add-ons

Our journey so far has been about what AWS Lambda is , and how we can build ,test, deploy, monitor, and log it. We also looked at some best practices for AWS Lambda in general and also for DevOps. So now, here in this chapter, it is time to bring them all together as one use case. Before we cover the use case for DevOps with AWS Lambda, let's start to first look at use cases where Lambda can be efficiently used and then let's look at how DevOps can make life easier for developers and business users.

AWS Lambda use cases

As we know, serverless architecture was introduced to help businesses to focus on application development and not to worry about the underlying servers. Reducing the cost and shortening the deployment cycle, the adoption rate for serverless is growing exponentially. Now lots of companies are adopting serverless as a way to ensure rapid auto scaling and descaling. Let's look at some of the useful applications of serverless that are being adopted across the industry.

Serverless website

The best model for serverless adoption would be websites that want to take advantage of AWS Lambda and AWS S3. Both of these resources provided by AWS are very cheap. Also, with AWS Lambda, it can scale on demand and descale as demand slows downs. So they do not have to pay big money for keeping a server up and running all the time. So we can consider hosting the static content or the frontend on the S3 bucket and these frontend applications can send requests to Lambda functions via the API gateway HTTPS endpoints and Lambda does all the heavy lifting of the application logic and persists the data to a a a fully-managed database service (**RDBMS (relational databases)** or **DynamoDB (non-relational databases)**). We can host our Lambda function within VPCs to isolate them from different other networks and it is also cheaper, as we pay only for the traffic incurred by AWS S3 and AWS Lambda with the extra cost for the database service.

Video and image processing

With Instagram becoming more popular, a lot can be done with images and videos, but it is equally expensive to process or resize them. The traditional way of editing the videos and images would be to host a VM that is always running and when an image or video arrives for editing then running the application within the VM. But we have to incur costs for running the VM 24/7 without it being used all the time. Serverless could be the best option for these types of jobs. Serverless services can be used to dynamically resize the image or change the video transcoding for different target devices.

Also, with serverless, we can tap into the Google Vision API or Amazon Recognition to recognize faces and images or flat inappropriate content. In the AWS chapter, we created a tutorial where an image is uploaded into one S3 bucket and then Lambda is automatically triggered when the image is uploaded to the S3 bucket to resize it and push it to another bucket.

Logs Processing and notification

We can use Lambda functions to harvest the logs from CloudTrail and CloudWatch, Lambda watches for specific triggers and log entries and invokes an SNS notification on the event. These notifications can be configured and sent to Slack, Jabber, or other support systems.

Controlling the IoT

The **Internet of things (IoT)** is the latest trend in the market, where lots of smart gadgets at home and in the office can be controlled through Alexa. But how do they work ? So, it is Alexa with Lambda that controls these smart devices. Say we have to light an LED bulb that is controlled by Alexa through a voice message, the event is triggered on the Alexa, and the Lambda function is invoked to perform the action to switch on or switch off the light. So, serverless could become the backend for all the IoT calls.

Backup and daily tasks

Lambda functions can plays an important role with backups and daily tasks. We can schedule the Lambda functions to do repetitive tasks, such as checking for idle resources, creating backups, generating daily reports ,and various other routine jobs. The old school involved installing a task manager application that was running on the server all the time and performing the task when required. But with Lambda, functions are invoked only at a certain event or schedule. They also scale horizontally when required and also it costs less.

Continuous integration and continuous deployment

The ability to rapidly iterate software is more important than it has ever been. CI/CD pipelines allow you to ship code in small increments, so that bug fixes and other updates can be shipped on a daily basis.

Serverless can automate many of these processes. Code check-ins can trigger website builds and automatic redeploys, or PRs can trigger running automated tests to make sure the code is well-tested before human review.

When you think about automation possibilities with serverless applications, it becomes easy to cut manual tasks out of your workflow.

So, we have looked at different use cases where we can use AWS Lambda functions that can perform better jobs than transitional servers or virtual machines. Currently we have a small number of serverless being used in real life, but this certainly will grow in coming years.

But as the use of serverless grows, managing them becomes really tedious. For example, if we use serverless for a share market portal or any ticketing application, then these applications will have many functions to work together, as the applications and functions have to be versioned, built, tested , deployed, and rolled back. This is where continuous integration and continuous delivery plays a role. So, our DevOps use case would be how to set up efficient CI/CD for Lambda functions.

Starting with development locally, the serverless framework provides an interesting plugin, which is **serverless offline.** This plugin emulates AWS Lambda and the AWS API gateway locally, which helps to develop and test code locally without uploading to the AWS Cloud before we have thoroughly tested our code locally.

To demonstrate this, I used our earlier task pipeline and modified it to work with serverless offline with DynamoDB in local node. Interestingly, AWS provides a downloadable version of DynamoDB files that allows us to set up the DynamoDB server locally on our development area. So, this will allow us to develop a DynamoDB application locally without paying for data storage and data transfer and it also does not need internet access. You can find more information about setting up this at the following link: `https://docs.`
`aws.amazon.com/amazondynamodb/latest/developerguide/DynamoDBLocal.html`.

I have simply used the serverless plugin name `serverless-dynamodb-local` to set it up locally. It is much easier to set up along with Jenkins. I created an extra stage within the Jenkinsfile. So, here in this stage, I am installing `serverless-dynamodb-local`, `serverless-offline`, and also `serverless-mocha-plugin`, which are required plugins for us to unit test our functions locally before we push them into the AWS Cloud. I have added the code snippet for this and have put the code in the Git repository (`https://`
`github.com/shzshi/aws-lambda-devops-usecase.git`):

```
#Jenkinsfile

stage ('Dev init')
{
    nodejs --version
    npm install serverless-dynamodb-local --save-dev
    npm install serverless-offline --save-dev
    npm install serverless-mocha-plugin --save-dev
```

```
    npm install
    serverless dynamodb install
    chmod 755 startOffline.sh
    chmod 755 stopOffline.sh
}
```

In the next Jenkins stage, I am installing DynamoDB locally and adding the path local API task endpoint to the Jenkins job and invoking the serverless test. I have updated the `serverless.yml` handle and also made sure to update `TASKS_ENDPOINT` within the Jenkinsfile, so the rest of the pipeline should be same as that in Chapter 3, *Applying DevOps to AWS Lambda Applications*:

```
# serverless.yml
plugins:
    - serverless-dynamodb-local
    - serverless-offline
    - serverless-mocha-plugin
custom:
    serverless-mocha-plugin:
        preTestCommands:
            - bash startOffline.sh
        postTestCommands:
            - bash stopOffline.sh
    dynamodb:
      stages:
        - dev
      start:
        migrate: true

# jenkinsfile
stage ('Dev init')
        {
            steps {
                deleteDir()
                checkout scm
                sh '''
                    nodejs --version
                    npm cache clean --force
                    npm install serverless-offline --save-dev
                    npm install serverless-mocha-plugin --save-dev
                    serverless plugin install -n serverless-dynamodb-local
                    npm install
                '''
            }
        }

        stage ('System Test on Dev') {
            steps {
```

```
                    sh '''
                        sls dynamodb remove
                        serverless dynamodb install
                        chmod 755 startOffline.sh
                        chmod 755 stopOffline.sh
                        export TASKS_ENDPOINT=http://localhost:3000
                        serverless invoke test
                    '''
                }
        }
```

And the Jenkins log should look something like this:

```
Installation complete!
+ chmod 755 startOffline.sh
+ chmod 755 stopOffline.sh
+ export TASKS_ENDPOINT=http://localhost:3000
+ serverless invoke test
Serverless: Tests being run with nodejs6.14,  service is using nodejs6.10.
Tests may not be reliable.
Serverless: Run command: bash startOffline.sh


  Create, Delete
    ✓ should create a new Task, & delete it (198ms)

  Create, List, Delete
    ✓ should create a new task, list it, & delete it (180ms)

  Create, Read, Delete
    ✓ should create a new task, read it, & delete it (133ms)


  3 passing (523ms)
```

And once the pipeline succeeds, it should look like the following diagram:

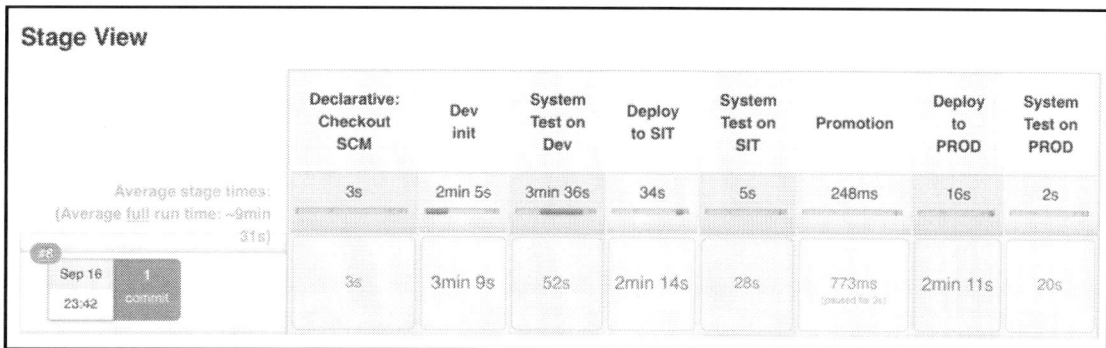

Stage View									
	Declarative: Checkout SCM	Dev init	System Test on Dev	Deploy to SIT	System Test on SIT	Promotion	Deploy to PROD	System Test on PROD
Average stage times: (Average full run time: ~9min 31s)	3s	2min 5s	3min 36s	34s	5s	248ms	16s	2s
Sep 16 23:42 — 1 commit	3s	3min 9s	52s	2min 14s	28s	773ms (paused for 3s)	2min 11s	20s

So, now we can develop and test our functions locally as a part of continuous integration and then move to the cloud for other non-production and production environments. But one thing that can further be automated is our Lambda API path over the cloud , as when the function is deployed to the AWS Cloud, then we will get the random hostname for the API gateway:

```
api keys:
  None
endpoints:
  POST - https://ax1hlqv0vl.execute-api.us-east-1.amazonaws.com/sit/mytasks
  GET - https://ax1hlqv0vl.execute-api.us-east-1.amazonaws.com/sit/mytasks
  GET -
https://ax1hlqv0vl.execute-api.us-east-1.amazonaws.com/sit/mytasks/{id}
  PUT -
https://ax1hlqv0vl.execute-api.us-east-1.amazonaws.com/sit/mytasks/{id}
  DELETE -
https://ax1hlqv0vl.execute-api.us-east-1.amazonaws.com/sit/mytasks/{id}
functions:
```

We have updated the task endpoint for the API hostname within our Jenkins pipeline Jenkinsfile. That is because the hostname provided by the API gateway is not static and also because every time we redeploy or remove our service the hostname will change and, accordingly, we have to to change it where ever we are using it. So, how to we resolve this problem? This can be automated through the dynamic allocation of the static domain. This is easily possible through the serverless framework, using one of its plugin, and that plugin is serverless-domain-manager. Let's look at how that can be achieved.

Before we start using the plugin, there are a few pre-requisites:

- We need to register a desired domain name through the following link: `https://docs.aws.amazon.com/Route53/latest/DeveloperGuide/registrar.html`
- We need to make sure we have have our domain name in the registered domain in Route 53 (`https://console.aws.amazon.com/route53/home?#DomainListing`)
- We need to request a new certificate for the domain we have created, which can be created through this link: `https://console.aws.amazon.com/acm/home?region=us-east-1#/wizard/`

Once the pre-requisites are successfully completed, we need to install the serverless domain manager plugin:

```
$ npm install serverless-domain-manager --save-dev
```

Then within the `serverless.yml` file, we add two sections. First we add `serverless-domain-manager` in the plugins block , and then we configure the plugin with `customDomain` via the **Custom** block. The `basePath` attribute will be prefixed to every route of our service. Say, for example, our function is `helloworld` and we add `basePath` as `serverless`, then the route that is registered as `/helloworld` will be accessed through `serverless/helloworld`.

For example, `https://api.<registered_domain_name>/serverless/helloword`:

```
plugins:
    - serverless-domain-manager

custom:
    customDomain:
        domainName: 'api.<registered_domain_name>'
        basePath: '<my_base_path>'
        stage: ${self:provider.stage}
createRoute53Record: true
```

We can also set up source code analysis by integrating SonarQube or ESlint within the Jenkins pipeline.

Monitoring

When we talk about monitoring serverless applications , we do not need to worry about monitoring CPU usage or memory usage, and we don't need to update our system package, as all these are managed by AWS. But the Lambda function still needs to be monitored for execution failures, because in a production environment one single function failure could be a disaster.

CloudWatch, by default, provides metrics for Lambda functionsand these metrics are:

- **Invocation**: Number of times the functions were invoked
- **Errors**: Number of times the functions failed due to various errors, timeouts, unhandled exceptions, memory problems, and other issues
- **Throttles**: Number of times functions throttled, as AWS limits the number of concurrent executions per function and if we exceed the limit the function is throttled
- **Duration:** Invocation time of the function

And errors and throttles are to be monitored 24/7 and we cannot be watching CloudWatch all the time, but we can set an alerti for all the errors and throttles. If we are using the serverless framework, then this can be managed through a plugin named `serverless-plugin-aws-alerts`.It makes it easy to set up alerts for the services.

To set up alerting, we need to install the plugin within our serverless framework service:

```
$ npm install serverless-plugin-aws-alerts --save-dev
```

Then we need to add it to the plugins sections and set the alerts details in the custom section within `serverless.yml`. So, this setup adds alerts to all the functions in our service when deployed to the production stage. Then we configure subscriptions for our SNS topics and each subscription has to have a protocol, which, in our case, is the email and endpoint, which is email address:

```yaml
# serverless.yml
plugins:
    - serverless-plugin-aws-alerts
custom:
    alerts:
        stages:
            - production
        topics:
            alarm:
                topic: ${self:service}-${opt:stage}-alerts-alarm
                notifications:
```

```
          - protocol: email
            endpoint: myemail@domain.com
      alarms:
          - functionErrors
          - functionThrottles
```

Static website

AWS Lambda function will play the role of the backbone of our web application. We also need a cosmetic frontend too to be deployed along with the Lambda function and there is a serverless framework plugin available that can perform this task with ease. That plugin is `serverless-finch`. This plugin will upload static assets of our web application into AWS s3.

Let's look at how it works. To use this plugin, we need to first install it and then configure it into our `serverless.yml` file:

```
$ npm install --save serverless-finch
```

So once the plugin is installed, we first need to create a distribution folder that, by default, would be `client/dist`, which is also configurable through a `custom` tag. So, all our static content will reside in the `client/dist` folder:

```
custom:
  client:
    ...
    distributionFolder: [path/to/files]
    ...
```

Then next we need to mention the S3 bucket name within the custom tag to which static files will be uploaded:

```
custom:
  client:
    bucketName: [unique-s3-bucketname]
```

So, ideally `serverless.yml` should look something like this, where we define the provider, add the plugin configuration for `serverless-finch`, and define the client details with the `custom` tag. The `indexDocument` parameter is for the index page and the `errorDocument` parameter is for the error page:

```
service: my-static-website

frameworkVersion: "=1.26.0"
```

```
provider:
  name: aws
  runtime: nodejs6.10
  stage: dev
  region: us-east-1
  profile: dev-profile

plugins:
  - serverless-finch

custom:
  client:
    bucketName: my-static-pages-bucket
    distributionFolder: client/dist
    indexDocument: index.html
    errorDocument: index.html
```

Finally, to deploy the content, we have run the following command and we should be able to see the location of the newly deployed website on the console output of the serverless application:

```
$ serverless client deploy
```

There are many more configuration parameters and features that are provided by this plugin. You can find them through at the link: `https://github.com/fernando-mc/serverless-finch`.

Warm-up

A cold start is one of the major issues with respect to serverless function. The warmer the functions are, the better performance we get. But how do we keep our functions warm all the time? The serverless framework provide a plugin to help us do that. The plugin's name is Serverless WarmUP Plugin. So, how does this plugin work?

The plugin creates a scheduled event Lambda that invokes all the service Lambdas we select in the time interval. So this plugin will keep the function warm by forcing the underlying container's to stay alive. To set up this plugin, we need to first install it:

```
$ npm install serverless-plugin-warmup --save-dev
```

Then in `serverless.yml`, we can configure it by calling it under the plugins section. We need to mention which environment warm-up should be run, which can be single or multiple. Then in the custom section, we need to define the configuration for the warm Lambda function to run. It can be further configured and details of those configuration can be found at the link: `https://github.com/FidelLimited/serverless-plugin-warmup`.

```
# serverless.yml
plugins:
  - serverless-plugin-warmup
functions:
  hello:
    warmup:
      - production
      - staging
custom:
  warmup:
    folderName: '_warmup' // Name of the folder created for the generated
warmup
    cleanFolder: false
    memorySize: 256
    name: 'warm-my-lambdas'
    role: myCustRole0
    schedule: 'cron(0/5 8-17 ? * MON-FRI *)' // Run WarmUP every 5 minutes
Mon-Fri between 8:00am and 5:55pm (UTC)
    timeout: 20
    prewarm: true // Run WarmUp immediately after a deploymentlambda
    tags:
      Project: foo
      Owner: bar
```

These are a few add-ons for Lambda functions that can help us to make things easier to create and maintain serverless functions.

Azure Functions add-ons

In DevOps, it is very important to make sure development is smoother and faster and that we deploy bug-free applications to production. It is possible if we can develop, debug, and test the application locally. But with respect to Azure functions, to test and debug the functions, we need to deploy it on the Azure Cloud each time. The good news is that, like AWS Lambda, Azure functions can be debugged and tested locally by means of the **Azure functions core tools** .

With Azure functions tools, we can create, develop, test, run, and debug the Azure functions locally. They can be installed on Windows, macOS, and Linux. We can visit the GitHub link for how to set them up: `https://github.com/Azure/azure-functions-core-tools`

After, we have installed the tools, we need to first create the`create function` app. By default, this will also create a local Git repository that can skipped by passing a parameter, `-n`:

```
$ mkdir my-local-azure-function
$ cd my-local-azure-function
$ func init -n
Writing .gitignore
Writing host.json
Writing local.settings.json
Created launch.json
```

The next step is to create the function by executing `func new`. We will be asked few options with respect to the type of function we want to create and what type of language we want choose for our function and then a function folder is created with three files, `function.json`, `index.js`, and `sample.dat`:

```
$ func new
Select a language:
1. C#
2. JavaScript
Choose option: 2
JavaScript
Select a template:
1. Blob trigger
2. Cosmos DB trigger
3. Event Grid trigger
4. HTTP trigger
5. Queue trigger
6. SendGrid
7. Service Bus Queue trigger
8. Service Bus Topic trigger
9. Timer trigger
Choose option: 4
HTTP trigger
Function name: [HttpTriggerJS] my-azure-func-use-case
Writing
/Users/shashi/Documents/packt/chapter4/tutorial1/mylocalfunction/myLocalFun
ction/index.js
Writing
/Users/shashi/Documents/packt/chapter4/tutorial1/mylocalfunction/myLocalFun
ction/sample.dat
```

```
Writing
/Users/shashi/Documents/packt/chapter4/tutorial1/mylocalfunction/myLocalFun
ction/function.json
```

As we have the function baked in through a template, we can now invoke the function locally by `func start` and this command will start the function app locally and provide us with the API URL:

```
$ func start
%%%%%%
 %%%%%%
 @ %%%%%% @
 @@ %%%%%% @@
 @@@ %%%%%%%%%% @@@
 @@ %%%%%%%%%% @@
 @@ %%%% @@
 @@ %%% @@
 @@ %% @@
 %%
  %
[09/20/2018 20:57:09] Reading host configuration file
'/Users/shashi/Documents/packt/chapter9/my-local-azure-function/host.json'
[09/20/2018 20:57:09] Host configuration file read:
[09/20/2018 20:57:09] {}
info: Worker.Node.769f18ed-34f3-4813-9e9f-b4d43ea01191[0]
 Start Process: node --inspect=5858 "/usr/local/lib/node_modules/azure-
functions-core-tools/bin/workers/node/dist/src/nodejsWorker.js" --host
127.0.0.1 --port 65058 --workerId 769f18ed-34f3-4813-9e9f-b4d43ea01191 --
requestId 964f6629-d61a-4006-a293-e0438da20e45
info: Worker.Node.769f18ed-34f3-4813-9e9f-b4d43ea01191[0]
 Debugger listening on ws://127.0.0.1:5858/0d0bfa98-
d2a3-4af2-8c5c-3a2cc346b1fc
info: Worker.Node.769f18ed-34f3-4813-9e9f-b4d43ea01191[0]
 For help see https://nodejs.org/en/docs/inspector
[09/20/2018 20:57:10] Generating 1 job function(s)
[09/20/2018 20:57:10] Starting Host (HostId=shashismacbookpro-628939497,
Version=2.0.11415.0, ProcessId=5072, Debug=False, ConsecutiveErrors=0,
StartupCount=1, FunctionsExtensionVersion=)
[09/20/2018 20:57:10] Found the following functions:
[09/20/2018 20:57:10] Host.Functions.my-azure-func-use-case
[09/20/2018 20:57:10]
[09/20/2018 20:57:10] Job host started
info: Worker.Node.769f18ed-34f3-4813-9e9f-b4d43ea01191[0]
 Worker 769f18ed-34f3-4813-9e9f-b4d43ea01191 connecting on 127.0.0.1:65058
Listening on http://localhost:7071/
Hit CTRL-C to exit...
Http Functions:
my-azure-func-use-case: http://localhost:7071/api/my-azure-func-use-case
```

What the function does when invoked from `http` is to retrieve request data via the `req` parameter and look for the `name` parameter in the request body and, on successful execution, add some response text:

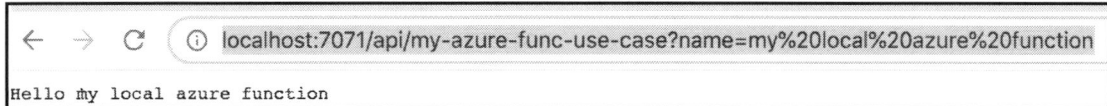

```
← → C  ⓘ localhost:7071/api/my-azure-func-use-case?name=my%20local%20azure%20function
Hello my local azure function
```

Google Functions add-ons

When we decide to move toward a cloud infrastructure or decide to use Google Functions, then we start with a proof of concept or minimal viable product, to prove our application can perform better in the cloud and that we do not have to worry about infrastructure. Also, if the number of the functions is small at the the time of POC, it is easier to develop, test, and deploy them manually, but as they grow, it become quite difficult to manage development, testing and development. Integrating them together to work as an application is another challenge. So, for smoother development, Google also has introduced the Node.js emulator for Google cloud functions. Although currently it is released as the alpha phase, it is still good to iron out quite a number of the issues locally.

The Node.js emulator for Google Functions is distributed as an npm standard package, so it has to be installed through the `npm` command:

```
$ npm install -g @google-cloud/functions-emulator
```

After installation there are many commands that can be used for setting up local environments for testing and debugging the Google Functions. More details can be found at `https://cloud.google.com/functions/docs/emulator`

In the chapter, *DevOps with Google Functions*, we learned how to deploy using Google Cloud's out-of-the box tools, but they can also be deployed in the serverless framework, which also provides templates to start with.

To use the serverless framework, we need to first install the framework plugin. The name of the plugin is `serverless-google-cloudfunctions`. So, if we need to do a quick start with Google Functions , then we should start with the following command that will create a simple `helloworld` Google Function with the filenames as `index`, `serverless.yml`, and `package.json`. Currently the serverless framework supports just Node.js at runtime:

```
$ serverless create --template google-nodejs --path my-service-name
```

In `serverless.yml`, we need to configure the Google project name and credentials. The credentials JSON file needs to be the absolute path. But for security reason, it should be kept somewhere really safe within the server path:

```
provider:
    name: google
    runtime: nodejs
    project: my-serverless-function-usecase
    # the path to the credentials file needs to be absolute
    credentials: ~/.gcloud/Serverless-SIT.json
plugins:
    - serverless-google-cloudfunctions
```

Then deploy it on to the google cloud through Serverless command

```
$ serverless deploy -v
Serverless: Packaging service...
Serverless: Excluding development dependencies...
Serverless: Compiling function "first"...
Serverless: Uploading artifacts...
Serverless: Artifacts successfully uploaded...
Serverless: Updating deployment...
Serverless: Checking deployment update progress...
..............
Serverless: Done...
Service Information
service: my-g-function-usecase
project: serverless-sit-217120
stage: dev
region: us-central1
Deployed functions
first
  https://us-central1-serverless-sit-217120.cloudfunctions.net/http
```

Once deployed successfully, we should get the API link in the deployment output and which can we used and in our we can browse it through the browser and the screen should display

Hello World!

Summary

In this chapter, we looked at some popular use cases for serverless and also some essentials that can improve the development and deployment. In the next and the final chapter, we will see how serverless will shape the DevOps and how DevOps has to change its track with the adoption of serverless.

10
DevOps Trends with Serverless Functions

Finally, our journey is coming to an end. Throughout this book, we have looked at various different serverless providers, and various ways to build, deploy, monitor and log the serverless functions and with different service providers. So, how will serverless change the course of DevOps? As we know, with IaaS and PaaS, we need to build the infrastructure, always monitor it, and scale it. We need to use configuration management tools to upgrade the servers from time to time, monitor, log and manage manual scaling and, when you consider serverless, all this does away. So in what direction does DevOps go, when we decide to use serverless ? Well there was a perception that DevOps won't be required if we adopt serverless, but that is not completely true which we have already learned through our chapters, that DevOps does not completely vanish. We still need to version the code, package it, deploy it, and monitor and log it too, but it is still easier then IaaS and PaaS.

This final chapter will cover two minor but very important topics:

- The impact of serverless on Ops
- The direction of DevOps with serverless

The impact of Serverless on Ops

DevOps, as we know, is actually a handshake between the developer and operations team to work together to build and productionize an application faster. DevOps has become very powerful in recent years, and its value has grown with acceleration and better enabling of the deployment of an application, and it has also contributed to the continuous improvement of the development and options process.

But developers are not really in favor of Ops, because they always have to deal with Ops for their code to function and perform as per the business requirement on the production. The whole idea of Operations was to provision the infrastructure, which is similar across the different environments (development, QA, pre-production and production), so that it makes life easier for the developer so they can just worry about building the application.

The job of the operator until now has been setting up infrastructure, which was eventually enhanced to configure the infrastructure through scripting. The operator has to manage the security, monitor, log, and many other daily routine jobs, so it takes lots of work, which pushed us toward Serverless computing. So the developer got back to their development, creating new functions and features, and worrying less about whether their code would work on the provided infrastructure, or whether they would have code application scaling within their code.

So, basically, serverless was technically un-ops-ing the developers, so the developer and the operations team could now be more focused on their task instead of spending time in troubleshooting the infra issues. So, how did the concept of serverless arrive? There are lots of components and reasons added to the birth of serverless, but one of the main components are popularisation of containers. Container did exist earlier but with docker and kubetenes it become much popular. Conceptually, serverless basically is, breaking the microservices into smaller chunks which can be called as nanoservices. So these nanoservices can fit perfectly to function within the containers so as to perform nano-function, and we also know that with Kubernetes, or other services like it, the management of containers has become quite easy. So this could be one of the reason why popularity of serverless is growing.

With the entry to the cloud provider, infrastructure has become stable and also cheaper, but with respect to virtual machines, we still have to provision and configure them. But with the introduction of serverless by cloud providers, ops teams do not have to worry about provisioning and configuring. So, virtually, ops team will vanish, but not fully. Instead of provisioning and configuring the infrastructure, they can fully focus on Monitoring, Logging, Orchestration of service deployments and management, Managing Security and much more. Though VM/container management is removed from the picture. The monitor of the performance, monitor security, and so on, in short they will have to upgrade their skills to align with cloud services.

The direction of DevOps with serverless

When there was no DevOps, development and operation worked in silos, leading to poor teamwork and a lack of transparency. Operations processes were painstakingly slow, with no control over environment consolidation, and with the DevOps team consolidated into one single team working together in the application lifecycle and automation through the technology stack and tooling. DevOps became the backbone of the organization and also an integral part of time to market.

But DevOps has its own challenges to implement. First and foremost, as DevOps is a vast area of expertise, it is very difficult to find or experts in every aspect of DevOps. Because of this, organizations find it difficult to adopt DevOps easily, and it also leads to confusion in proper implementation.

Tool selection for DevOps is another challenge on it own. Continuous deployment, continuous testing, and collaborative reporting makes DevOps successful. But many organizations fumble tool selection, and that leads to wrong tool selection which eventually adds to failure.

Many managers doubt that DevOps can be successful. They are worried about whether DevOps will deliver with the required transparency to the customer and organizations.

The bigger the company, the harder it is to work collaboratively, as the workers are different and teams are independent, and this creates barriers and walls. But it is imperative to make the team understand how to bring down these walls, and collaborate.

DevOps team mostly spend their time supporting development teams with builds, setting up and maintaining the development environment, and troubleshooting deployment issues, but they end up giving more attention to operations side.

But serverless has helped to overcome these challenges. It has freed up space for the operations team to spend their time wisely and add improvements to the existing ecosystem. Business agility is possible with serverless computing because you can create an environment where there is a continuous improvement of development.

With no need to worry about infrastructure, the DevOps teams can improve on other aspects of development, such as automating deployment, adding process to code versioning, automating deployment metrics, adding more value to applications (such as introducing different dashboards), and application performance management.

As serverless is still in its growth stage, there is a lot to achieve in terms of language or runtime support, vendor locking, security, and also, currently, not all the applications are serverless compatible. Also, there are lots of open source serverless architectures coming onto market such as OpenWhisk, OpenFaaS, FN, Kubeless and Iron.io (`https://www.iron.io/`). There is a long journey toward maturity in terms of serverless, and also with DevOps tools around serverless.

Lots of banking customers and government organizations are wary of cloud services, due to security reasons, and also due to their slow adoption of cloud technologies. But, technology such as Kubernetes is gaining lots of popularity and its performance, functionality, and support with respect to forums, is improving as days pass. Therefore, government organizations and banking domain customers might lean more toward the same, as microservices and Kubertenes can be combined together to perform as serverless functions. So DevOps would surely play an important role here.

So there would be a requirement to set up technologies such as Kubernetes on-premises, provision and configure servers, upgrade infrastructure, monitor and log, and add infrastructure when needed for support scaling.

But, if some companies choose to use cloud providers for their serverless needs, then the track for the DevOps would change. With respect to development, the cloud operation engineer and developer roles would fuse into one, as there would be no underlying infrastructure to take care of. But, we would need the services of continuous integration, continuous deployment, monitoring, and logging.

DevOps will very much be needed to set up deployment pipelines, automated metrics notification, automate logging, and monitoring. But when everything is automated and streamlined, then DevOps' workloads will decrease, which will eventually be the same for any type of infrastructure.

But job responsibility will surely change, and lots of roles will change. For instance, we would need fewer network and infrastructure engineers. So, before moving to serverless, it is recommended that we evaluate the IT operations. If we don't, then adoption of serverless architecture might slow things down and become a bottleneck for operations.

So, to conclude, as serverless is still improving, it is difficult to speculate how DevOps will play its role in terms of serverless adoption. The direction might change, but the journey will still continue.

Summary

The journey has come to an end, but only for this book. With respect to serverless, the journey has just begun and, through this journey of maturity, we will see lots of improvements in terms of service, and also in terms of technology and new vendors. With that, we will see lots of maturity with DevOps tools and processes for serverless applications. So, here, we finish this book, with the hope of the growth of serverless and DevOps alongside serverless.

Other Books You May Enjoy

If you enjoyed this book, you may be interested in these other books by Packt:

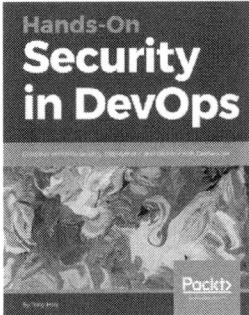

Hands-On Security in DevOps

Tony Hsu

ISBN: 978-1-78899-550-4

- Understand DevSecOps culture and organization
- Learn security requirements, management, and metrics
- Secure your architecture design by looking at threat modeling, coding tools and practices
- Handle most common security issues and explore black and white-box testing tools and practices
- Work with security monitoring toolkits and online fraud detection rules
- Explore GDPR and PII handling case studies to understand the DevSecOps lifecycle

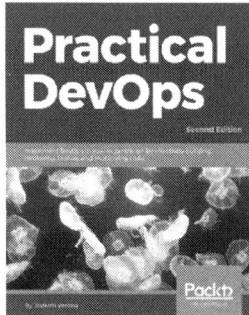

Practical DevOps - Second Edition
Joakim Verona

ISBN: 978-1-78839-257-0

- Understand how all deployment systems fit together to form a larger system
- Set up and familiarize yourself with all the tools you need to be efficient with DevOps
- Design an application suitable for continuous deployment systems with DevOps in mind
- Store and manage your code effectively using Git, Gerrit, Gitlab, and more
- Configure a job to build a sample CRUD application
- Test your code using automated regression testing with Jenkins Selenium
- Deploy your code using tools such as Puppet, Ansible, Palletops, Chef, and Vagrant

Leave a review - let other readers know what you think

Please share your thoughts on this book with others by leaving a review on the site that you bought it from. If you purchased the book from Amazon, please leave us an honest review on this book's Amazon page. This is vital so that other potential readers can see and use your unbiased opinion to make purchasing decisions, we can understand what our customers think about our products, and our authors can see your feedback on the title that they have worked with Packt to create. It will only take a few minutes of your time, but is valuable to other potential customers, our authors, and Packt. Thank you!

Index

Printed in Great Britain
by Amazon